Argentina and the United States

A Conflicted Relationship

Twayne's International History Series

Akira Iriye, editor
Harvard University

ARGENTINA AND THE UNITED STATES

A Conflicted Relationship

Joseph S. Tulchin

TWAYNE PUBLISHERS • BOSTON
A DIVISION OF G. K. HALL & CO.

Published by Twayne Publishers
A division of G. K. Hall & Co.
70 Lincoln Street, Boston, Massachusetts 02111

Twayne's International History Series No. 5

Book design by Barbara Anderson
Book production by Janet Z. Reynolds
Copyediting supervised by Barbara Sutton
Typesetting by Huron Valley Graphics, Ann Arbor, Michigan

Printed on permanent/durable acid-free paper
and bound in the United States of America

Library of Congress Cataloging-in-Publication Data

Tulchin, Joseph S., 1939–
    Argentina and the United States : a conflicted relationship /
Joseph S. Tulchin.
        p.   cm. — (Twayne's international history series ; no. 5)
    Includes bibliographical references.
    ISBN 0-8057-7900-0. — ISBN 0-8057-9204-X (pbk.)
    1. United States—Foreign relations—Argentina.   2. Argentina—
Foreign relations—United States.   I. Title.   II. Series.
E183.8.A7T85   1990
327.73082—dc20   89-26847
                                                                        CIP

0-8057-7900-0 (alk. paper) 10 9 8 7 6 5 4 3 2 1
0-8057-9204-X (pbk., alk. paper) 10 9 8 7 6 5 4 3 2 1
First printing 1990.

To all my Argentine friends,
for whom this book was written

CONTENTS

illustrations   ix
foreword   xi
preface   xiii
introduction   xv

chapter 1
First Contacts   1

chapter 2
The Clash of Global Visions   16

chapter 3
World War I   30

chapter 4
Between the Wars: Collapse of the Argentine Growth Model   46

chapter 5
An Argentine Dilemma: Between Europe and America   62

chapter 6
World War II and U.S. Persecution of Argentina   81

chapter 7

Cold War Relations   99

chapter 8

Argentina as Pariah in the International Community   132

chapter 9

Reinsertion into World Affairs   163

chronology   179
bibliographic essay   183
index   187

ILLUSTRATIONS

Illustrations follow page 80.

1. Estanislao Zeballos, foreign minister under three presidents before World War I.

2. Honorio Pueyrredón, foreign minister under Hipólito Yrigoyen and ambassador to the United States.

3. Carlos Saavedra Lamas, foreign minister under Augustín P. Justo and winner of the 1937 Nobel Peace Prize.

4. Diplomatic rivals Spruille Braden and Carolos Saavedra Lamas.

5. José María Cantilo, foreign minister under Roberto Ortíz.

6. Enrique Ruíz Guiñazú, Ramón Castillo's foreign minister.

7. Orlando Peluffo, member of the military junta that took power in 1942.

8. Juan Carlos Bramuglia, Perón's chief foreign affairs advisor.

9. Hipólito Jesus Paz, one of Perón's foreign ministers.

10. Mario Amadeo, one of Perón's foreign ministers.

11. Carlos Florit, foreign minister under Arturo Frondizi.

12. Cartoon by Clifford Berryman, the *Washington Star*, 1944.

FOREWORD

    Twayne's International History Series seeks to publish reliable and readable accounts of post–World War II international affairs. Today, nearly fifty years after the end of the war, the time seems opportune for a critical assessment of world affairs in the second half of the twentieth century. What themes and trends have characterized international relations since 1945? How have they evolved and changed? What connections have developed between international and domestic affairs? How have states and peoples defined and pursued their objectives, and what have they contributed to the world at large? How have conceptions of warfare and visions of peace changed?

    These questions must be raised if one is to arrive at an understanding of the contemporary world that is both international—with an awareness of the linkages among different parts of the world—and historical—with a keen sense of what the immediate past has brought to civilization. Hence Twayne's *International History* Series. It is hoped that the volumes in this series will help the reader to explore important events and decisions since 1945 and develop the global awareness and historical sensitivity required for confronting today's problems.

    The first volumes in the series examine the United States' relations with other countries, groups of countries, or regions. The stress on the United Stated is justified in part because of the nation's predominant position in postwar international relations, and also because far more extensive documentation is available on American foreign affairs than is the case with other countries. The series addresses not only those interested in international relations, but also those studying America's and other countries' histories, who will find here useful guides and fresh insights into the recent past. Now more than ever before, it is imperative to understand the linkages between national history and international history.

This volume offers an extremely valuable discussion of U.S.-Argentine relations. It is unique in the series in that close to half of the text is devoted to developments before 1945. Such an emphasis on the historical background is justified because, as the author shows, contemporary Argentine perspectives on international affairs and on the United States are profoundly affected by history, especially early Argentine dealings with North America and European powers. Joseph S. Tulchin, who has written extensively on Latin American affairs, enables the reader to see U.S. relations with Argentina as a story of mutual misperceptions and often frustrating encounters, which in turn are related to domestic political and social developments in the two countries. Such a dual perspective is much needed today.

Akira Iriye

PREFACE

I had been writing this book for many years without even intending to. I had been at work for years on a socioeconomic study of Argentina, publishing bits and pieces as I went along. More as a hobby than anything else, I began writing essays on Argentine relations with the United States. It began twenty years ago when, through an intermediary, Ambassador Adolfo Scilingo brought me a copy of a piece he had done on the so-called Non-Belligerancy Proposal of April 1940. Scilingo felt that a great deal of animosity had been created in the United States as a result of Argentina's neutrality in World War II and that little was known in this country of the Argentine effort to get the United States to join in a hemispheric effort. Scilingo, who had been a junior official in the Argentine embassy in Washington, provided me with access to copies of Argentine documents and to Filipe Espil, ambassador in Washington at the time. Both men spent hours with me talking about Argentine foreign policy.

Other diplomats generous with their time were Miguel Angel Cárceno, Roberto Levillier, and Carlos Muñíz. Given the spare quality of Argentine diplomatic archives, their recollections were especially valuable. Many other Argentines contributed to my understanding of their country's worldview. Worthy of mention is Roberto Etchepareborda, whose work on three time Foreign Minister Estanislao Zeballos was cut short by his death. Jorge Balan, Carlos Escudé, and Roberto Starke read the manuscript and offered valuable help. Heraldo Muñoz and Alberto van Klaveren, two Chilean scholars, read chapters and shared with me their insights on hemispheric relations.

In the United States I want to thank Gary Wynia and Akria Iriye for reading the manuscript and helping me improve it. Martin Gonzalez was a resourceful and patient research assistant. Leona Pallansch facilitated her compilations of U.S. aid data. Rosalie Radcliff and Barbara Holliday were heroic in their repeated efforts to retype my drafts (thank God for the PC!). And, any scholar who is married, as I am, and has children, as I do, owes his family a debt of gratitude for putting up with some very strange behavior while he is writing a book.

Joseph S. Tulchin

University of North Carolina at Chapel Hill

INTRODUCTION

The history of relations between the United States and Argentina is one of repeated misunderstandings, extended periods of tension, and missed opportunities for cooperation and friendship. The difficulties have recurred for nearly two centuries and in governments of various sorts: civilian or military, populist or oligarchic in Argentina and Democratic or Republican, isolationist or internationalist in the United States. This persistent pattern, in the face of hemispheric pressures for cooperation, suggests that there may be some underlying causes for the difficulties, some structural factors that account for the inability of the two nations to establish a firm basis on which to construct friendly relations of mutual benefit.

The obvious, simple fact, too often lost from view because it is so obvious, is that the two nations have had different historical experiences from their very beginnings as colonies and as independent nations. Building upon those experiences, they have continued to see the world from different perspectives as they evolved and developed, and as each was inserted into the world system. Geography is another factor dividing the two nations. They are quite far apart. It is nearly twice as far between Washington, D.C., and Buenos Aires as it is between Washington and London or Paris. Travel between the two countries never has been easy and, to this day, continues to be relatively difficult. For the last one hundred years, economics have been another factor that set the two nations against one another, as they have produced the same goods for the international market.

The roles in world affairs that each nation has attempted to play have changed with time. The United States was not always a world power, nor did it always aspire to exercise influence and dominion over other peoples and polities. Argentina, now a middle-rank power confronted with staggering economic problems and suffering through a period of prolonged political instability and international impotence, once was considered on the verge of becoming one of the world's major states.

Argentina, first as part of the Spanish empire and then as a major player in the informal economic empire under British influence in the nineteenth century, was more fully and effectively integrated into the international system than it is today or than it has been at any time since World War II, when the power struggle among nations focused severely on an East-West axis in the northern hemisphere and the United States became the uncontested leader of the Western bloc. As Argentina considered itself one of the world's great powers, at least potentially, and as a "European" or Western nation in the cultural sense, it did not immediately see a role for itself in the postwar world. It did not want to become part of the Third World. Thus, for reasons that are as much exogenous as endogenous, Argentina has had a serious international identity problem for the past half century or more, and that has contributed to the tensions in the relationship with the United States.

On the other side, since 1945, the United States has been preoccupied—some would say obsessed—with the perceived threat from the Soviet Union. This led to an appealing simplification in the perception of the world—it was divided into opposing power blocs, East versus West, and into those who sided with the United States and those who didn't. From the U.S. perspective, Latin America was reduced en masse to a region supporting the United States in its struggle-crusade against the advance of Soviet influence and international communism. Nations that did not support the United States or that suffered endemic instability represented potential threats to U.S. security as pockets of subversion. In this context, Argentina simply was too far away to matter very much. In geopolitical terms, since the end of the war, with few exceptions, it has been outside the arena of contention, significant only in its capacity to cause trouble.

There have been instances in which Argentina attempted to impose itself on the attention of U.S. leaders and to alter their simplified thinking on world affairs. The persistent, often strident efforts by Juan D. Perón (1946–55) to create for Argentina a role as autonomous intermediary between the power blocs amounted to very little, an irritating annoyance that could be ignored. Similarly, in the 1960s, after the regime of Fidel Castro had been identified as an enemy of the United States, efforts by President Arturo Frondizi (1958–62) and subsequent Argentine leaders to establish contacts with Cuba were a source of irritation to the United States. While they might have been intended as a challenge to U.S. power, they did little to alter U.S. policy or Cuba's position in the hemisphere or the general trend of declining Argentine significance in U.S. policy planning. The 1982 war in the Islas Malvinas (or Falkland Islands) temporarily drew attention to the geopolitical importance of Argentina as a key player in the South Atlantic. But the administration of Ronald Reagan (1981–89) soon turned its attention back to the East-West issues in which Argentina plays only a marginal role. This neglect or disregard is a source of frustration to Argentines and another source of friction between the two nations.

The persistent tension in the relations between Argentina and the United States following World War II can be understood only in the context of the long history of misunderstanding between the two nations. The difficulties facing the two nations today and the problems Argentina is having in reintegrating itself into the family of nations following a long period of being outcast during the military dictatorship of the 1970s are in large measure the product of the prolonged pattern of dissonance in the relations between the two countries. Relations reached a crisis during World War II, when Argentina remained neutral until the very last moment. That episode precipitated excruciating pressure on Argentina by the United States and left a bitter legacy that colors relations between the two countries to this day. The wartime crisis is the centerpiece of this volume, chapters 5 and 6. However, Argentina's neutrality and the crisis in bilateral relations was itself the product of nearly a century in which the two nations saw the world from different perspectives and developed very different foreign policies. Without understanding the long development of the pattern in Argentine-United States relations as well as the crisis during the war, the modern period is virtually incomprehensible. For that reason they are the subject of the first five chapters of this book. Throughout the book, I have sought to present the Argentine point of view on events, something with which most North American readers will not be familiar.

chapter 1

FIRST CONTACTS

The first contacts between Argentina and the United States came when both were still colonial units within farflung global empires. Those contacts—made at the beginning of the eighteenth century and sporadic and of minor importance for both colonies—were partly the result of imperial rivalry between Spain and Great Britain, and partly the result of individual entrepreneurial zeal in one British colony or the other. Merchants from the British colonies participated with increasing frequency in the contraband trade with the Spanish colonies, often providing the materials requested or facilitating the re-export of British goods to Buenos Aires. Whalers from the New England colonies stopped at Buenos Aires or at the Malvinas Islands for provisions. The British fomented these contacts to undermine Spanish mercantilism in the Americas. In this endeavor, they were aided by Spain's declining economic strength, which rendered it incapable of maintaining its role as metropolitan power, as well as by its military ineptitude and maladroit diplomacy. The combination would prove fatal for Spain's empire.

The economic and political changes that occurred during the eighteenth century had markedly different impacts in North and South America. The British colonies of North America participated as direct protagonists in many of the principal episodes, while the Spanish colonies at the southern extreme of South America were marginal to events in Europe. They virtually had no impact on those events and felt very little repercussion from them. By the end of the century, the two regions appeared quite different and looked upon the world in very different ways. Most of the territory in the colonies that were to form the United States was settled at the time of independence. Boston, New

York, Philadelphia, and Charleston—although still provincial by European standards—did provide for most of the creature comforts associated with urban living, and fully developed commercial and financial systems were in place to service the colonies' expanding economic activity. The total free population of the United States was around six million at the end of the century, most of which had come from the British Isles, although there were important minorities from Germany, France, the Low Countries, and Sweden. There also was a pluralism of religious beliefs that had led to a pragmatic, even indispensable tolerance of the beliefs of others.

The situation in the River Plate was quite different. Total population there was scarcely half a million, and almost all of it had come from Spain. Catholicism was officially recognized by the state as it was in all of Spain's dominions, and tolerance of the beliefs of others was never conscious or deliberate. The settlement pattern was erratic. There were modest cities along the old trade route on the way to the Altiplano—Salta, Jujuy, Tucumán, and Córdoba. But by the end of the century, even Buenos Aires, the only portion of the colony experiencing growth, was still a fairly rude urban center, with unpaved streets that ran with mud in the rainy season. The harbor could not compare in size, quality, or activity with any of five or six ports in North America. There were a few tiny settlements farther south, along the coast, but the vast portion of the territory included within the administrative unit of the River Plate was unsettled.

By the time the thirteen British colonies began their armed struggle for independence, they had been active participants in European diplomatic and military conflicts for nearly half a century. They were disturbed by that role, but it had served to build the confidence of their leaders and to give them a sense of their importance in world affairs. The new nation's leaders assumed for themselves a role in international affairs that the colonies already had been playing. They did not have to create that role.

The most traumatic experience for an entire generation of North American colonists was the French and Indian War, 1756–63. Many fought in it. The peace settlement, negotiated in Europe, made geographic expansion extremely difficult, although almost all colonists considered such expansion natural and necessary. They took as a lesson from the war that monarchies were naturally predatory and that having a rival on your borders inevitably would lead to difficulty. Propinquity would create tension, and it was important to protect the frontiers of settlement from politically hostile forces as well as from the more traditional threat of hostile Indians. Another lesson reinforced by the war was that the European nations appeared to act more rationally or predictably in the definition and protection of their commercial or economic interests. These ideas would be reflected in the comportment of the new nation and summarized in the most famous foreign policy statement of the independence period, George Washington's Farewell Address.[1]

The contrast with the colonial experience in the River Plate is broad and significant. If it was certainly true that the Spanish colonists, the creoles, were pawns in an international power game, it is hard to find an instance in which representatives of the River Plate settlements played a prominent role in any of the power-political games in which the fate of the colonies was determined. Nor is it possible to find examples in which the interests of the creoles influenced Spanish policy toward other nations in Europe, and very few instances in which they figured prominently in Spanish thinking about the colonies in America as a whole. From their beginnings in the sixteenth century, the settlements in the River Plate had been strategic points at the outermost reaches of the empire, to be defended as the broader interests of empire required.

The products, almost entirely pastoral, of the River Plate, were never the sort to fire the imagination of the Spanish rulers. Trade in the area was largely contraband and carried almost exclusively in non-Spanish bottoms, most of which were British. In other words, though the economic activity in the region rapidly was acquiring international significance in the eighteenth century, it had little political impact on the formal organization of the colony or on the colony's relationship to the mother country, except to emphasize the creoles' disdain for imperial regulations. Furthermore, since so much of their economic activity was clandestine, it did little to provide the region's leaders with valuable international experience. Without that experience and without clear linkages between internal activities and international events, it was hard for the creoles to formulate clear ideas concerning the appropriate behavior of their territorial unit in international affairs.

The creoles' experience suggested a separation between formal or political linkages, in which they took little part, and informal (not to say illegal) or commercial linkages, and that the latter could be sustained even in the face of explicit restrictions against them, as long as the official, imperial authority could not enforce its sovereignty. Colonists in southern South America had experiences similar to those of their counterparts in British North America, but the leaders of the new nation reached different conclusions from their experiences. They seem to have been convinced that it was necessary to have a powerful patron, a patron with whom the region or the nation might establish effective, natural commercial ties.[2]

Once the British colonists had made good their independence as the United States of America, contacts with the Spanish colonies increased rapidly. Now the United States was a freewheeling, if modest, player in the international game, sending out consular agents to represent its interests— although Spain refused to recognize these officials. In the River Plate, the expanded trade consisted mainly of flour, lumber, and furniture from the United States in return for hides, tallow, and wool. Spain joined in the war for independence as a means of getting even with Great Britain. As part of the ongoing effort to curb British trade with its colonies, Spain gave the United States privileged access to certain colonial markets. But this proved a short-lived and even illusory benefit for the North Americans. Spain itself was cut off from the colonies by the British fleet, and the North Americans fared only slightly better.

Expansion of U.S. trade with the River Plate was inhibited by two major obstacles. First, the British simply were too powerful. Great Britain was, after all, far and away the richest nation in the world, with the most elaborate banking and trading infrastructure, and with the largest navy and merchant marine at the service of this economic machine.[3] The United States could not compete and could only gain advantage in particular markets when the British were distracted by diplomatic or political complications in Europe. The second inhibition was more complicated, because it involved domestic or internal political issues in the United States. Beginning with its own independence, the United States developed a significant trade with peninsular Spain, a trade that rivaled in importance the trade with Spain's colonies. The government did not want to put the peninsular trade at risk by forcing open on behalf of private interests markets in Spain's colonies. If trade with the River Plate prospered, it was not the result of diplomatic or political nurture. U.S. leaders were anxious to propagate republicanism but only in an abstract fashion, and they expressed their sympathy in general terms with Latin American lobbyists such as Francisco de Miranda. There seemed to be no good reason to become any more specific.[4]

The United States continued to be indecisive in the early years of the new century. Trade with Spain by 1810 represented 12 percent of U.S. exports, nearly $13 million. In just five years that trade had gone from representing one-fifth the value of U.S. trade with Latin America to three times the value of trade with Latin America. Thus, while the purchase of the Louisiana Territory had relieved the pressure for access to the Mississippi River, the trade with Spain replaced it as a factor inhibiting the U.S. government in its dealings with Latin America. On the other hand, it was not at all clear that the Spanish colonies would become cooperative republican neighbors. It seemed highly likely that one or more of them would fall into the hands of some predatory European monarchy, thereby becoming far more of a threat to the United States than they were in the hands of Spain. Furthermore, U.S. interest in Florida was growing to the extent that Presidents Jefferson and Madison, despite their obvious sympathies for republican movements, were unwilling to take a forward position on the question of independence in any of the Spanish colonies.[5]

Almost as soon as the Cabildo Abierto in Buenos Aires had declared its refusal to be governed either by Joseph Bonaparte or by the Junta acting in the name of Ferdinand VII, on 25 May 1810 the United States sent an agent, Joel Roberts Poinsett, to the River Plate. Poinsett also was told to visit Chile and Peru

to diffuse the impression that the United States cherish the sincerest good will towards the people of Spanish America as neighbors, as having a mutual interest in cultivating friendly intercourse; that this disposition will exist whatever may be their internal system or European relations, with respect to which, no interference of any sort is pretended; and that in the event of a political separation from the parent country and of the establishment of an independent system of National Governments, it will coincide with the sentiments and policy of the United States to promote the most friendly relations and the most liberal intercourse.[6]

Poinsett's principal task was to help U.S. commercial interests, especially against British competition.

The authorities of the early governments in Buenos Aires, acting in the name of the United Provinces, soon sent their own agents to the United States to purchase arms and to secure U.S. diplomatic and material support. The first mission was fairly successful and secured what might be considered recognition of their beligerency status. United States efforts to strengthen ties with the River Plate virtually ceased after 1811, when the war with Great Britain threatened its own independence. The independence of the Buenos Aires Junta was threatened at about the same time by Royalist troops in Montevideo and by the failure of the expeditionary force they had sent north to the Altiplano. Governments in Buenos Aires changed frequently. Several of them solicited support from the United States, but Madison was unwilling to do more than express his general sympathy for the republican governments in South America.

Once the hostilities in Europe and the war between the British and the North Americans had ended, the potential danger to the United Provinces of the River Plate grew. The United States on the other hand, felt relatively free of foreign threats and now was concerned primarily with the control over the Florida peninsula. Trade with Latin America expanded while the grain trade with Spain declined. The government in Buenos Aires increased its pressure for support. On 9 July 1816 it declared its formal independence from Spain and informed the U.S. Consul in Buenos Aires a few days later that "It can not be forgotten that in this hectic revolution the people of the Union have had their eyes fixed in advance upon that great Republic that exists in North America. The United States since their glorious liberty have been as a luminous constellation pointing the way opened by Providence to the other people of this part of the Globe."[7] The only U.S. response was to name a fact-finding commission to visit the area and report back to Washington.

The lessons of the independence period for Argentina cannot be considered constructive in terms of preparing the new nation for its role in international affairs. Its two logical allies, the United States and Great Britain, displayed persistent and annoying caution in their diplomacy. Protesting their sympathy for the independence movements, neither would come forward even to declare its unqualified support. The British fleet, unchallenged around the world, did not intervene to protect the new republics, although individual British naval veterans, such as Lord Cochrane, played vital roles in the naval campaigns against Spain. The United States demonstrated its support by a most tolerant attitude toward commercial agents from the new governments and toward privateers sailing under their flags. This caution in London and Washington was the result of concern for events in Europe, their desire to placate Spain and, until 1821, a pessimistic evaluation of the independence movements. It was far from clear that the former colonies could sustain their independence or what form their new governments would take. In the case of the United States, internal political differences strengthened the government's disposition to caution.

For Washington the greatest danger was a concerted intervention by the European monarchies on behalf of Ferdinand. In this, the North Americans supported British diplomacy. A secondary preoccupation, increasing in importance after 1815, was the acquisition of the Florida territory. Under no circumstances was Spain to be driven to turn the territory over to another power, as had happened in the case of Louisiana. Recognition of the colonies or blatant support of their struggle for independence could only anger the Spanish Crown and embarrass the efforts to consummate the delicate negotiations for transfer of Florida. By the policy of keeping the Europeans out of Latin America, thought Secretary of State James Monroe in December 1818, "we have lost nothing, as by keeping the Allies out of the quarrel, Florida must soon be ours, and the Colonies must soon be independent, for if they cannot beat Spain, they do not deserve to be free."[8] As president, Monroe never doubted the virtue of recognizing the independence of the Latin American nations. For him, it was essentially a question of time and timing, because the central issue was liberty. The United States was the stronghold of liberty in the world, and his duty as president was to strengthen the country at home and increase its influence abroad.[9]

From the Argentine perspective this caution was maddening. It undermined efforts to raise funds and to purchase arms, without which it would be difficult if not impossible to consolidate the various territorial units that had comprised the viceroyalty of the River Plate. In fact, the decade produced a series of military campaigns in which the government in Buenos Aires successively failed to assert its control over Paraguay, Uruguay, and Bolivia. Although an Argentine, José de San Martín, was the leader of the rejuvenated military struggle against the Spanish forces in Chile and Peru, none of his successes added to the territory of the United Provinces or augmented the international role of its government. The political legacy of this experience is a powerful latent desire to recover lost territory that refers to the "territorial dismemberment" of the independence period and that serves as a chip on the collective Argentine shoulder in its dealings with neighboring countries. This territorial pathology has been reinforced over the years in Argentine education virtually creating a myth of what might have been.[10]

Of course, the painful instability of the government in Buenos Aires did not enhance the Argentine cause. The kaleidoscopic changes in leadership were an important factor in reducing the confidence foreign governments might have had in the United Provinces being able to discharge their international responsibilities. No Argentine government considered its own ephemeral nature a valid excuse for the standoffish policy of foreign governments. Nevertheless, on more than one occasion the U.S. government used this instability, together with recurring dalliances with monarchism and the obvious failure to control the territory they claimed to represent, to fob off insistent advocates of recognition. If we compare the Argentine experience with that of the United States at their moments of independence, it is remarkable to see in retrospect how seriously the North Americans took their own weakness, their international vulnerability, into account in their dealings with foreign powers. The Argentines seem not to have dealt with the problem, at least not in public discussion.

The timing of U.S. recognition of Argentina and of the rest of the Latin American nations was determined by the undeniable success of the independence movements in the region after 1821, and by the complex web of diplomacy in Europe. By 1822 the Monroe administration was prepared to recognize the new nations and submitted a bill in this sense to Congress in March. French intervention in Spain, to prop up Ferdinand yet again, raised the possibility that the French or some combination of reactionary forces in Europe might extract from Ferdinand some special privilege in Latin America as compensation for their support. The North Americans sought to gain British support in frustrating any such designs, and for a period of months in 1822 and 1823 it looked as if Foreign Minister George Canning was prepared to join the United States in keeping the rest of Europe out of South America. At about the same time, in mid 1823, the Russians announced the exclusion of all foreign powers from the territory they claimed on the west coast of North America, and Canning extracted from the French minister, the Count de Polignac, written assurances that the French had no designs on any part of Latin America. News of the Polignac memorandum, which arrived in Washington in November 1823, served to confirm the government's determination to act independently of the British and to make a strong public statement of U.S. foreign policy principles that would serve simultaneously as the reply to the Russians, the French, and the British. That statement was made in President Monroe's message to Congress of December 1823, known as the Monroe Doctrine.

The specific case of the United Provinces did not enter into the protracted deliberations that led to the formulation of the Monroe Doctrine. Nevertheless, for a short while it appeared as if relations between the two nations would flourish as a result of it. The government in Buenos Aires received news of the North Americans' intentions to recognize the Latin American governments with great enthusiasm. Foreign Minister Bernardino Rivadavia spoke eloquently of U.S. moral influence in world affairs, and numerous public statements heralded the many ties that would bind the two nations. But these grand words were premature.

The first official U.S. representative, Caesar A. Rodney, fell ill during his trip south and died in May 1824, not long after presenting his credentials. He was not replaced until 1854, although John Forbes was appointed chargé d'affaires in April 1825, and there always was at least a commercial agent in Buenos Aires. The first Argentine representative to the United States, Carlos María de Alvear, a hero of the wars for independence, stayed in the United States only a short time. After his departure, in January 1825, no replacement was appointed until 1838, when he again was named minister. Full diplomatic discourse was not restored until 1844.

The Argentine government attempted to invoke the principles of President Monroe's message in their conflict with Brazil over Uruguay. Rivadavia asked Forbes if the United States would come to Argentine aid and prevent European intervention in the dispute. After nearly two years' delay, Secretary of State Henry Clay told Rivadavia in 1827 that the principles of policy could not be invoked by a foreign power, that the United States would remain strictly neutral in the dispute between the two American nations, and that, in any event, the principles did not seem to apply in the present case. Efforts to strengthen diplomatic ties were further undermined by severe internal difficulties in Argentina during most of the 1820s and 1830s, as well as by the constant fact of life that trade with the United States never approached in value that with Great Britain. The final blow to efforts to improve relations was the grave offense taken by Argentine authorities at actions by a U.S. naval vessel in the episode that led to British occupation of the Malvinas Islands in 1833.

The Malvinas archipelago had been a whaling station and a haven for fisherman of many nations for at least a century when French settlers established a colony there in 1764 and gave the islands their name. Undeterred by this action, the British asserted their formal possession of the islands which they named the Falklands, in the following year and proceeded to establish their own colony, on the second of the major islands within the group. The Spanish Crown declared the complete exclusion of all foreign fishing and whaling vessels but left to the new viceroy of the recently established viceroyalty of the River Plate to carry out this declaration and to settle the islands as best he could. Spanish settlement never could be considered effective, and the islands reverted to their traditional role as a friendly haven for all those mining the riches of the South Atlantic.

Upon assuming authority over the government of the River Plate in 1810, the Cabildo Abierto of Buenos Aires formally demanded that the Spanish colonists on the islands leave or recognize the authority of the new government. They left. In 1820 the government of the province of Buenos Aires sent a frigate to assume formal possession of the islands. Three years later it appointed a civilian governor. Adopting a technique the Spanish had used with very little success along the northern frontier of the empire, the government of Buenos Aires, acting on behalf of the United Provinces, attempted to solidify its sovereignty on the islands through a series of contractual arrangements with entrepreneurs who undertook to settle the islands and pay the government a royalty in exchange for specific commercial privileges, the most important of which was the right to levy a fee on those engaged in sealing, whaling, or fishing in the waters around the archipelago.

The most ambitious and successful of these impresarios was Lewis Vernet, who expanded his influence on the islands to the point where he convinced the governor of Buenos Aires, Juan Lavalle, to name him political and military governor in 1829. Armed with this new power, Vernet attempted to enforce his concessionary monopoly on foreign vessels that sailed into the harbors of the islands. Few, if any, of the fishermen paid him any heed. After appealing to Buenos Aires for a warship to patrol the waters around the islands, Vernet was moved in 1831 to seize three ships from the United States. One quickly escaped and sailed back to the United States where it sounded the alarm. The captains of the other two struck a bargain with Vernet in which one was set free on condition it continued to fish only in the west coast sealing grounds, while the third, the *Harriet*, proceeded to Buenos Aires with Vernet on board. Unfortunately for amicable relations between the two nations, the *Harriet* landed in Buenos Aires at a most inopportune time. Internal political conditions in the United Provinces made it particularly difficult to deal with the nation's foreign relations with calm deliberation. To make matters worse, the affairs of the United States were in the hands of Consul George W. Slacum, who had assumed those responsibilities upon the death of Chargé Forbes in June. Slacum had no specific instructions from his government concerning this or any other matter, and his behavior can only be described as tactless and counterproductive.

Slacum demanded that the *Harriet* be set free and that the government in Buenos Aires disavow the actions of Vernet, which he labeled piracy. He denied that Argentine officials on the islands had the right of seizure or that they or anyone else had the right to limit the rights of U.S. citizens to use the fisheries, which were open to the fishermen of all nations by virtue of uninterrupted custom. Minister of Foreign Affairs Tomás Manuel de Anchorena was dubious about Slacum's credentials to conduct such a negotiation and was certain that he was displeased with the tone of the consul's notes. He replied that the appropriate authorities were looking into the matter and that he anticipated an amicable settlement. Not backing down, however, he took the occasion to remind Slacum that the United States had no rights to the islands or to the fisheries. He undoubtedly was moved to make such an assertion by the surprising intrusion of the British into the dispute, when British Chargé Woodbine Parish informed the Minister that the British had not surrendered their claim to the islands by their withdrawal in 1774, and that the Argentines had no legitimate grounds for the settlement of the islands.

While the Argentine government was studying the matter further, the U.S.S. *Lexington*, under the command of Silas Duncan, sailed into the dispute. After brief consultation with Slacum, Duncan determined to defend the rights of U.S. citizens. Using Slacum as an intermediary, he told Minister Anchorena that unless the government of Buenos Aires suspended the right of seizure and promised restitution of the *Harriet* and other stolen property, he would sail for the Malvinas and carry out justice himself. When no reply was received in the time stipulated, Duncan sailed for the islands. A few days later Anchorena delivered his reply to Slacum. In it he reasserted Argentine rights to the islands and to the fisheries there. But in omitting any claim to exclusive rights in the fisheries and by insisting that the dispute was a private litigious affair, he certainly had backed away from his original position and provided all that Slacum reasonably could have asked. To save diplomatic face, Anchorena told Slacum that his government did not recognize the consul as authorized to conduct such negotiations and would deal directly with Washington. By this time, however, events were moving much faster than the pace of communications in the early nineteenth century. Duncan arrived at the islands at the end of December without knowledge of the Argentine note and sacked the settlements, taking prisoners with him to Montevideo, promising to release them as soon as the Buenos Aires government satisfied his demands. Governor Juan Manuel de Rosas decided to wait for a new diplomatic representative from the United States before continuing negotiations.

The new chargé d'affaires, Francis Baylies, who arrived in June 1832, was a close political friend of President Andrew Jackson and had no diplomatic experience. Even if he'd been a seasoned diplomat it is doubtful he could have prevented what was to follow. His instructions indicate that the Jackson administration, having been informed by the captain of the vessel that escaped from Vernet and by Slacum's dispatches, had evaluated the facts of the episode and made up its mind about the necessary solution. Vernet was a pirate because the decree under which he claimed to act either had no official status or, if it had, had not been communicated formally to the diplomatic representative of the United States, therefore it was of no effect. Furthermore, the rights of U.S. citizens to the fisheries were of long standing and could not be limited unilaterally. Secretary of State Edward Livingston reminded Baylies that the U.S. government did not claim these rights exclusively for its citizens, but that they were universal and belonged to the citizens of all nations participating in ocean fishery. Baylies was authorized to sign a treaty with the Argentine government recognizing these rights and to demand restitution of the captured vessel, indemnification for the captured property, and disavowal of Vernet's actions.

Given the nature of these instructions, based as they were on extremely sketchy information of what actually had transpired, it is little wonder that Baylies conducted himself in an intemperate manner. His opening note to the acting minister of foreign affairs, Manuel Vicente de Maza, in June 1832 was close to an ultimatum. De Maza answered a few days later that the gravity of the situation required that it be referred to Governor Rosas. Baylies considered this nothing but evasion, which indicates how little he knew of Argentine politics of the time. Rosas finally responded in August, with his own ultimatum. His government would refuse to negotiate further with Baylies and, in any event, would not resume negotiations until there were "prompt and complete satisfaction for [the] outrages [committed by Duncan], and reparation and indemnification, not only to the Argentine Republic, but to Commandante Vernet, and the Colonists . . . for all the damages and injuries."[11] Considering matters at an impasse, Baylies demanded his passport and left Buenos Aires in September. De Maza and Rosas were taken aback by this attitude and resolved to continue talks in Washington, through their own minister, Carlos María de Alvear, who would assume his responsibilities "soon." The Jackson government also thought there were grounds for accommodation as it awaited the promised minister in Washington to resume the "suspended" talks.

At this point the British stepped in and seized control of the islands, effecting settlement at the end of 1832, which they have refused to relinquish in the face of diplomatic and military pressure ever since. The Argentines protested but could do little else. The nation was not particularly effective at conducting its foreign affairs in the 1830s, as internal discord occupied all the attention of its leaders. Still, Rosas did send Alvear to Washington in 1838, with instructions to settle the dispute on the basis of official U.S. disavowal of Duncan's actions. That was impossible. No substantive reply came from the U.S. government until Secretary of State Daniel Webster suggested that it was premature for the two nations to discuss a settlement of the claims of either against the other until the question of sovereignty between Argentina and Great Britain had been settled. Until that time, he proposed that the nations resume full diplomatic relations. Alvear indicated that he had no instructions for such a step and retired. Full diplomatic discourse was restored in 1844, when the United States finally sent a minister to Buenos Aires. The Argentines, for their part, periodically placed their claims before the United States government. The response was either that Duncan's actions were justifiable because Vernet's were unjustifiable, or that no discussion of the matter could be entertained until the Argentines and British settled the question of sovereignty.

In the century and a half since the Lexington sacked the Vernet colony on the Malvinas, Argentines have blamed the United States for their loss of the islands and for allowing the British to usurp control over them. Given the long history of difficulties between the two nations, perhaps it is indicative of their mutual distrust that the Argentines should blame the United States for the loss of the Malvinas as much as, if not more than, they blame the British, who took them and still hold them. For the rest of the nineteenth century the controversy over sovereignty in the Malvinas was more of an obstacle to friendly relations with the United States than it was to relations with Great Britain.

Following the episode on the Malvinas the United States and Argentina entered a prolonged period of mutual disinterest. In both, the central cause of their quite conscious failure to exert any effort to strengthen ties between them was a determined focus on internal affairs, which included territorial expansion and civil war. Throughout much of this period the U.S. government appeared as if it simply couldn't muster the energy to do more than insist on its friendly disposition toward the Argentine republic. Despite repeated requests, it did not bother even to send a diplomatic representative to replace Baylies until 1844 or to send a minister until 1854. The lack of such a representative rendered its diplomacy ineffective during the period of French and then Anglo-French pressure against the Rosas government. This pressure included a naval blockade that interrupted U.S. commerce in the River Plate, which for some implied the threat of European intervention. Despite provocation, the U.S. government never thought of invoking the Monroe Doctrine or of doing more than protecting the rights of U.S. citizens under difficult circumstances. It declared its strict neutrality and ignored suggestions or requests for a more active role. The Polk administration even went to the point of disavowing aggressive actions by local naval officers and disciplining Captain P. F. Voorhees, who had actually captured some Argentine vessels he accused of violating the rights of U.S. shipping in the blockade of Montevideo. By contrast, both the Buchanan and the Johnson administrations declared their willingness to use naval force to secure their short-term diplomatic objectives in the River Plate, especially against the Lopez regime in Paraguay; this belligerence appeared totally out of place in the region and was almost totally ineffective.

Argentine foreign policy throughout most of the period was extremely defensive. Until 1862, when the nation was reorganized under the centralizing hegemony of the province of Buenos Aires, the foreign affairs of the United Provinces were conducted by the province of Buenos Aires in the name of all of the provinces, or, after 1854, when the province seceded from the confederation, by the province for itself. Once the question of independence and recognition had been settled, the international relations of the new nation were conceived essentially as a matter of international trade on the one hand, and as a matter of defining its boundaries on the other. The former was generally a commercial matter involving the nations of Europe primarily and the United States to a lesser degree. The 1820s saw a brief flurry of bond issues and capital investments, but these collapsed by the end of the decade, and relations with Europe became almost entirely commercial.

The other dimension of Argentina's international relations in the half century after 1830 was a direct extension of the nation's internal political difficulties. Either it involved power struggles among the various provincial bosses (or *caudillos*) of the interior and the leaders of Buenos Aires, or it involved efforts on the part of Buenos Aires and the United Provinces to recapture control over elements of the former viceroyalty of the River Plate. In strictly commercial matters, Argentine governments could be flexible and pragmatic. In matters having to do with their meddling in the affairs of neighboring states, Uruguay and Paraguay, which had been parts of the viceroyalty, Argentine governments could be obdurate and belligerent. When the two dimensions intersected, the belligerent style or posture held in the face of severe pressure by larger and more powerful states. This was consistent with the nation's perspective on world affairs. The definition of the nation's boundaries was an affair of vital national interest. Short-term commercial interests had to be subordinated to the nation's territorial integrity. Besides, since trade relations were considered natural, it was assumed they would be maintained in the face of diplomatic disputes, no matter how serious.

In 1852 Justo José de Urquiza overthrew Rosas. Urquiza began his campaign by attacking Rosas's ally in Uruguay, Manuel Oribe, in 1848 and then offering recognition to Carlos Antonio Lopez in Paraguay. Finally, in conjunction with Lopez, he offered the European powers free navigation of the inland waterways. He also joined forces with Brazil, so that by the time he flushed Rosas out onto the field of battle at Caseros in 1851, it was an international campaign. In the succeeding decade Urquiza, as head of the Argentine Confederation, attempted to use foreign powers to break the resistance of the province of Buenos Aires and force the province to join the new union. In one sense he failed, and the consolidation of the nation was realized under the hegemony of the province of Buenos Aires when the governor of the province, Bartolomé Mitre, became president in 1862. In another sense Urquiza was successful as a transitional figure crucial to the evolution of his nation in the new international system. Himself a rancher and *saladero,* in the mold of Rosas, although from an interior province, he recognized that the regime Rosas represented had stagnated and that it was necessary to open Argentina to the outside world and to accommodate the nation to the changes already occurring in Europe and North America. To achieve those changes, universally called progress, it was necessary to establish internal order and to adopt a diplomatic style more congruent with the dominant style in Europe.

For the most part, the United States remained aloof from international intrigues in the River Plate. In 1866 Secretary of State William Seward tried to mediate the War of the Triple Alliance, in which Paraguay faced Brazil, Argentina, and Uruguay, but he backed away when his offer was spurned, despite the urging of the U.S. minister in Rio, James W. Webb, who insisted that it was in the Latin Americans' "interest and their duty to look to the United States for protection and advice," and that the United States should assume "her right to interpose in all international conflicts on this continent."[12]

These were brave words in 1866. They would be echoed thirty years later by Secretary of State Richard Olney, to greater effect in the dispute over the boundary between Venezuela and British Guiana. Seward knew that U.S. trade in the River Plate region was not significant and that U.S. capital was virtually absent from the early stages of the economic development that had begun following national consolidation. There was no direct steamship link between the two countries. And to make matters worse, when Congress began to impose protective tariffs on a growing list of products, one of the first, in the law of 1867, was wool, then the primary export of Argentina. The Argentine government protested the terms of the tariff and the minister in Washington exerted considerable effort in Congress and in the national press to change the provisions of the bill. No changes were made. The executive did nothing to prevent damage to Argentine interests or national pride. Apparently the State Department did not consider the trade and the goodwill of Argentina worth the effort required to intervene in the legislative process.

NOTES

1. See Felix Gilbert, *To the Farewell Address* (Princeton, N.J.: Princeton University Press, 1961).

2. Ricardo Levene, ed., *Historia de la Nación Argentina* (Buenos Aires: Universidad de Buenos Aires, 1947); Ricardo Piccirilli, *Rivadavia y su tiempo* (Buenos Aires: Peuser, 1960); and Tulio Halperin Donghi, *Tradición Política Española e Ideología Revolucionaria de Mayo* (Buenos Aires: Editorial de le Universidad de Buenos Aires, 1961).

3. See H. S. Ferns, *Britain and Argentina in the Nineteenth Century* (Oxford: Oxford University Press, 1960); W. W. Kaufman, *British Policy and the Independence of Latin America* (New Haven, Conn.: Yale University Press, 1951); and R. A. Humphreys, *Liberation in South America, 1860–1827: The Career of James Paroissien* (London: Athlone Press, 1952).

4. The British were as indecisive as the United States. Castlereagh decided that Britain would seek no territory in the region and would concentrate its efforts on trade and investment. See Charles K. Webster, *The Foreign Policy of Castlereagh 1815–1822* (London: Bell, 1925).

5. See A. P. Whitaker, *The United States and the Independence of Latin America, 1800–1830* (Baltimore: Johns Hopkins Press, 1841).

6. William R. Manning, ed., *Diplomatic Correspondence of the United States concerning Independence of the Latin American Countries* (Washington, D.C.: Carnegie Endowment, 1932), 1:4.

7. Ibid., 1:345.

8. Quoted in Whitaker, *Independence,* 211.

9. This period of U.S. history has been studied in detail. See S. F. Bemis, *John Quincy Adams and the Foundations of American Foreign Policy* (New York: Knopf, 1956); Dexter Perkins, *The Monroe Doctrine* (Baltimore: Johns Hopkins Press, 1941); Bradford Perkins, *England and the United States,* 3 vols. (Berkeley: University of California Press, 1955–58); Charles K. Webster, ed., *Britain and the Independence of Latin Amer-*

ica, 1812–1830 (London: Bell, 1930); Whitaker, Independence; Webster, The Foreign Policy of Castlereagh; H. W. V. Temperley, The Foreign Policy of Canning 1822–1827 (London: Bell, 1925); Kaufmann, British Policy; Ferns, Britain and Argentina; E. R. May, The Monroe Doctrine (Cambridge, Mass.: Harvard University Press, 1975); and Humphreys, Liberation.

10. Carlos Escudé, Patología del nacionalismo. El caso argentino (Buenos Aires: Editorial Tesis, 1987).

11. Manning, Correspondence, 1:151.

12. Foreign Relations of the United States, 1866, 2:320. For an Argentine view of the war see Ramón J. Cárcano, Guerra del Paraguay, 3 vols. (Buenos Aires: Domingo Viau, 1941).

chapter 2

THE CLASH OF GLOBAL VISIONS

Argentina's growth and development in the half century after 1860 was remarkable. At the time of the centennial in 1910, historian and politician Juan Balestra wrote to President-elect Roque Saenz Peña, "No one, even in his wildest dreams, had anticipated the greatness of the Argentine people. . . . It has generated enough electricity to illuminate an entire century. Today, a new era has begun."[1]

Evidence of the nation's progress, strength, and vitality was everywhere at hand. The federal capital was being transformed—remodeled with graceful broad avenues connecting strategic points and with sanitary engineering the equal of any in the world. Elegant townhouses had been built or were going up in the fashionable Barrio Norte. There were fine restaurants, lively cultural centers, a world-famous grand opera, and even a subway—all the glitter and glamour of a great modern metropolis.[2]

The transformation of the countryside was just as dramatic. In little more than a generation, the vast internal land mass known as the pampa had been settled and put into production, creating a world-famous grainery and pasture. In Europe the cliché "as rich as an Argentine" bespoke the existence of fabulous personal fortunes. Both public and private coffers swelled with revenues accumulated from producing agricultural staples on the pampa and trading them in the international marketplace. By 1910 Argentina had become one of the world's great agricultural nations, exporting a higher percentage of its agricultural goods than any other nation in the world.

In the half century since 1860 the area under cultivation was increased from 580,000 hectares to 24 million hectares, on which there was produced

2.850 million tons of wheat, 6.684 million tons of corn, and 938,000 tons of linseed. The railroad network had grown from 10 kilometers to nearly 34,000 kilometers. British investments had increased from £2 million to £450 million. All of this meant prosperity. In 1892 the value of Argentine exports was $257.65 million (m/n or paper pesos); twenty years later it was $1.140 billion (m/n), 90 percent of which came from the agricultural sector. At the beginning of the period fewer than one thousand ships stopped in Buenos Aires in any year; fifty years later the total had risen to nearly ten thousand, making Buenos Aires a major port in the hemisphere, second only to New York.[3]

The growth experience was not without its difficulties. Even as the Argentine people celebrated their centennial, serious social disturbances forced the government to declare a state of siege for several months. Acts of violence were frequent, generally attributed to anarchists and to labor unions attempting to bring the claims of the working class to the attention of the nation's leaders. And even as books were filled with accounts of the glory that was theirs and the glory still to come, a few isolated voices, some even within the ruling elite, attempted to point out that the growth model, so proudly trumpeted by the oligarchy, was in fact not being carried out in several crucial aspects in both the country and the city.

The usual response to such critics was that the "social question," as these problems were called, was the result of nefarious foreign influences, that the wrong sort of immigration had been allowed, and that the crowding and other evidence of social inequalities would be eliminated in due course through the workings of the marketplace. The important thing was to eliminate the antisocial influences from the body politic and allow time for the marvelous healing process of growth and increasing national wealth to solve the social question. Anyone who thought otherwise was antinational. The vast majority accepted the idea that their nation's golden future was guaranteed by the exports of meat, grains, wool, and hides.[4]

The expectations of Argentine greatness were shared by foreign observers. At the end of the century *Harper's Weekly* forecast that Argentina "promises soon to become the greatest wheat producing country in the world."[5] By 1909 it was exporting more grain than any other nation. Four years earlier its meat exports to Great Britain exceeded those by the United States for the first time. Argentina did not produce more than any other country, but it exported a higher portion of its production than any other nation, and by 1910 it had the highest per-capita international trade in the world.

Argentines' projections of their nation's greatness anticipated that they would equal or even surpass the level of material accomplishment of the United States. Former president Domingo F. Sarmiento predicted in 1888, "We shall be America, as the sea is the ocean. We shall be the United States."[6] Just a year later Alois E. Fliess assured the Sociedad Rural Argentina, the nation's leading cattlemen's organization, "that Argentina had material conditions superior to the United States of America, and would some day be greater than that nation."[7] At the end of the centennial Estanislao Zeballos wrote somewhat testily that Argentina was destined to be "the colossus of the southern continent" and therefore did not need any tutelage or help from the United States.[8] Going further, some Argentines felt that they had the same missionary destiny, the same civilizing mission in the other nations of Latin America as the United States asserted for itself in the Caribbean. In 1896 *La Prensa* asserted on behalf of the Argentine nation, "This powerful land is destined to undertake in the southern continent a democratic and humanitarian mission as great as that of the country of Washington."[9]

The nature and the speed of Argentine development during this period often has led to comparisons with the United States and other nations of recent settlement, such as Canada, Australia, and New Zealand. In the case of the United States and Argentina, the comparison is tantalizing. Both had to deal with an internal frontier and used the frontier experience as an integral part of national consolidation. Both attracted large numbers of immigrants to settle their wide open spaces and struggled to assimilate those immigrant masses into their society. Almost unique among the Latin American nations, the population of Argentina was predominantly of European origin. The nature of their populations and the success of their development processes created in both an attitude of exceptionalism many have called manifest destiny—the notion that the nation had a special, predestined role in world affairs, a role that emphasized its influence or potential greatness.[10]

These similarities have led generations of scholars and politicians to compare the historical evolution of the two societies, a comparison that, since 1930, has not been favorable to Argentina. The inevitable question "What went wrong?" is misleading. The similarities to which people have pointed obscure far more the nations' significant differences, which can account for the divergent growth patterns and historical evolutions. The point is not that the nations were different after 1930, but that they were different from the very beginning of their historical development.[11]

The nature of development in the two countries is a function of the timing and the mode of the entry of each into the world system. The United States' insertion came with independence and continued uninterrupted. From the very beginning the state gave strong, unequivocal stimulus to local entrepreneurial efforts that encouraged the accumulation of capital within the country and supported the early articulation of a financial and commercial infrastructure that was in the hands of North Americans and responsive to their needs. This infrastructure was in place even while the United States was a debtor nation, still dependent upon imported capital and immigrant labor for its development.

In addition, as early as the first half of the nineteenth century the United States diversified economic activity into manufacturing, even while its growth was being fueled primarily by the production and export of primary agricultural products, particularly wheat and cotton. This, too, was supported by the state. This diversification made the United States the third largest industrial power in the world by the end of the nineteenth century—a time when the reigning orthodoxy in Argentina was to avoid "artificial" incentives to industry on the grounds that such products could be purchased cheaper and more efficiently from nations specializing in the production and sale of such products.

The transportation network in the United States served to stimulate the growth of an internal market and the incorporation of newly settled territory as well as to facilitate the export of certain products. Where necessary, the state provided incentives to the participation of private capital that ensured the service and interconnection of population centers of whatever size. In Argentina the state provided incentives to railroad builders, but not to connect population centers. The result was a network like the fingers of a human hand, designed to drain from the fertile pampa those exportable foodstuffs in the most effective manner. The railroad was rarely used as the instrument of demographic expansion to consolidate Argentine territorial pretensions, nor was it conceived as a means of integrating the national community. Once the original export economy that had defined the nature of the railroad network had been rendered archaic in the 1930s, the network proved inflexible and unsuited to other stages in the development process, and neither international nor domestic capital was available to make the necessary changes.

But the amazing speed and success of the Argentine insertion into the world economy reinforced the assumptions on which the development project had been based and converted those assumptions into an ideology or orthodoxy that became harder and harder to dispute as the capital and labor poured into the country, and the quantity and value of the nation's exports rose vertiginously. The nation's role in world affairs was understood almost entirely in terms of the free traders' model of the international division of labor. Other nations, presumably better suited to the task, would provide the shipping to move those foodstuffs from Argentine ports to consumers. Others, too, would provide the capital to construct whatever infrastructure might be needed and determine its configuration. With the revenues from the international sales, the nation would purchase whatever might be necessary to improve the production of the primary products or to improve the quality of life of the people who came to live in the country.

The worldview adopted by Argentina as a reflection of its growth and development specifically sought to distance Argentina from the United States and to distinguish as clearly as possible between the national experiences of the two countries. It was not that Argentina set out to compete directly with the United States or to confront U.S. power in the international arena. Rather, Argentine leaders sought to establish for their nation an image, a role, a niche as trading partner of Europe that obviously and deliberately differed from that of the United States. If circumstances brought the two nations together, either in the same forum or the same marketplace, then

Argentina was willing to run counter to the policies or objectives of the United States, should that prove necessary, in order to avoid any semblance of domination by that country and in order to avoid any action that would embarrass their commitments to Europe. Those commitments were perceived as the chief cause of the economic benefits that flowed to Argentina during its period of expansion and as the guarantor of the nation's privileged position in world affairs.

From the perspective of the governing elite in the United States, the rise to world-power status of their nation in the half century after the Civil War did not bring them or the public to think often or hard about Argentina. There were a number of occasions on which the government was sensitive to differences with the Argentine government, and several efforts were made to reduce the structural incompatibilities between the two economies, but Argentina never figured in policy planning or the thinking of the policy elite in the United States to the same degree or in the same manner as the United States figured in the thinking of Argentines. That asymmetry would lead to repeated confrontations and complicate the relations between the two nations even when there were no specific problems or issues dividing them.

Until the Civil War the United States confined its expansionist urges to territories contiguous to its boundaries and on the continent of North America. After the war successive governments sought to project U.S. influence beyond national boundaries and outside the continent.[12] One of the first comprehensive strategic visions of an imperial United States with global responsibilities and opportunities was put forward by Secretary of State William H. Seward. His was the integrated plan, the grand design.[13] He wanted the United States to take possession of 1) Caribbean islands to protect the isthmian trade route to the Pacific, 2) Alaska and the Aleutians to provide an entrée to Asia in the north, and 3) Hawaii to provide a stepping stone to Asia in the south. Of these, we managed to acquire only Alaska.

Little more than a decade later, Naval Captain Alfred Thayer Mahan added a geopolitical or strategic dimension to the grand design for U.S. global expansion. Mahan considered it unthinkable to expand the nation's international trade without planning on the naval strength to protect that trade. Without the naval might to back it up, the nation's export trade would suffer discrimination or even exclusion from foreign markets. Mahan never expressed an interest in what he referred to pejoratively as the European imperialistic desire for territory, but he did spell out the minimum territorial requirements for U.S. access to markets and for coaling stations. These stations were necessary as fuel suppliers to the U.S. Navy, which patroled the seas to defend U.S. trade and to protect what now were called "strategic interests."

Parallel to Mahan's efforts, intellectuals stressed an apocalyptic vision of world history that supported an expansionist foreign policy. Frederick Jackson Turner announced the closing of the frontier as if it were the death knell of civilization as his generation had known it. Brooks Adams warned that unless the country turned overseas to continue its expansion it would run out of energy and soon collapse.

The proponents of empire in the United States put forward a curious combination of faith in social Darwinism and U.S. exceptionalism that harkened back to the Puritan concept of the City on the Hill. John Fiske, Josiah Strong, and others made a moral case for the good expansionism, the good imperialism. Writers and public figures in the United States at the turn of the century displayed a broad consensus in seeing for their country "nothing less than the moral and material leadership of the world."[14]

The global reach of U.S. aspirations was reflected in its naval power, its trade, its missionary zeal, and its sense of manifest destiny. The United States was to form part of a world order in which major states competed for influence or power, and those well advanced on the road to progress were destined to carry the benefits of that progress—civilization—to all areas of the globe.

All the industrialized nations of Europe were engaged in the game being played or attempted to participate as best they could. European nations displayed their power in industrial production, public works, and increasing numbers of larger and larger naval vessels, which represented industrial capacity, technological advances, financial security, and military power. Their construction went along with public pronouncements declaring the will to use these symbols of the nation's power. The diplomacy of the last quarter of the nineteenth century and the first decade of the twentieth focused on the jockeying for advantage among the members of what slowly evolved into two great contending blocs of nations. The rhetoric of competition between the blocs as well as the labyrinthine commitments and arrangements among their members ultimately led to violent conflict, first in the Balkans and then, tragically, throughout Europe.

The consensus in the United States that international trade was vital to the nation's well-being emerged slowly. Few supported Seward's grand design in the 1870s, but time was on his side. U.S. exports increased from $316 million in 1860 to $1.37 million in 1900. Total foreign trade in the 1860s accounted for a fairly low 6.7 percent of gross national product, but by the 1890s it had grown to such significance—per-capita exports increased threefold from 1860 to 1900—that it was impossible to ignore in the political sense. In addition, foreign trade spawned organizations such as the National Association of Manufacturers (1895) to lobby on its behalf, to support it, and to legitimize it in the eyes of the public.

Throughout the 1890s advocates of stimulating international trade as the principal means of ensuring the nation's health and enhancing its influence in the world focused on Latin America and China. Latin America was envisioned as an area of U.S. hegemonic influence, while the best the United States could aspire to in China was equal access, to avoid being excluded by the European and Asian powers that had gotten there first. Trade with Latin America increased from $90 million in 1860 to $300 million in 1900. U.S.

exports to China rose from $4 million in 1890 to $6.9 million in 1896 and to $11.9 million in 1897. Exports to Japan went from $3.9 million in 1894 to $7.6 million in 1896 and $13 million in 1897. By comparison, exports to Argentina at the same time were $4.68 million in 1885, $4.46 million in 1895, and $11.6 million in 1900.

The investment of U.S. capital outside the country was slow to follow trade. The degree of financial involvement in the Western Hemisphere seemed loosely correlated with proximity although distance clearly was not a factor in deterring or stimulating the interest of investors in China. They and their government noted the inferiority of their stake to that of the European powers, especially Great Britian. The first concrete proposal to deal with the threat of European predominance was put forward by Secretary of State James G. Blaine in 1881, although it was frustrated when President Garfield was assassinated and Blaine was forced out of the cabinet.

When he returned to the Department of State in 1889, Blaine was delighted to find that Congress had resurrected his plan for a Pan American Conference and had ordered that invitations be sent to all nations of the hemisphere. The ultimate objective was a customs union that would facilitate trade among the nations of the hemisphere and leave the Europeans in an inferior position. As steps to the desired goal, the U.S. delegation would place before the representatives of the other American republics proposals to establish common weights and measures, a common monetary unit, a juridical mechanism to settle disputes, a transportation network, and a central office or bureau that would collect and disseminate information of interest and value to the membership. Any progress on any of these would improve the position of the United States in the hemisphere vis-à-vis their European competitors. As Andrew Carnegie wrote Secretary of State Blaine, "Let the country be told it will cost money, but that the time has arrived when the republic must . . . secure the greater portion of the trade of its southern neighbors."[15]

The U.S. delegation did not anticipate much debate or any significant opposition to these proposals.[16] They were not prepared for the persistent contrariness of the Argentine delegates who, from the opening session, did their best to scuttle every initiative by the U.S. delegation. Virtually single-handedly the Argentines managed to nullify or reduce to the barest minimum every proposal put before the conference. Through their interventions, which ran the gamut from parliamentary gambits to filibustering, it was patently obvious that they were simply opposed to any multilateral arrangements in which, by virtue of its superior size and power, the United States would have a significant role.

The Argentine delegates to the conference in Washington, Roque Saenz Peña and Manuel Quintana, represented the thinking of the newly consolidated oligarchy that was firmly in power in Buenos Aires. Their speeches during the conference and their later reflections on the experience define clearly and give public expression to the emerging consensus concerning the Argentine position in world affairs and the consequences for the international relations of the nation of its recent insertion in the world market. Just before the centennial, Saenz Peña reflected on this policy to the historian Adolfo Saldías:

> I tell you that to the bottom of my heart—and without intending to alienate us from America, my leanings are toward Europe, in the sense of our cordiality toward the great powers of the Old World, from whom we have nothing to fear and much to hope. This tendency naturally will not prevent continental solidarity if we should be confronted by aggression from Europe; but that is so remote as to be considered impossible in the present state of affairs.[17]

When reflecting on their nation's accomplishments and power, Argentines adopted the language of discourse then in vogue in Europe. They spoke of being "a factor in human affairs" and serving as "a directing force in civilization."[18] It was important to Argentines that they had become or were becoming one of the civilized nations of the world. Through their trade they expected to participate in the march toward progress. As an editorial in *La Nación* put it, "The Argentine Republic now has an established personality in the civilized world. From this moment forward one may say that Argentina will be highly esteemed because we have made known the rich products of our soil, of our industry, and of our intelligence."[19] Repeatedly, Argentine leaders insisted that they must not be lumped in with the other nations of Latin America in the eyes of Europe and that they must not allow themselves to be treated like the nations of Africa and Asia. The aggressive assertion of U.S. hegemony in the hemisphere in the Venezuelan boundary dispute, 1895, and the revolution in Cuba, 1895–98, elicited strong criticism from many Argentines and unequivocal insistence that the nations of South America were different from those of the Caribbean basin.[20] Publicly, the government declared its adherence to the "principles" of international relations—principles that favored the peaceful settlement of disputes between states.[21]

Given the existing pattern of Argentine trade, the widespread attitude toward Europe, and the seemingly divine order of the international division of labor, it should not be surprising that Argentina's leaders reacted with something less than enthusiasm to U.S. efforts to create a Pan American Union and enhance its own influence in the hemisphere through the operations of such an organization. Aside from the fact that the nations appeared to be rivals, the United States did not make any serious effort to improve trade between the two. The protective tariff structure of the United States seemed to operate with particular prejudice against Argentine products. Wool, Argentina's principal export for most of the second half of the nineteenth century, was virtually excluded from the U.S. market. When the

United States sent a trade commission around Latin America in 1884 it stayed only twelve hours in Buenos Aires. Trade between the two nations a year later amounted to 10 million gold pesos, whereas Argentina's trade with Great Britain in 1885 amounted to 48 million gold pesos, out of a total trade of 176 million. That year, more than one thousand steam vessels arrived in Buenos Aires from England or departed from Buenos Aires for British ports.

If U.S. economic diplomacy in dealing with Argentina in the 1880s and 1890s proved ineffective or worse, private business methods were also less than adequate. The U.S. minister frequently lamented that, compared with representatives from the European countries, U.S. businessmen came to Argentina unprepared. They did not know their own products well, they did not know anything about the market in which they wanted to operate, and they did not come willing to offer the short-term credits indispensable to open trade with Argentine customers. To make matters worse, there were no U.S. branch banks in Argentina until 1914 and few direct investments by U.S. capital until the early years of the new century.

Privately, Argentines expressed considerable hostility toward the United States. In January 1909 the United States minister to Argentina, Edward O'Brien, approached Ricardo Pillado, an official in the Ministry of Agriculture and a confidant of President de la Plaza, with an informal inquiry as to how their two nations might improve the trade between them. Pillado's response was scathing, inquiring in a sarcastic tone why the United States purchased goods in Europe it could purchase more cheaply in Argentina. He closed by informing the minister that if the United States wanted to improve relations, all it had to do was buy more from Argentina.[22] When Theodore Roosevelt visited Buenos Aires after his presidency in 1910 he was lionized publicly, but privately many Argentines took his visit as the occasion to express their disdain for the United States. The writer María Rosa Oliver, then a young girl, was much taken by the charismatic Roosevelt, although she found him ugly. When she expressed her opinion, her grandfather chided her, shouting, "Don't you know that those people want to swallow us?"[23]

After 1895 U.S. exporters appeared to take more interest in the Argentine market. Not by accident, Argentine exports to the United States increased significantly for a few years at the end of the decade when the duty on wool was cut. This era of commercial goodwill culminated in the years just prior to World War I when, in 1913, the U.S. tariff was amended to allow the import of Argentine beef, including chilled beef, the most profitable of the Argentine exports. U.S. exports also increased that year, as did direct investments. In 1914 the first U.S. branch bank was opened in Buenos Aires. These were the natural relations of which Saenz Peña and Quintana had spoken in Washington twenty-five years earlier. The war aborted this beginning, so it is impossible to say what might have happened had trade between the two countries continued to expand.

Argentine foreign policy remained remarkably coherent and consistent throughout the prewar period of rapid economic expansion. That policy, which asserted as the nation's highest priority the maintenance of fluid and open commercial ties to its natural markets in Europe, implied potential conflict with the United States. Curiously, that conflict was not understood in the terms normally used to describe interstate rivalry. The nation's leaders assumed that successful execution of the policy would lead inevitably to the nation's achievement of greatness and recognition as an international power or player. This is curious because, having demonstrated on innumerable occasions that they understood the European discourse on the nature of national power and its use, Argentine leaders never worked to provide their nation with the universally recognized symbols of that power, nor did they attempt to project Argentine influence on the global scale, in competitive terms. When they complained of a lack of maritime connections between ports in the United States and Argentina, they asked the U.S. government to provide the subsidies necessary to create such a link. They never proposed building their own merchant marine or providing subsidies for vessels bearing the Argentine flag to carry Argentine products to ports in the United States, or anywhere else. Argentine leaders aspired to greatness and to influence in world affairs but refused to compete with the other great powers on the usual terms. As a consequence, the Argentine view of world affairs became unrealistic even as it became entrenched in the thinking of the nation's leaders.[24]

The principal index of progress among the civilized nations in the decades prior to World War I was industrial capacity. And yet the Argentine government deliberately and repeatedly rejected all proposals to diversify the economy through the development of national industries. It also refused to face the very serious issue of the persistent cyclical illiquidity of the agricultural economy. The liquidity necessary for the successful functioning of the economy was provided by British and other European banks. Efforts to create Argentine banks that could provide the necessary liquidity and thus facilitate the process of capital accumulation in Argentina were systematically rejected by the oligarchy. In this and in countless other ways, the thinking of Argentine leaders on how greatness was measured and appreciated appeared strangely out of step with that of the rest of the world. They recognized that the European nations were powerful because of their industrial and financial capacity as well as their military might, and that even the United States had become great through the acquisition of these characteristics or capacities. But they did not consider it necessary for Argentina to acquire coaling stations for its navy or to build a navy to protect its trade. They assumed that trade would be protected by the self-interest of the buyers, who included the most powerful nations in the world. They never had a global sense of their national interest.

The confidence with which Argentine leaders contemplated the workings of the international system appears to have been a consequence of the timing of their insertion into the international market and the dizzying speed with which they had established their niche in it. They were left with an almost religious faith in the international division of labor, which they expected to increase their wealth and, somehow, to create for them a role in the international arena no less significant than that of the United States or of any of the other major powers. How this was to come to pass was not discussed during the period. Even opponents of the regime and those few critics of the liberal growth model failed to deal explicitly with this problem.

Exemplary of Argentina's curious methods for acquiring influence in world affairs is the campaign to buy—not build—modern naval vessels. The decision in 1908 to buy two Dreadnaughts for the Argentine navy at a time when the country had virtually no merchant marine was the manner in which Argentine leaders adapted the rules of the international power game to their perspective and to their understanding of the nation's strategic interests.[25] The timing and the nature of the Argentine arms buildup was a reaction to developments in Brazil. For a brief period, between 1906 and 1909, the two nations engaged in an arms race and a rhetorical escalation that brought them to the brink of war, just as the European nations were competing with one another and would soon go to the brink of hostilities and then cross beyond the brink. But Argentina backed away from the confrontation, and refused to participate in a regional or continental balance of power. They considered theirs to be a European role and refused to define their international status in terms of their relations with other American states.

At no time in the debate over the naval arms race did the influential public in Argentina propose or contemplate the use of the naval power to open new markets to Argentine products or to force access to coaling stations in far-flung oceans so that Argentine trade would be assured of naval escort. Estanislao Zeballos was a prominent exception to this consensus, appealing repeatedly for an assertive foreign policy. He attempted to proselytize his colleagues among the oligarchy on behalf of an expansionist policy, a policy that would place Argentina among the civilized, imperialistic nations of the world on the same terms as the United States was being accepted and was participating in world affairs. Zeballos wanted to accumulate economic and military power for Argentina and use that power to make explicit the nation's influence over its neighbors and throughout Latin America. He told British Ambassador Sir Reginald Tower that Argentina would absorb Uruguay and Paraguay and that Brazil did not have the power to prevent it.[26] His voice, while not totally alone, found little echo.[27]

Although Zeballos served in the cabinet of three different presidents and enjoyed the confidence and friendship of powerful members of the oligarchy, including Saenz Peña, he never managed to bring any other major figure to his way of thinking. Zeballos's writings and his correspondence make it impossible to sustain the argument that the generation of 1880 was oblivious to events that did not touch directly upon trade with Europe or that they did not understand the implications of power politics. They did. They chose consciously and deliberately to follow a line of policy that would keep Argentina at the margin of the international power struggle. And, yet, many indicated their belief in a strong nation. That was their error and the fundamental error of Argentine foreign policy in the twentieth century: to aspire to the exercise of power in world affairs and to insist on the recognition of its role as a powerful and influential nation when it had little power and scant influence.

Argentines did not want the reponsibilities of world power. They did not want to take up the white man's burden in Africa or Asia. Quite a few appeared willing to shoulder it in South America, but all but a very few backed away immediately when asked to deal with the consequences of such a posture as in the conflict with Brazil. They confided in the support and even the protection of the European powers who were their best customers. That support or protection, they believed, would come to them when necessary in order to preserve the international division of labor that benefited their customers as much as it benefited them. In this way, the oligarchy constructed the relations of dependency that would distort their nation's development for the next century. Even in this early period it is clear that the Europeans did not expect Argentina to become a world power, in the sense that the United States had been admitted into the club. The British, who maintained the most intense relations with Argentina, revealed in their foreign policy that they expected Argentina to remain a faithful supplier and market, a role that assured Argentina the status of subordinate in the international scheme of things. Argentines did not see their role in the same light.

In a sense, the Argentine oligarchy was prepared to march slightly out of step with the other nations of the Western world, but they believed that such a position would not prejudice their security, their prestige, or their national interests. It almost certainly would bring them into conflict with the United States, but they believed that the confrontation would be held within acceptable limits, deferred by their own growing power in the marketplace or by their European customers and natural allies. Until that time, Argentine policy would be directed toward frustrating U.S. ambitions in South America and preventing any hemispheric projects that might compromise Argentine commitments to Europe and the international division of labor. The war in Europe would demonstrate painfully the limits of such a policy by exposing the extent of Argentine dependence within the international market, the new power of the United States, and the considerable costs of confronting the United States in a situation in which the colossus of the north was disposed to use its overwhelming power.

NOTES

1. Miguel Angel Cárcano, *Saenz Peña: La Revolución por los Comicios* (Buenos Aires: Talleres Gráficos Cepeda, 1963), 8; my translation.

2. For a sample of the most useful works on Argentine development see Carlos F. Díaz Alejandro, *Essays on the Economic History of the Argentine Republic* (New Haven, Conn.: Yale University Press, 1970); Laura Randall, *An Economic History of Argentina in the Twentieth Century* (New York: Columbia University Press, 1978); and Aldo Ferrer, *The Argentine Economy* (Berkeley: University of California Press, 1967).

3. Data from Alejandro, *Essays,* 436–41 and 475, and from *Banco de la Nación Argentina en su Cincuentenario* (Buenos Aires: Guillermo Kraft, 1941), 368.

4. James R. Scobie, *Argentina* (New York: Oxford University Press, 1964), 123. On the social question see J. L. Romero, *A History of Argentine Political Thought* (Stanford, Calif.: Stanford University Press, 1963); and Carl Solberg, *Immigration and Nationalism* (Austin: University of Texas Press, 1970).

5. Cited in Thomas F. McGann, *Argentina, the United States and the Inter-American System* (Cambridge, Mass.: Harvard University Press, 1957), 128.

6. Cited in ibid., 61.

7. Cited in ibid., 61.

8. *Revista de Derecho, Historia, y Letras* 8, no. 31 (1910). On the concept of progress in Argentina see R. Cortés Conde, *El Progreso Argentino, 1880–1914* (Buenos Aires: Sudamericana, 1979), and N. R. Botana, *El Orden Conservador* (Buenos Aires: Sudamericana, 1977).

9. Cited in McGann, *Argentina,* 197.

10. Roberto Cortés Conde, "Some Notes on the Industrial Development of Argentina and Canada in the 1920s," *Serie Documentos de Trabajo* 120 (Buenos Aires: Instituto T. DiTella, 1986); John Fogarty, Ezequiel Gallo, and Héctor Dieguez, eds., *Argentina y Australia* (Buenos Aires: Instituto T. DiTella, 1979).

11. To sample the hand-wringing literature see Tomás Roberto Fillol, *Social Factors in Economic Development. The Argentine Case* (Cambridge, Mass.: MIT Press, 1961); Centro de Estudios Nacionales, *Introducción a los problemas nacionales* (Buenos Aires: Centro de Estudios Nacionales, 1965); Álvaro C. Alsogaray, *Bases para la acción política futura* (Buenos Aires: Editorial Atlantida, 1969); and Juan C. de Pablo, *Macroeconomia. Replanteo del enfoque convencial: la problemática argentina y latino-americana* (Buenos Aires: Amorrortu editores, 1973).

12. The literature on U.S. expansion is vast. For a variety of perspectives see Milton Plesur, *America's Outward Thrust. Approaches to Foreign Affairs, 1865–1890* (DeKalb: Northern Illinois University Press, 1971); Walter LaFeber, *The New Empire. An Interpretation of American Expansion, 1800–1898* (Ithaca, N.Y.: Cornell University Press, 1963); Foster Rhea Dulles, *Prelude to World Power. American Diplomatic History, 1860–1900* (New York: Macmillan, 1965); and Ernest R. May, *American Imperialism. A Speculative Essay* (New York: Atheneum, 1968).

13. LaFeber, *The New Empire,* 15–25.

14. David F. Healy, *The United States in Cuba, 1898–1902* (Madison: University of Wisconsin Press, 1963), 247.

15. Cited in McGann, *Argentina,* 128.

16. The best discussion of the conference and of the entire period from the Argentine perspective is McGann, *Argentina,* passim. For other views see Russell H. Bastert, "A New Approach to the Origins of Blaine's Pan-American Policy," *Hispanic American Historical Review* [HAHR] 39 (August 1959); "Diplomatic Reversal: Fre-

linghuysen's Opposition to Blaine's Pan-American Policy in 1882," *Mississippi Valley Historical Review* (March 1965); and Plesur, *America's Outward Thrust.*

17. Saenz Peña to Saldías, 21 August 1908, AGN, Archivo Saldías, 3-6-10; my translation. Unless otherwise noted, all translations in this chapter are mine.

18. *La Prensa,* 5 August 1914, 5:5, and Saenz Peña to de la Plaza, 20 November 1908, AGN, Archivo Saenz Peña, 22-21-15.

19. 30 October 1889, cited in McGann, *Argentina,* 119.

20. *La Prensa,* 18 December 1895, cited in McGann, *Argentina,* quoting former president Julio Roca, p. 184. See also Hebe M. García de Bargero, "Repercusión en la república argentina de la controversia entre estados unidos y gran bretaña, acerca de la frontera entre venezuela y la guayana" (Córdoba: V Jornadas de Historia y Literatura Argentina y Norteamericana, 1970), and Ricardo Caillet-Bois and Ernesto Annecou, "La política argentina y el conflicto hispano-norteamericano en 1898" (Mendoza: III Jornadas de Historia y Literatura Argentina y Norteamericana, 1968).

21. Carlos Escudé refers to this posture as *principismo* and considers it to have had a negative effect on Argentine foreign policy for the past century (*La Argentina ¿Paria Internacional?* [Buenos Aires: Belgrano, 1984]).

22. Pillado to O'Brien, 28 January 1910, AGN, Archivo de la Plaza, 4-6-1.

23. María Rosa Oliver, *La Vida Cotidiana* (Buenos Aires: Sudamericana, 1969, 15.

24. Carlos Escudé argues that Canada, Australia, Switzerland, and other nations participate effectively in international affairs without the trappings of power. The difference is that they do not delude themselves concerning their influence or power. The problem, says Escudé, resides in the unrealistic goals set by Argentine leaders and the illusory effects of their reliance upon *principismo* (personal communication with the author, 25 July 1988).

25. Robert N. Burr, in *By Reason or Force: Chile and the Balancing of Power in South America, 1830–1905* (Berkeley: University of California Press, 1967) and "The Balance of Power in 19th Century Latin America," *HAHR* 35, no. 1 (1955), suggests that Argentina focused on a regional power struggle because it was too weak to participate in a global balance of power and that the same was true for Chile and Brazil. At the same time, the European powers were prevented from dominating South America politically. Thus South American nations were in a position to assume roles with relation to one another that they could not play with any hope of success on a world stage. Although this is probably correct and a realistic analysis of the limited potential of the South American states, there is no evidence that the Argentine leaders consciously adopted policies designed as adaptations to their power level or their geographical area of patterns of thinking or action adopted by European powers on a world stage.

26. See Tower's no. 93, 9 December 1911, in Public Record Office, Foreign Office 371/1295, file 971.

27. For Zeballos's view of the events, see his letter to Saenz Peña, 27 June 1908, AGN, Archivo Saenz Peña, 22-2-14. A different view is Cárcano, *Saenz Peña* 224–25. Support for the mission is in Saenz Valiente, chief of naval operations, to Saenz Peña, 11 August 1910, and Juan P. Gomez to Saenz Peña, 12 August 1910, both in AGN, Archivo Saenz Peña, 22-2-18.

chapter 3

WORLD WAR I

The Great War was a devastating shock to the international system. Faith in the underlying concepts of reason, civilization, progress, and the free exchange of goods in the marketplace were shattered by events. Many hoped that the broad oceans would protect the nations in the Americas from the contagion of intrigue that had led to the outbreak of hostilities and the brutal carnage that ensued. All the nations of the hemisphere declared their neutrality in the conflict and consulted among themselves, informally, as to how best to protect the rights of neutrals in a modern war.

In the case of the United States, modern technology in combination with the extraordinary cost of the conflict and the significance in the world economy of the nation's financial and industrial resources made strict neutrality all but impossible. Within a year, the British turned to the United States for the capital to pay for its war effort, quickly converting the United States from one of the world's great debtors to its principal creditor. In another year, the British fleet was totally dependent on U.S. petroleum to remain afloat. The Anglo-American interpretation of the rules of neutrality allowed the free flow of capital, petroleum, and industrial goods. The Germans, whose surface fleet was not a factor in the war after the battle of Scapa Flow, relied upon submarine warfare to alter the role of the United States, preferring to risk inciting a declaration of war by the United States to allowing the continuation of a situation that almost certainly would lead to their defeat.[1]

Argentines expected that the significance of their foodstuffs in the world economy would cause the combatants to do whatever might be necessary to maintain the flow of meat and grains from the pampa. The war, however, shifted the relations of power between the United States and Great Britain, irrevocably altering Argentina's position in the international system. After 1918 U.S. hegemony would extend throughout South America as the British proved incapable of maintaining the role they had assumed during the period of Argentina's rapid growth.

After the initial shock of the news wore off, most Argentines looked upon the outbreak of war in Europe as a great opportunity. Editorialists for the major Argentine newspapers thought that the British, who quickly demonstrated their naval dominance and capacity to interrupt merchant traffic, would allow Argentine trade with Germany to continue uninterrupted because it was not in British interests to hurt Argentine trade.[2] Indeed, it appears that the British thought that way for a while at the beginning of the war. The Board of Trade argued that rigorous enforcement of the enemy trading restrictions on the neutrals, especially on Argentina, would do more harm than good. That view held for about a year until, toward the end of 1915, the Foreign Office and Board of Trade agreed that the pressures of the war were such that strict enforcement was imperative, even if it did hurt Argentine trade.[3] Argentines did not react. Even when the first imperial preferences were actually put into effect in 1918, the Argentine consul general in London, J. García Uriburu, assured the foreign minister that the British could not possibly cut the Argentines out of their trade.[4]

Those in charge of the daily operations of the Argentine government felt the impact of the war immediately, as they were unable to fill orders for machinery or other goods required to carry out the mandate of their ministries. They turned to Foreign Minister José Luis Murature for help. His response was to instruct the ambassador in Washington, Rómulo Naón, to make every effort to stimulate trade with the United States and to encourage people in the United States to invest their capital in Argentina. The lack of capital was particularly frustrating and led the government to take an uncharacteristic, positive approach to the Pan-American Financial Conference called by the United States in Washington in 1915.[5]

But this overture toward the United States was fraught with ambivalence. No one in the government looked with favor on the prospect of U.S. penetration, and several important groups remained implacably hostile to any policy that favored the United States at the expense of the nation's traditional ties, despite the fact that those ties were strained by the war. On more than one occasion, Murature had to curb the enthusiasm of Naón, who became a strong advocate of closer relations to the United States during his tenure as ambassador.

On balance, and compared to his predesessors, Murature maintained a positive stance on cooperation with the United States, despite strong negative pressure from domestic groups. He encouraged Naón to engage in discussions with other representatives of American states in Washington of a possible common defense of their neutral rights. He encouraged public discussion of a proposal to declare a nonbelligerency zone around the hemisphere by extending neutral rights to all inter-American trade. He engaged regularly and without hesitation in conversations with the U.S. ambasssador dealing with technical questions arising from the testing of neutral rights. He even indicated his willingness to use the Pan-American Union to defend neutral rights. Most extraordinary of all, he joined his Brazilian and Chilean colleagues in mediating the dispute between the United States and Mexico, at the Niagara Falls Conference in 1915. His purpose was to strengthen neutral rights through an act of Latin American solidarity and increase Latin American influence while diminishing their dependence on the United States.

Although the Niagara Falls mediation was successful, its impact on Argentine policy was ephemeral. It was an approach that won few supporters among the political groups in Argentina and would not again be repeated until the early days of World War II.[6] One of the nation's most influential specialists in international law, Carlos A. Becú, published an extended pamphlet to denounce the entire effort and ridicule the Pan-American movement, even though he, too, recognized that the mediation "marked the entry onto the world stage of a new force."[7] This may be one of the reasons Becú was chosen by President-elect Hipólito Yrigoyen in 1916 to be the first foreign minister in the new Radical government. One of Becú's first acts as minister was to instruct Naón to have nothing to do with the Pan-American Union because the organization was dominated by the United States.[8] At the same time, a few members of the oligarchy, including former President Roca, feared the United States might look upon Argentina as a candidate for intervention, much like Mexico, if the election of a Radical led to internal chaos.[9]

The advocates of progress were the most optimistic in their appraisal of the opportunity presented by the war. Members of the Club de Progreso and the Unión Industrial Argentina saw the interruption of normal patterns of trade as a blessing. It would provide Argentina with the opportunity to diversify its economy, establish an industrial base, and finish putting together all the elements necessary to make Argentina the great nation everyone anticipated it should become. In a more traditional manner, the Argentine representative in Rio de Janeiro saw the difficulties that Europe's war occasioned in that country and reported gleefully that Argentina could take over the Brazilian market and assert its preeminence in South America through trade. The representative did not make clear where Argentina was going to get the goods with which to supply the Brazilian market.[10]

The war proved to be a deceptive opportunity. The optimism felt in Buenos Aires in August 1914 soon faded in the face of disturbing shortages and even more disturbing decisions by the British and the Allies to cut supplies to the neutrals in order to assure supply of their own armies. The first bitter realization that Argentina was not as important in the calculations of the British as Argentines had anticipated came at the end of November when the streetlights of Buenos Aires had to be dimmed because of a lack of coal to keep the power turbines going. Two years later fuel for electricity and heat would become an obsession with the porteños, and the fate of shipments of firewood from the north was the subject of daily front-page headlines.

Fuel was just the first problem, not the last nor the most serious. By the middle of 1915 the Allies had begun to restrict shipping to neutrals, and the German submarines threatened what little tonnage was allowed to make the long journey from Buenos Aires to channel ports. This puzzled and infuriated the Argentines.[11] The disillusionment was sharpened by the fact that the United States appeared to be prospering at the expense of the combatants and the neutrals. Even *La Nación*—voice of the cattle fatteners, mouthpiece for de la Plaza in foreign policy matters, the most optimistic of the major papers—noted that the situation was not what it might be. Despite this note of doubt, the paper held tenaciously to the view that the nation's problems were temporary and would be solved by the *industrias madres* and by the workings of the international market. Their faith, and that of a majority of the National Congress, that the nation's economic problems were temporary and self-correcting, was unshakable.[12]

The problems presented by shipping and fuel raised for the first time in public debate the question of Argentina's economic dependence. No one denied that the war had pointed out some embarrassing weaknesses in the Argentine model and that external control was a threat to national sovereignty, but there was no agreement over the appropriate response to the dilemma. As the war dragged on, it became increasingly obvious that Argentina was dependent upon decisions taken in London or Berlin and, after February 1917, in Washington. Particularly annoying was the fact that decisionmakers in those capitals did not appear to take Argentine interests much into account in formulating their policies.

The wartime lessons of dependence, already clear to some, were driven home after the United States entered the war. Now, decisions on what ships would visit Argentine ports, what strategic materials would be allowed to go to Argentina, and what materials would be shipped from Argentina were made by the alphabet soup of war boards that met in Washington.[13]

The problem of shipping is a good case to illustrate the progression of Argentine thinking on their dependence during the war and the way in which the growth model, so deeply entrenched, inhibited policy innovations. Argentina had little merchant tonnage of its own and most of that was restricted to the coastal trade. Discussion of the issue before the war was limited to modest proposals by advocates of progress, such as Estanislao Zeballos and Ricardo Pillado, for enhancing the coastal shipping capacity. No plan to build the nation's own merchant marine was put forward. In 1913 Pillado managed to place a bill before the National Congress to strengthen the coastal shipping fleet. The bill died in committee. The chairman of the congressional committee commented that Argentina didn't need its own merchant marine because the transport of Argentina's exports was a job for the maritime nations of the world, which would do a better job and at a lower cost than Argentina could. Sudden, sharp increases in cargo rates, such as had occurred during the British coal strike of 1912, and as would occur again after August 1914, were the result of temporary aberrations to be solved over time to Argentina's advantage by the natural actions of the market. The iron laws of the international division of labor indicated that Argentina should stick to producing foodstuffs.[14]

The problem became so acute during the war that, in 1917, a number of people advocated the acquisition of a national merchant marine in order to guarantee the nation's economic independence.[15] Few spoke against the measure, and yet it aroused little enthusiasm. Perhaps people realized it was too late. There was no tonnage available on the market, and Argentina didn't have the liquid capital necessary to buy it even if it had been available. The fact that the United States seized the opportunity to build a merchant fleet and dominate hemispheric carrying trade disturbed some congressmen but not enough to get the bill out of committee.

The shipping problem was only one of many that brought about a domestic consensus that Argentina was unprepared to take advantage of the opportunity presented by the war, no matter how that might be interpreted. Another shortcoming was the lack of a professional diplomatic and consular service.[16] The deficiencies in the diplomatic corps became more evident and painful after the outbreak of war because the activities of the combatants made virtually all international activities state-to-state relations. Keeping up with the increasingly complex web of wartime regulations laid down by the combatants expanded the sphere of international relations and threatened the relaxed, gentlemanly, unprofessional style in which the nation had conducted its international affairs. Foreign policy, per se, was becoming a matter of concern to the entire government bureaucracy.[17]

Murature tried to minimize the demands on his ministry and on the nation's diplomatic corps by adhering to as strict a concept of neutrality as he could.[18] But his cautious legalism alone could not extricate the Argentine government and its citizens from the difficult situations the war created. When the British seized the *President Mitre*, flying the Argentine flag, in international waters off the Argentine coast, it was an unacceptable affront to Argentine sovereignty, and Murature demanded an apology and full explanation from the British. Privately, he admitted that he was powerless, for Argentina was not about to declare war on the British. Moreover, his legal adviser found considerable merit in the British claims against the ship and its cargo, bound for Germany. Murature accepted the British terms for release of the vessel and trumpeted the great success of his administration in defending Argentine sovereignty. The opposition press railed in anger against the sellout and shameful trampling of the nation's pride.[19]

The British blacklist of enemy firms presented the Argentine government with much the same dilemma. Frequent complaints were lodged with the government, and Murature himself considered the concept of a blacklist to be an outrageous interference in Argentina's domestic affairs. He tried, without success, to get other Latin American nations to join him in protesting its application in the region. Again, he admitted privately that Argentina had limited recourse and instructed the nation's representatives in London to present their protests with extreme caution and tact.[20] It turns out that Murature's protests did not fall on deaf ears. The Foreign Office realized that it had made a mistake in treading clumsily on the national pride of a friendly neutral and vowed to exert every effort to be more considerate in the future. Argentine trade was important to Britain, although not as crucial to the war effort as the goods and capital coming from the United States, and not nearly as important as the Argentines believed.[21]

Whereas most Argentines preferred to wait out the war patiently, believing that the world would return to normal at its conclusion and that their country would resume its certain rise to international power and influence, there was no such passivity in the United States. For the first time, attention was focused specifically on Argentina as a challenge and opportunity. More generally, the United States hoped to replace the Germans as suppliers and investers throughout Latin America. Government leaders and businessmen realized that Britain was entrenched in Argentina and that it would be a special case, but they were enthusiastic about trying. The government came to the service of the private sector, largely as a result of the wartime conditions and partly to take advantage more efficiently of the vast Latin American market. From 1914 to 1916 trade with Argentina increased from $95 million to $302 million and would continue to increase throughout the war.

Just as in Argentina, the United States' governance of international affairs became infinitely more complicated because of the war. The State Department was less successful than its Argentine counterpart in coordinating the new activities for several reasons. First, Secretary of State William J. Bryan was not an administrator with a strong sense of territorial imperative. Second, the scale of United States' activities was so vast and so complex that coordination and control were difficult under the best of circumstances. Finally, until his reelection in 1916, President Woodrow Wilson's preoccupation with Mexico made it hard for the State Department to exercise any real authority over economic or commercial intercourse with Argentina.

During the war two significant changes occurred in the way in which the United States perceived international affairs and, more specifically, in its relations with Latin America. Both changes would affect U.S. relations with Argentina, and both were the result of U.S. experiences during the war, first as a neutral and then as a combatant. The first change was the extension of the definition of strategic interest beyond the limits laid down by Alfred Thayer Mahan nearly thirty years earlier. The United States decided that it was vital to the national interest to maintain under U.S. control, private or public, adequate supplies of fuel required by the navy and a communications network free of foreign control. It also decided to avoid financial commitments that would compromise U.S. security. The second change, a corollary to the first, was the greatly expanded geographic scope of U.S. strategic interests. The fuel resources would or could come from any place in the world, but the United States would do everything within its power to make sure that foreign powers did not control fuel resources within the Western Hemisphere. The communications network should be global, but at the very least it must reach throughout the hemisphere. And no foreign power should be allowed to use financial pressure to undermine the sovereignty of an American nation and thereby threaten the security of the United States. These changes were made when the United States was neutral and took clear shape when it became a combatant, and it was in this later period that the expanded definition of U.S. strategic interest clashed with the new administration of Hipólito Yrigoyen, who was in the process of defining a more nationalistic posture in world affairs for Argentina.[22]

The Yrigoyen administration was as carefully neutral as its predecessor in its dealings with the combatants. The government was determined to maintain the vital commercial links with England, but it was not willing to have its national interests sacrificed by either of the warring parties. From the perspective of bureaucratic politics, the continuity across the two administrations was remarkable. The professional staff of the Foreign Ministry remained the same, with the single exception of the new subsecretario, Diego Luis Molinari, a young, energetic member of Yrigoyen's party, the UCR, who enjoyed great influence over Yrigoyen's foreign policies. Similarly, the principal diplomatic posts were not altered. The Ministry's legal advisers, who prepared briefs for the subsecretario and the minister on all matters of policy, remained the same and followed the same logic as they had since August 1914, whether they were dealing doggedly with the British to secure coal for the German-owned electric company, or with the Germans in securing an apology and the promise of reparations for the sinking of the *Monte Protegido*, *Toro*, and *Oriana*.[23] If anything, the foreign ministry after 1916 betrayed a slightly greater disposition to take umbrage against the imperious tone adopted by the representatives of the British government and to lodge slightly stiffer complaints against the application of the blacklist to Argentine firms. These minor changes might well have been a function of growing impatience in the face of repeated insults to national pride.[24]

The German declaration of unrestricted submarine warfare in January 1917 created a difficult situation for the Argentine government. From the moment they had taken office, the Radicals had exerted every effort to distinguish themselves from their predecessors, to whom they referred scathingly as the oligarchy or the regimen. The neutrality policy of the de la Plaza administration they described as "passive." The new government would adopt an active policy, defending the principles of Argentine policy and Argentine interests with vigor. Emboldened by these public declarations, the U.S. government invited the Argentines to join them in protesting the German note. Ambassador Naón warmly endorsed the U.S. proposal, and Ambassador Stimson went directly to the president to urge him to join with his government in denouncing this latest threat to the rights of neutrals. Whether it was because he sensed that the United States was on a collision course with Germany for reasons of its own or because of his deep distrust for the United States, Yrigoyen told Stimson that as much as he admired the stance taken by President Wilson, the differences in geographical, commercial, and political situations between the two countries would necessarily lead Argentina to make a different response to the German government.[25]

This posture caused expressions of dissatisfaction in Washington and in the Allied capitals. It also caused widespread confusion among the staff of the ministry, who were at a loss as to how to apply the policy implied in the president's statement. It led to consternation among the senior members of the diplomatic corps, who expressed their discrepancies with their government's policies.[26] The confusion and consternation only increased when, in response to the United States' declaration of war in April, Yrigoyen sent Wilson an effusive telegram praising the moral strength of his actions, while maintaining the stance that Argentina's different circumstances would determine a different action. This was the policy of *principismo*—following principle rather than mere interest.[27] The U.S. government did not hide its displeasure at what they took to be an evasive response, and one that some State Department officers took to be confirmation of rumors of the new government's pro-German leanings.

Yrigoyen never was pro-German. At the same time he was praising Wilson's note to the Germans, he was approving a stiff note to Berlin demanding an apology, full reparations, and a salute to the Argentine flag for sinking the *Monte Protegido*. He got everything he asked for. Two months later, on 22 June 1917, a German submarine sank the *Toro*. Again, the Argentine government demanded a full apology and reparations. This time, the Germans were slow to respond. Molinari prepared the text of an ultimatum delivered through Minister Molina, in Berlin. He also prepared the text of a declaration of a severance of relations, and secured the president's approval of it, to be made public if the German government did not provide Molina with the specified apology within a matter of days.[28]

Having made his point and having won public confirmation of Argentine sovereignty, Yrigoyen pulled back from the brink of hostilities with Germany. When the *Oriana* was sunk in July, and the cables of the German Minister Luxburg were published in which he called Foreign Minister Pueyrredón "a notorious ass and an anglophile," Yrigoyen rejected the arguments of his legal advisers and refused to make either incident the pretext for the escalation of tension.[29] The same month the Argentine government behaved in a most unneutral fashion by accepting a lengthy visit from a U.S. naval squadron under Admiral Caperton, during which the government declared itself to be "morally identified with the international attitude of the government in Washington."[30] The U.S. government was grateful for the reception accorded Caperton, but officials in Washington took Yrigoyen's rhetoric with a grain of salt.

Yrigoyen's rhetorical and administrative style represent a dilemma for the historian. Taken at face value, they suggest a significant departure in Argentine foreign policy—an aggressive posture in relations with nations outside Latin America and a definite nationalistic trend in the approach to foreign affairs. Specific actions that mark this trend include his call for an American organization without the United States, his public declaration of a need for a national merchant marine, and his stated desire to have Argentina exploit its own petroleum reserves. His administration consistently set itself against U.S. pretensions of leadership in hemispheric affairs, especially after the United States entered the war. Yrigoyen shared the deep-seated distrust of the United States common among members of the oligarchy.

At the same time, it is just as clear that Yrigoyen never attempted to alter the basic pattern of Argentine dependence upon Great Britain, either in its international or in its internal facets. He accepted the assumptions underlying the traditional growth model and the foreign policy derived from it, despite the painful lessons concerning Argentine dependence that were taught by the war. During the public discussion of the sale of the wheat harvest to the Allies, *La Época* commented that no commercial treaties with European nations were necessary because "Europe needs Argentine products and European markets are the most convenient for Argentine trade."[31] A month later the government rolled out the red carpet to welcome a trade mission from the United Kingdom headed by Sir Maurice de Bunsen of the Board of Trade and described the relationship between the two nations in terms reminiscent of Saenz Peña or Roca, twenty years earlier: "The Bensen [sic] mission has highlighted the position in the world conquered by our republic, a position conquered by its impartial and measured conduct in world affairs. The good relations between Great Britain and Argentina are the result of reciprocal benefit."[32] Even when the British cabinet discussed an imperial preference scheme that would discriminate against Argentine products, the Argentines concluded that there was no cause for alarm, as there would be a market for their products in Great Britain "for many years to come."[33] After the war Foreign Minister Pueyrredón expressed the government's desire to return to the status quo ante in encouraging British investments in Argentina.[34]

In his attitude toward Argentina's position in world affairs and in his hostility toward the United States, Yrigoyen was a traditionalist. His specific projects to reduce Argentine external dependence, which, together with his exalted rhetoric, form the basis for the case made for him as a strong nationalist, came to nothing. The conference of neutrals excluding the United States was a failure. The administration did not even pursue its original invitation. The bills for a merchant marine were never pushed even when the UCR enjoyed a majority in the National Congress. The party leaders in the legislature evinced no interest in the project. The desire to protect the nation's natural resources, central to the nationalist platforms in many Latin American nations, was not taken up with energy during the president's term in office.

To a U.S. observer, Yrigoyen's idealism appears similar to Wilsonianism, with the principal difference being that his assertions were not directly connected to the projection of his nation's power beyond its borders. In fact, Yrigoyen's code of conduct was derived from his personal beliefs, not from any faith in a specific political system or form of government. He was a follower of Karl Krause, the German philosopher who had been widely influential among Spanish republican intellectuals at the end of the nineteenth century. Krause expressed the belief in the divine presence in all human acts. He argued that individuals were bound by moral obligations and love, and that peoples were united by the same principles as individuals. International peace would be achieved by the successful projection of these moral values into the relations between states. The few public pronouncements by Yrigoyen on international affairs reveal these spiritualist convictions. His followers, then and since, insist that he pointed out a new way for nations to solve their problems, by insisting that morality must be the basis for such relations. They also claim that this moral posture was the first assertion of Argentine nationalism, rejecting dependence upon the United States and enhancing the nation's prestige in world affairs.[35] But if we put aside Yrigoyen's rhetoric, his Krausismo is very similar to the *principismo* asserted by Saenz Peña and other conservative leaders. Except in style, he was a traditionalist in his view of Argentina's position in world affairs.

Foreign observers did not know what to make of Yrigoyen's rhetorical flourishes. At best, they considered him an idealist, which was not a complimentary description in the thinking of European diplomats. Sir Maurice de Bunsen summarized the consensus among foreign observers:

> It is impossible to speak with certainty regarding Yrigoyen's true sentiments. . . . My impression, which I believe agrees with Sir Reginald Tower, is that he has never realized the vast importance of the issues of the war; that he is profoundly ignorant on foreign affairs; and that he cares only for social questions. . . . Very likely President Yrigoyen now wishes he had taken up a distinctly pro-Ally attitude and finds it difficult to "evolve" in that direction.[36]

The British and United States officials most informed about Argentina agreed with this view.[37]

As the war drew to a close, Argentine protestations of pro-Allied sympathies became more and more frequent, as if there was an uneasy sense that having remained neutral would have a political cost after the war. The protestations in *La Época* were expressed in a tone of hurt pride, stemming from the conviction that Argentine neutrality had benefited the Allies. One British diplomat, looking back, agreed. He felt that the Argentine stance, especially the sale of the wheat harvest of 1918, was "far more useful than going to war on the side of the Allies." The Foreign Office recognized the benefits to the Allies of Argentine trade, but there was considerable bitterness at the end of the war both in London and in Washington because of that neutrality.[38]

Krausean gestures by the Argentine government continued after the war, with most, though by no means all, directed at the United States.[39] Of course, the most important gesture was Yrigoyen's insistence that the League of Nations conform to its own principles of organization and his refusal to participate in it when it failed to live up to those standards. The dramatic exit of the Argentine ambassador from the first meeting of the new organization's assembly created a brief stir around the world. But in the final analysis, it accomplished nothing concrete, either in the organization of the League or on behalf of Argentine principles. It certainly did not enhance Argentina's influence in the postwar world, which was the central goal of *principismo*.

The gesture had positive consequences on domestic politics, however. All nationalists supported Yrigoyen's policy, and all of the internationalists, traditionalists, and progressives did as well.[40] U.S. rejection of the peace treaty and of participation in the League made continued participation by any of the Latin American nations difficult, since it specifically recognized the Monroe Doctrine as a regional understanding, something no Argentine government would accept. U.S. withdrawal from the League meant Argentine activities there received little or no comment in Washington.[41]

It is difficult to explain Yrigoyen's moralistic gestures as part of a coherent foreign policy; they can only be seen as elements in a consistent effort to establish an international personality for Argentina and to enhance the nation's prestige. They were designed to fix for the nation a role as moral leader by taking advantage of episodes that did not affect the core of the nation's strategic interests. The gestures and the role were designed in such a way that they would complement and not conflict with the nation's central concerns and interests—those elements of its foreign relations that had to do with international trade, investments, marketing the nation's primary products, and Argentina's position in the world economic system. They had virtually no impact on policy-making in any European nation or in the United States, or for that matter on the international system. But however empty the gestures may appear in retrospect—and despite the fact that in the long run they did to the nation more harm than good—all of them, together with the rhetoric and the administrative style, had the effect of enhancing the Radical party's nationalist credentials at home, which was one of Yrigoyen's fundamental objectives in his first administration.

While it is possible to argue that Yrigoyen established the basis for modern

Argentine nationalism, it never was a coherent policy and it never questioned the Anglophilic assumptions underlying the traditional policy that had been rendered inappropriate by the war. Yrigoyen's government failed actively to seek industrialization, failed to touch the core of the matter, the structure of Argentina's international dependence on the British market and British capital that compromised the very essense of national welfare that Yrigoyen claimed to be strengthening. The policies Yrigoyen formulated in regard to the nation's petroleum reserves, the efforts to build a merchant marine, and the stiff approach to problems with the nation's railroads were features of a budding nationalism that, sooner or later, would create a serious conflict with the groups most closely linked to the British and those most dependent upon the British market for British goods. But during his first administration, Yrigoyen did little to push these policies and avoided conflict with the Anglophilic oligarchy.[42] When special British representative Lord D'Abernon visited Argentina during Yrigoyen's second administration at the end of the 1920s, Yrigoyen chose to strengthen its ties with Britain, thus postponing for another decade any Argentine efforts to effect independent and autonomous decision-making in international affairs.[43]

Most Argentines who participated in public affairs assumed that the prewar international division of labor would be restored in 1919, which meant *principismo* still could be asserted without risk. At the Second Pan-American Financial Conference in 1920, the Argentine government displayed the same disdain for U.S. initiatives as Saenz Peña had thirty years earlier, even to the point of refusing to answer the invitation. In one speech, the Argentine representative actually invoked language from Saenz Peña's famous speech at the earlier conference, in order to explain Argentina's European orientation and its rejection of hemispheric agreements.[44]

Some progressives understood that the war had changed the terms of success in the international system. They assumed Argentine leaders would recognize that fact and predicted that in the next forty years Argentina would enjoy industrialization equal to or greater than that of the United States during the preceding forty years.[45] This group of progressives favored close relations with the United States in order to speed the diversification of the economy. They were still a tiny chorus at the end of the war, but they drew strength from the obvious power of the United States.

The majority of Argentines refused to see the shift in relative power from Great Britain to the United States, which demonstrated that Argentina's international behavior was becoming irresponsible or unrealistic in the sense that it was not calculated on the basis of the likely reactions of other nations. At the next crisis in the international system, in 1930, the traditional assumptions underlying the nation's foreign policy were rendered totally dysfunctional. By that time the nation's leaders were at a loss as to how to formulate a new policy. Independence of action had been a series of gestures designed to define a stance with meaning in domestic politics, not the heart of a policy reflecting a new approach to the nation's insertion in the international system. It focused on prestige, not national interests.

From the U.S. perspective relations with Argentina had changed very little as a consequence of the war. Yrigoyen's neutrality merely confirmed or strengthened official suspicions about Argentine unreliability. Attitudes in the United States toward Argentina as a world power or possible rival indicated that Argentina had declined significantly in their estimation. The Argentine market was important, and Argentines were considered among the more advanced and civilized of Latin Americans, but the nation was not to be taken seriously as a factor in world affairs. After the war the United States turned its attention to Europe, although it was Europe within a global framework of strategic concerns. In strategic terms, Latin American policy was consistent with general policy, except that the region was taken as a special preserve for U.S. interests, a proposition that no other major power was willing or able to dispute. In such a framework Argentina did not warrant special attention or a policy that distinguished it from other nations in the hemisphere. That was a cruel blow to Argentine pride, and it guaranteed that relations between the two nations in the years following the war would continue to be marked by tension and misunderstanding.

NOTES

1. E. R. May, *American Isolation* (Cambridge, Mass.: Harvard University Press, 1959).

2. De la Plaza to Minister Lucas Ayarragaray, Rio de Janeiro, 18 August 1914, AGN, Archivo de la Plaza, 6-3-32; *La Prensa*, 2 November 1914, 5:2; *La Nación*, 6 February 1915, 8:1.

3. Tower's no. 246, 11 August 1915, in Public Record Office (PRO), Foreign Office (FO) 368/1205, and the Minutes appended thereto.

4. García Uriburu's no. 211, 6 August 1918, Archivo del Ministerio de Relaciones Exteriores (MRE), caja 8, legajo 1, e, 3.

5. The correspondence is MRE, caja 52, legajo ix, c., and caja 70, legajo 20, a, 8. For internal discussion of the problems created by having the normal British sources of supply cut off, see MRE, caja 1512, carpeta 10; materials on the financial conference are in caja 121, expediente 120.

6. See MRE, caja 1512, carpeta 16, and caja 15, legajo 1, bis; Murature to E. B. Moreno, 23 November 1914, AGN, Archivo Moreno, 12-3-3; *La Nación*, 11 February 1916, 11:2; *La Prensa*, 14 August 1915, 5:5; *La Argentina*, 23 May 1915, 4:2. British concern over U.S. penetration is in Tower's no. 73, 15 March 1915, PRO, FO 371/2240, file 43377. A Chilean view of the Niagara Falls episode is Cristian Guerrero Y., *Las conferencias de Niagara Falls* (Santiago: Universidad de Chile, 1968).

7. Carlos A. Becú, *El ABC y Su concepto político y jurídico* (Buenos Aires: La Facultad, 1915), 40.

8. Becú to Naón, 10 January 1917, MRE, caja 20, legajo 2, d, 7.

9. R. Weinmann, "La política neutralista argentina durante la Primera Guerra Mundial," master's thesis, Köln University, 1984. This splendid study is the best and most complete on the subject. It is in the process of being expanded into a doctoral dissertation and should be published soon.

10. Report by Chargé Paulino Llambí Campbell, June 1915, MRE, caja 1551, carpeta 4.

11. La Nación, 17 July 1915, 9:2; La Prensa, 21 January 1915, 5:5; MRE, caja 67, legajo 17; caja 30, legajo 2.

12. La Nación, 29 September 1914, 9:1; La Prensa, 8 October 1914, 5:5. Of course, the pro-German La Unión had been critical of the British since the beginning of the war. On the local anxiety and the British echo of it, see Norman's commercial 227, 25 August 1914, PRO, FO 368/928, file 51366; and Tower's no. 246, file 60999. Argentine concern is in MRE, caja 1513, carpeta 100. For a sample of the financial press see El Cronista Comercial, 1 November 1916. For faith in the system see La Época, 18 May 1918, 2:4, and La Nación, 9 September 1916, 9:5. For congressional comment see Diario de Sesiones, Diputados, 1916, vol. 2.

13. Joseph S. Tulchin, Aftermath of War (New York: New York University Press, 1971); Stanley's 22 March 1918 PRO, MAF 60/59, file 3996; Bill Albert, South America and the World Economy from Independence to 1930 (London: Macmillan 1983); Joseph S. Tulchin, "The Argentine Economy during the First World War," Review of the River Plate 147, nos. 3750–52 (19 June, 30 June, and 10 July 1970); Tulchin, "Latin America and the War," History of the First World War 7, no. 14 (1971). The most interesting Argentine discussion of this issue is in Guido Di Tella and Manuel Zymelman, Las etapas del desarrollo económico argentino (Buenos Aires: Editorial de la Universidad de Buenos Aires, 1967). For some contemporary views, see La Prensa, 26 October 1918, 6:4–5; Alejandro Bunge, Los Problemas Económicos del Presente (Buenos Aires: n.p., 1919); Diario de Sesiones, Diputados, vol. 2 1917; Alejandro de Olazabal, Hacia la emancipación económica (Buenos Aires: n.p., 1920).

14. Diario de Sesiones del Congreso de la Nación, Diputados, vol. 1 1913; Pillado to E. B. Moreno, 1 November 1913, AGN Archivo E. B. Moreno, 12-3-3; La Nación, 19 April 1915, 8:2–3.

15. La Prensa, 17 March 1917, 6:2–3; Tower's no. 306, 10 September 1916, FO 371/2601; file 201143; DS, Diputados, vol. 5 1916–17.

16. SP to de la Plaza, 20 November 1908, AGN Archivo SP, 22-21-15. For other correspondence on the subject, see Archivo de la Plaza, 4-5-10; Zeballos to SP, 27 June 1907, AGN Archivo SP, 22-2-14; H. Moreno to E. B. Moreno, 23 September 1912, AGN Archivo Moreno, 12-3-2; and La Prensa, 25 October 1915, 4:4.

17. MRE, caja 67, carpeta 17–1; caja 1561, carpeta 5(Holanda); caja 1461, carpeta 714.

18. MRE, caja 16, legajo 2, b, 2; caja 17, legajo 2, c, 1.

19. MRE, caja 78, legajo 21, a, e. La Nación, 13 January 1916, 7:4, is a defense. La Prensa, 14 December 1915, 6:3, is an attack.

20. MRE, caja 28, legajo 2, i, 2, and 3.

21. FO Minutes, 20 March 1916, FO 371/2061, file 154591.

22. Tulchin, Aftermath of War.

23. Documents on these episodes are in MRE, caja 79, legajo 21.

24. See, for example, MRE, caja 24, legajo 2, f and caja 29, legajo 3, i, and *La Época*, 23 January 1918, 1:2.

25. MRE, caja 15, legajo 1, bis 4. This policy did not begin in a memorandum by the legal adviser. Most likely it was the result of conversations between Molinari and Yrigoyen in the day between Naón's cable and Stimson's interview with the president.

26. MRE, caja 11, legajo 2, 1; caja 15, legajo 1, bis 4.

27. MRE, caja 13, legajo 1, 1.

28. MRE, caja 78, legajo 21, c; Molinari, *Acto de Chapultepec* (Buenes Aires: Senado de La Nación, 1946); *La Época*, 28 August 1917, 1:1.

29. MRE, caja 79, legajo 21, b, 1.

30. *La Época*, editorials, 16, 24, and 26 July 1917.

31. 18 May 1918, 2:4.

32. 1 June 1918, 2:5.

33. MRE, caja 8, legajo 1, e, 3; *La Prensa*, 21 May 1918, 5:6.

34. *Monthly Journal of the British Chamber of Commerce* 1, no. 5 (January 1921).

35. Manuel Galvez, *Vida de Hipólito Yrigoyen* (Buenos Aires: Tor, 1959); Felix Luna, *Hipólito Yrigoyen* (Buenos Aires: Raigal, 1957). Official interpretations of his foreign policy are Lucio Moreno Quintana, *La diplomacia del gobierno de Yrigoyen* (La Plata: Editorial Inca, 1928), and Gabriel del Mazo, "Prologo," in *Pueblo y Gobierno* (Buenos Aires: Raigal, 1956), 7:16–17.

36. Minutes, 28 May 1918, FO 371/3131, file 178126; Frederick J. Stimson, *My United States* (New York: C. Scribner's Sons, 1951), 56–65. Argentine diplomat and historian Roberto Levellier expressed the same opinion in an interview with the author, 9 July 1967. Cables from Ambassadors Alvear (Paris) and Naón suggest they held the same opinion. See MRE, caja 79, legajo 21, a, 2; caja 15, legajo 1, bis 4. De la Plaza used similar language in a private letter to Naón, 18 January 1919, AGN, Archivo de la Plaza, 6-3-8.

37. The State Department's view is in the conversation between the secretary of state and Uruguayan Minister Brum, 27 August 1918, RG 59, 710.11/385; the Foreign Office opinion is in the Minutes of 25 October 1918, FO 371/3131, file 184551. For supporters of Yrigoyen's view, see *La Época*, 12 April 1917, 1:5; *El Diario*, 13 April 1917, 4:1; Chargé Carlos Acuña to Minister Ruiz de los Llanos (Rio), 14 September 1918, AGN Archivo de la Plaza, 4-5-3. The most significant gesture of Argentine independence was the conference of neutrals. Radical party historians call it a "revolutionary challenge" to the United States. See, Del Mazo *Prólogo* 29–36; and Luis C. Alen Lascano, *Hispano-America en el pensamiento de Yrigoyen* (Buenos Aires: Propulsion, 1959), 68. For another view see Tulchin, *Aftermath*; the official Argentine view is in MRE, caja 13, legajo 1, 1; and in the pages of *La Época*.

38. The positive view is Millington Drake, in the *Review of the River Plate*, no. 3743 (10 April 1970); the Foreign Office views are in Minutes of 18 August 1916 FO 371/2601; and Tower's no. 350, 5 December 1918, FO 371/3503. The Washington view is Stimson's 6 November 1918, RG 59, 763.72/12100. Protestations of sympathy for the Allies are in the editorials of *La Época* throughout 1918, and in Legal Adviser Sarmiento Laspiur, 2 June 1918, MRE, caja 52, legajo 9, b.

39. MRE, caja 1780, legajo 29.

40. *La Prensa*, 27 November 1919, 5:4; *Nosotros*, various articles from 1919 to

1924; *Revista Argentina de Ciencias Políticas,* articles from 1919 to 1923; and Oscar Troncoso, *Los nacionalistas argentinos* (Buenos Aires: Editorial Saga, 1957), 17–40.

41. Tulchin, *Aftermath.*

42. David Rock, *Politics in Argentina, 1890–1930* (Cambridge: Cambridge University Press, 1975), and Paul B. Goodwin, *Los ferrocarriles Británicos y la UCR, 1916–1930* (Buenos Aires: La Bastilla, 1974).

43. Even sympathetic observers Carlos A. Mayo and Fernando García Molina in "Yrigoyen 1928: Top Secret," *Todo es Historia* no. 83 (April 1974), consider the pact "a bad deal."

44. MRE, caja 124, exped 82.

45. Bunge, in *Pan-American Magazine* 33, no. 5 (1921). A similar view is expressed by C. A. Tornquist in the same journal, 30, no. 5 (March 1920).

chapter 4

BETWEEN THE WARS:
COLLAPSE OF THE ARGENTINE GROWTH MODEL

The reactions in Washington and Buenos Aires to the end of the Great War point up how differently the two nations perceived and understood the world. In the United States was a widespread popular rejection of the idealism represented by Woodrow Wilson and his project for a League of Nations to preserve the peace. First the Congress rejected the League of Nations, and then the people rejected Wilson's party at the polls and chose as president, instead, a charming political hack who promised that he would return the nation to "normalcy."

The normalcy to which Warren G. Harding referred meant shunning formal commitments of U.S. power overseas, a return to the doctrine of no entangling alliances. It never meant and never was intended to mean a reduction of U.S. ties with other nations or the reduction of U.S. private and public activities abroad. On the contrary, Republicans and Democrats alike accepted with enthusiasm the new position the United States had won in world affairs as a result of the war. Except for a very few social critics on the Left, the attentive public and the political leadership of the nation accepted the privileges and responsibilities that accompanied the new power the nation enjoyed. Through the decade there was a constant and gradual increase in the informal or behind-the-scenes support by the government for private-sector interests operating overseas.[1]

In Buenos Aires it was both the fervent hope and deeply felt conviction that the international market would return to its status quo ante as soon as the hostilities had ended. And there was considerable evidence to support such a view in the first years after the war. The British returned to their former markets with energy, and the Germans and other European nations looked as if they would be able to recapture their place in the Argentine market. At the same time, the United States suffered a short, sharp recession following the war and was so wrapped up in the debate over the League of Nations and the Treaty of Versailles that it appeared as if the nation was not ready or able to play a dominant role in world affairs. As far as the Argentine leadership was concerned, nothing had changed in the balance of forces in the world, so that it was not reasonable to expect any significant changes in the nation's foreign policy. That policy, as it had been since the previous century, was based upon a set of assumptions concerning the nature of the country's economic growth, which held that Argentina would soon become one of the world's major powers and that its future development would allow it to equal or replace the United States as the dominant power in the hemisphere. The Argentine perception of the world did not agree with the view of the world from Washington—or from Rio or any other capital in Europe or in America.[2] The United States came out of the war with a vastly expanded economy and with an equally expanded sense of its strategic requirements. The Democrats, in the last years of their administration, were as persistent in their efforts to project U.S. influence overseas through the mechanisms of the private sector as were their Republican successors. Although most Argentines either denied it or ignored it, the capacity and the will to project U.S. power throughout the hemisphere increased dramatically as a result of the war.

Several changes in the world economy at the end of the war had a profound effect on Argentine well-being. First, the British position in world trade declined sharply, never to recover fully. Second, that position was taken by the United States, for whom trade was never as important as it had been to Great Britain. Perhaps worse for the Argentines, the British did not have the same surplus of capital to sink into economic activities in Argentina. If Argentine governments were going to balance their budgets with short-term loans, as they had before the war, they would have to get those loans in New York, not in London. If Argentines wanted to stimulate direct investment in industrial activities, that, too, would have to come from the United States. Although not immediately apparent at the time, the worst consequence of the war for the Argentines was the sharp and continuing loss of competitiveness suffered by British exports, expecially in the most dynamic sectors of the economy.[3]

Now as the Argentine economy expanded and diversified it became more dependent upon the United States for both capital and equipment. This meant that those who favored industrialization tended to favor trade with the United States, and that created grave difficulties for Argentine nationalists. Trade between the two became ever more unbalanced as the Argentines tried time after time to penetrate the U.S. market, with grave consequences for Argentine prestige.

The new ambassador to the United States, Honorio Pueyrredón, although not the United States' warmest friend, came to his task in 1922 with energy and with the support of the Alvear administration and of the principal exporters' associations. In addition, he was supported by the industrialists and by the economists who urged the government to encourage the diversification of the economy in order to save Argentina from a vulnerable posture in the international market and to prepare the country for the next stage in its economic development. Nationalists who demanded that Argentina reduce its dependence upon external forces welcomed the diversification of the nation's markets, although they tended to be leery of any dealings with the United States, which they considered the evil empire. This was a very broad consensus, and it emboldened Pueyrredón to state his country's case in a forceful manner.

Pueyrredón served in Washington for six years. By the time he returned to Buenos Aires at the end of the Alvear administartion, he was as convinced as Saenz Peña ever had been that Argentina could not do business with the United States and that it would only damage its national interests in attempting to do so. He managed to win the attention and the support of the State Department. He even earned a general statement of encouragement from Secretary of Commerce Herbert Hoover, generally considered the most influential member of the Harding and Coolidge cabinets. Despite this support, he saw repeated Argentine campaigns to increase exports rejected on one pretext or another.

First, the Department of Agriculture, responding to the Texas beef lobby, informed the State Department that any import of Argentine beef, except processed meat in cans, was inconvenient because hoof-and-mouth disease was endemic in Argentina. This imputation was infuriating to an Argentine representative, especially one like Pueyrredón, who raised and fattened cattle and sold them to U.S. and British meat packers for export. Were the British less particular about their health than the United States? Were U.S. packers indifferent to questions of health? Clearly, Pueyrredón argued in a lengthy series of memoranda to the secretaries of state and agriculture, the allegation was without foundation. Successive secretaries of state, Hughes and Kellogg, expressed their sympathy and professed to be convinced themselves, but they insisted that they could do nothing on behalf of Argentine beef in the face of persistent opposition from the Department of Agriculture and the support for ` the beef lobby in Congress. What galled Pueyrredón most was the realization that the state of relations with Argentina was of such low priority for the U.S. goverment that the State Department could not or would not exert enough pressure on other executive departments or marshall enough influence in Congress to preserve Argentine honor, not to mention its trade.[4]

Throughout the 1920s U.S. farmers succeeded in protecting their markets from all foreign competition by encouraging Congress to enact a series of high tariffs that effectively barred from the U.S. market Argentine and other foreign agricultural products with a comparative advantage. Pueyrredón had no more success in getting the State Department to tear down these tariff walls or even to poke small, temporary holes in them than he had in winning access to the United States for Argentine beef. The crowning blow that drove the ambassador to distraction was the episode in which the Department of Agriculture, while agreeing to allow a modest amount of Argentine alfalfa seed to be imported in order to cover an anticipated shortfall, insisted that the Argentine seed must be colored a bright orange so that U.S. farmers could distinguish it easily from the native product.[5]

Pueyrredón vented his spleen at the Pan-American Conference in Havana in 1928. In many ways his was a vintage Argentine performance. There were instructions from his government only on the issue of U.S. intervention in Central America, and no special preparations by the Alvear administration for the conference. In support of a committee resolution by El Salvador, Pueyrredón delivered a ringing denunciation of U.S. imperialism, including the practice of trade discrimination. The chief of the U.S. delegation, Charles Evans Hughes, who had been secretary of state and knew that intervention would be a sensitive issue at the conference, was completely surprised by the source and the vehemence of the attack. His reply, delivered the next day, was a noble attempt to defend U.S. policy in the Caribbean by emphasizing the duties of states as well as their rights. More important, the members of the U.S. delegation worked hard in the halls between sessions to make sure that few other nations supported the Argentine initiative.

Their work was made easier by the fact that Pueyrredón did not try to follow up on his lead and win other delegations to his side. As Saenz Peña and Quintana thirty years earlier, and as Yrigoyen had done so many times during his presidency, Pueyrredón appeared content to make his point and walk out—*principismo* without compromise. In this case he walked out because President Alvear specifically refused to support his policy on the economic relations among states and urged him to modify his stance and to sign the general convention upholding the Pan-American Union (PAU). Pueyrredón refused, left Havana, and resigned his ambassadorship. The foreign ministry, fearing that he would use the episode in the forthcoming elections, published the correspondence.[6]

For the most part, Yrigoyen, who was reelected in 1928, despite encroaching senility, reacted in a traditional manner. In relations with the United States and in dealings with the PAU, the second Yrigoyen administration simply ignored correspondence and refused to participate in conferences. This stance, fairly effective twenty or thirty years earlier, was now counterproductive. Without a positive objective and without persistent efforts to win support from other nations in the hemisphere, Argentina could not influence policy within the hemispheric organization. It could not prevent action by either obstinance or abstention as it had in the past. Argentine silence in the face of invitations to hemispheric cooperation was a source of frustration to a series of U.S. ambassadors; but in Washington State Department officers merely chalked up additional evidence of Argentine obstructionism and went about their business. The costs of *principismo* already exceeded the benefits of such a policy.

At the end of the 1920s the British increased their efforts to shore up their position in Latin America and warned of restrictions against Argentine exports. Given the fact that capital flows from the United States had slowed and the price of wheat had softened, Argentine leaders were nervous about how to generate the dollars to pay for increasing imports from the United States and to pay debts incurred in the U.S. bond market. Fearful of U.S. domination, Yrigoyen preferred to strengthen Argentine ties to its traditional trading partner, Great Britain, even though the British were no longer able to play the role in the Argentine economy that they once had. In the trade pact he signed with Lord D'Abernon in 1929, in the London Wheat Conference of the following year, and in a series of Anglophilic executive actions, Yrigoyen turned his back on the free-trade philosophy that had dominated Argentine thinking for so long and accepted a closed bilateralism. In doing so, he paved the way for a policy of formal state-to-state links with Great Britain to maintain Argentine exports in the face of the ever-widening repercussions of the depression that threatened to restrict world trade. This policy would be extended by the Conservatives who governed the country during the 1930s and legitimized in the infamous Roca-Runciman Pact.[7]

The Argentine strategy undoubtedly was based on past experience that Argentine sales in Great Britain increased with British sales to and investments in Argentina—the apparent result of the political influence of the Anglo-Argentine community, especially the railroad executives and grain exporters. What Yrigoyen did not see was that while Argentine dependence on the British market remained much as it had been for fifty years, the Argentine market was less important to the British than it had been, being only 4 percent of British exports by 1930. The coal and textile industries no longer enjoyed a central position in the British economy, and surplus capital was no longer available for investment abroad or to make up for trade imbalances with short-term loans. These and other changes in the British economy and within the commonwealth made the British less responsive to Argentine needs.

The United States clamored for greater access to the Argentine market but showed no inclination to fill the complex supportive role the British had played for more than half a century. After the Great War U.S. investors increased their stake in the Argentine economy and U.S. exporters sold more goods at the right price. The Americans complained, however, that they did not sell as much as their comparative advantages warranted and did not enjoy the same influence as the British. This was true. Argentina unofficially and officially continued to favor the British and to defer to them because of their perception of the complementarity of interest they shared with the British and the strong reinforcement provided by the network created by the deeply rooted Anglo-Argentine community.

Despite these advantages and despite Argentine favors, the Foreign Office was pessimistic about British chances of recapturing the Argentine market in 1929. Diplomatic officers lamented the apparent inability of British industry and commerce to take advantages of the opportunity presented by the D'Abernon mission and U.S. protectionism, particularly the rigidity of the British economic structure, which made it difficult for exporters to combine with shippers, or shippers to combine with bankers. The organization of the British government also was considered an obstacle.[8] As if this were not a sufficient handicap, British enjoyment of official favor in Argentina was undermined by the government's political difficulties beginning in 1929 and culminating in the golpe of 6 September 1930.

As Yrigoyen had been openly anti-American, it seemed only logical to anticipate an about face in foreign policy from the men who ousted him. Such were the expectations of the U.S. business community in Argentina and U.S. Ambassador Robert Woods Bliss, who urged the state department to "help our situation in Argentina" by early recognition of the provisional government. He submitted as convincing proof of his argument the assurances of Provisional Foreign Minister Ernesto Bosch that the new government wanted to restore good relations with the United States, so badly damaged by the "unreasonable attitude of Yrigoyen."[9]

When the news of the revolution in Argentina first reached London, the reaction of the press was concern bordering on alarm. Within a week the Economist could balance the good that had resulted from the revolution with the bad, and by the end of September the Foreign Office observed philosophically that while they would miss Yrigoyen, they expected the same factors that made him pro-British would "inspire his successor." Appreciation of these factors undoubtedly accounted for the State Department's reserve in dealing with the new government. It was a question of weighing pious public promises about cooperation with the United States and the Pan-American Union against the widespread "depression and consternation" in Argentina caused by the Smoot-Hawley Tariff, which raised U.S. tariffs to historic highs and virtually excluded Argentine beef, combined with a decade of protests against U.S. protectionism.[10]

The State Department's caution was well-founded. The new government's enthusiasm for the United States was based entirely upon the hope that expanded trade between the two nations would save Argentina from the effects of the depression and the threatened loss of the British market.[11] The land-owning oligarchy had been thrown into a panic by the prospect of sharply reduced participation in the world economy, and most of the corporatist or fascist models favored by advisers to General José F. Uriburu, the leader of the golpe, called for a turn toward economic autarchy and economic self-sufficiency.[12] But only a few small groups were willing to accept such a dramatic shift in economic priorities. The majority of the export-oriented elite had little stomach for such radical change and threw their support behind General Augustín P. Justo, who replaced Uriburu in a bloodless golpe in 1932, and his program of "controlled democracy." While the Justo government considered diversification the only viable defense of national independence in the long run, for the moment, it decided to do whatever was necessary to guarantee the country's export markets, including active intervention by the state in the production and commercial process. Justo adopted the package of solutions proposed by the technicians Uriburu had recruited, aiming at making the economy more efficient. The cult of efficiency had an apolitical quality congenial to the military professionals, whose support was indispensable to the new government, and in the public mind government by technicians compared favorably to the notoriously venal cronyism of the Radicals.[13]

The Argentines knew their ties to Great Britain were to undergo significant change.[14] The Argentine ambassador in London importuned the foreign secretary to give his goverment advanced information on the British wheat quota and urged special consideration for Argentina in view of the British investments there; the Argentine Rural Society urged the president to make special tariff concessions to Great Britain in order to save the Argentine meat industry. In a sense these efforts were anachronistic, based on a perception of complementarity and mutuality of interest that no longer existed. More to the point, though considered of less immediate value, the Foreign Ministry began secretly to sound out all of Argentina's trading partners on the possibilities of reciprocal trade agreements that would preserve the status quo in international trade; and in a much-publicized move the president appointed a blue-ribbon commission to study trade with Great Britain.[15] Such efforts were undermined by the persistent belief among many that this crisis, too, would pass, and that the international division of labor somehow would be restored.

Such a view did have supporters in Great Britain. A vocal lobby consisting of British exporters and the Anglo-Argentine Committee of Investors argued that Argentina and Great Britain were tied by mutually advantageous bonds. In the words of Sir Malcolm Robertson, former ambassador in Buenos Aires, "Argentina must be regarded as an essential part of the British Empire. We cannot get on without her, nor she without us." The worst Argentines expected was a tariff policy based on reciprocity. Proudly confident, La Prensa warned Great Britain in February 1932 to eschew discrimination or Argentina would reduce its food exports to Great Britain and sell its surplus products elsewhere.[16] Within a matter of months these brave words would have a hollow ring.

As the preparations for the 1932 Ottawa conference went forward, information reached Buenos Aires that the dominions most certainly did consider Argentina one of the "foreign" countries and that Great Britain probably would have to demonstrate its commitment to the empire by extracting material concessions from the Argentines. The new foreign minister, Carlos Saavedra Lamas, responded with a flurry of initiatives touting the benefits of commercial reciprocity. What had been Argentina's worst fear now appeared its best hope.

Manual Malbran, Argentine ambassador in London, on home leave, offered British ambassador Macleay the "same preferential treatment as might be accorded . . . by any of our Dominions or even better." This is what the Foreign Office had been looking for. It had been very pessimistic about the chances of establishing bases for trade with Argentina if the imperial conference insisted on discriminating equally against all foreign nations. Here was an opportunity to extend to members of the informal empire the benefits of formal empire. Now, Macleay concluded, the Foreign Office would be able to protect the Argentine position vis-à-vis the dominions. The response from Ottawa was a resounding defeat for the Foreign Office viewpoint and a mortal blow to Argentine trade, allowing no room for doubt, as shown in the following cable from London to Macleay: "suggestion that any any foreign country can obtain the same advantages as those given to the Dominions runs counter to the whole question of Imperial Preference link of Empire. Any suggestion that the Argentine could participate in Preference would never be entertained by delegations of the Dominions and to put it forward would destroy all prospect of agreement. Tell British Ambassador in Buenos Aires this to avoid false hopes."[17]

The details of the Ottawa accords were not immediately available in Buenos Aires, although Macleay carried out the instructions in the quoted telegram. In what must be considered another case of wishful thinking, Secretary of Agriculture Antonio de Tomaso reassured the crowd at the annual Palermo stock show that Great Britain would resist the pressure to build high tariff walls. Because of the great quantity of British investments in Argentina, the high quality of the food Argentina sent to England, the British shipping interests involved, and the "indestructible moral bonds uniting the two nations," he said, "we have never doubted that whatever agreements might be made with the Dominions Argentine produce would continue to enjoy the welcome in that market which it has always received hitherto." The Foreign Office minutes noted dryly, "Doctor de Tomaso is perhaps more optimistic than the facts justify."[18]

Malbran returned to his post to extract formal trade commitments from Great Britain in order to blunt the effects of colonial competition, but he got nowhere. By the end of the year he was ready to quit. At this juncture, in February 1933, the Foreign Office forced a confrontation at a cabinet meeting and managed to move the Department of Agriculture and the Board of Trade to accept a limitation on the restrictions to be placed upon Argentine meat imports. At the same time it persuaded Malbran to close his eyes to the diminution of Argentine sovereignty implicit in control of the meat export quota by foreign private corporations. With these two obstacles removed, the way was cleared for formal negotiations, and Vice President Julio A. Roca, Jr., sailed to London to conduct talks with Sir Walter Runciman, president of the Board of Trade.

The formal trade talks were as painful for Argentina as the preliminary talks had been, with the added disadvantage that the public was fully aware that they were talking place. Roca's primary objective was to formalize by treaty the minimum requirements of complementarity that had existed naturally under informal empire. Within a matter of days the central issue was defined as a straight bargain of a meat quota for an exchange guarantee. Foreign Minister Saavedra Lamas sought to strengthen his representatives' bargaining position by another round of diplomatic initiatives in search of new markets. His trump card would be an agreement with the United States, where President Franklin D. Roosevelt and Secretary of State Cordell Hull were committed to freer trade policies than their predecessors had pursued. The Foreign Office was sensitive to the danger this implied, and there is little doubt that the Argentine negotiating posture was strengthened in March 1933, by the Democrats' reciprocal trade policy. Ambassador Felipe Espil in Washington pressed insistently for a commitment to trade talks, while in Buenos Aires there was significant improvement in the official allocations of exchange to U.S. importers.

This gambit, too, came to naught. Hull quickly disabused Espil of the idea that there could be bilateral talks before Congress had approved the president's general policy. All the trumps now belonged to Runciman. His principal concern was an orderly market. He felt that his department and agriculture had made a major concession in admitting the principle of limiting restrictions on Argentine meat imports and turning a deaf ear to the potent Texas beef lobby. Now, the Argentines would have to knuckle under. Aside from the brutal calculus of political influence, in which Argentina and the Foreign Office counted for very little, Runciman hammered on the extremely unfavorable balance of British trade with Argentina and the fact that British exports to Argentina represented 4 percent of the British total, whereas Argentine exports to Britain amounted to 37 percent of all Argentine exports.[19]

By the beginning of April the position of the Roca mission was untenable. The Argentines were even prepared to break off negotiations. Political pressure at home was mounting against the continuing disgrace of Roca's failure to get what he had gone after. At last the Argentines accepted the British terms. The Argentines granted a final concession on the exchange issue and left apportioning the meat quota in the hands of the foreign packers. In return, Argentina was guaranteed access to the British market. The key to the agreement, when push came to shove, was that Argentine exporters, ranchers, farmers, economic experts, and government leaders all wanted an orderly market as much, if not more, than Runciman. Besides, as one of the members of the mission put it, linking the Argentine quota to shipments from the dominions was the best security for Argentine trade, and the terms could have been much worse.

Nationalists of the Left and Right in Argentina then and later assailed the Roca-Runciman Pact as a sellout. They argued that Britain called the tune on the meat trade and, through exchange preferences perpetuating British imperial domination over the Argentine economy, locked Argentina into the dependency role of a primary product exporter. The meat trade provisions of the Roca Pact were, in fact, not favorable to Argentina. On the other hand, it cannot be shown that the Argentine government had the means to extract further concessions from Britain or that refusing to sign the treaty would have benefited the nation. No other markets were available for the exportable surplus of beef and grains, and trade opportunities in the 1930s were shrinking, not expanding.[20] Further, the actual pattern of trade with Great Britain was not unfavorable to Argentina after 1933; the treaty saved Argentina from further cuts and restrictions.

The argument that the tariff and exchange provision of the treaty extended or intensified British imperial control over Argentina simply is not true. There is no question that the British talked familiarly of their special relationship with Argentina and that the Foreign Office had a patronizing attitude. However, as early as 1931 both the British and the Argentines came to realize that the combination of exchange controls and inconvertibility of the peso put the Argentine government in a position to bankrupt the British firms by starving them of exchange, or by refusing to allow the railways to raise their fares, or by making them carry government goods at uneconomic rates (half price), or by encouraging in Buenos Aires alternative methods of public transport.[21]

By the end of 1935 trade between the two was nearly balanced. This meant that there was no exchange available to facilitate remittances by British corporations, nor could there be expansion of British exports to Argentina without a corresponding expansion of Argentine exports to Britain. In short, the British were willing to sacrifice the investments that the Argentines held hostage behind the wall of exchange control, and they even came to support Argentine efforts to nationalize the railroads.[22] The Ottawa policy was triumphant. Argentina was sacrificed to the lions of dominion trade preference.

President Justo, the senior diplomats in the Foreign Ministry, the team of economists at the Central Bank, the bureaucrats at the treasury, and the engineers at the agricultural ministry were acutely aware that the imperial relationship was ended or about to end. Their problem was that in decolonizing Argentina, the British could not automatically change the colonial status of the Argentine economy. Nor, for their part, could Justo and his aides instantaneously diversify production and decrease dependence on the export of a few agricultural commodities. Until diversification could be achieved, their central concern and the concern of their successors under President Roberto Ortiz had to be market stability—to sell fairly predictable amounts of goods at fairly predictable prices. Without such stability, the consequences for the national budget and the level of economic activity generally were frightening to contemplate. Given the continuing structural dependence upon exports, Argentine policymakers chose to seek their minimum market stability through a treaty with a major trading partner, though the terms of dependence might appear onerous, rather than to rely on an utterly unpredictable, frivolous world market that became more anarchic as the decade wore on. There is adequate evidence to indicate that Argentine officials considered the Roca-Runciman Pact a palliative at best. They sought constantly to explore other options. A treaty with their other major trading partner, the United States, seemed the most logical alternative to the lapsed imperial relationship with Great Britain, and foreign policy efforts to achieve this goal went on for a decade. This, too, proved to be a source of bitter frustration to Argentina.

The Justo administration made no bones about its interest in talks for a reciprocal trade treaty with the United States and frankly admitted using exchange discrimination as a lever. The State Department hoped first to conclude a series of treaties with countries like Brazil whose trade offered no thorny domestic political problems. Ambassador Espil took his case directly to Roosevelt in July 1933 and won a promise to include Argentina on the list of nations with which the United States intended to negotiate. To appease Saavedra Lamas and save face for Espil, the department consented to have Argentine experts come to Washington to discuss the possible topics for trade talks, but at the end of 1936 Hull told Saavedra Lamas he feared "certain interests [that] might secure legislation in Congress defeating our purpose."[23] Hull had no sympathy for the beef lobby. When a modest proposal to exempt Patagonia—a region considered free of aftosa—from the sanitary exclusion ran afoul of pressure in Congress and in the Department of Agriculture, Hull told a press conference, off the record, that the exclusion was "an absurdity."[24]

As in the case of Argentina's frustration in seeking satisfaction from Great Britain, the explanation for failure to work out a deal with the United States lies in the configuration of domestic political forces opposed to admitting Argentine agricultural products into the U.S. market, as well as in the structural incompatibility of the two economies. Neither Roosevelt nor the State Department—both sincerely desirous of advancing the government's general trade policy, of satisfying what they considered legitimate Argentine requests, and of aiding the cause of U.S. economic interests in Argentina—was able to win the case for a trade treaty or any partial trade concessions. What went wrong? The principal difficulty was that satisfying Argentina's needs had repercussions for the entire farm program. Failure to conclude a treaty with Argentina did not undermine the administration's trade policy, whereas at one point it looked as if further pressure in support of Argentine interests would destroy the coalition that Roosevelt depended upon to support his farm program, irreparably alienate his secretary of agriculture, and stir up a hornet's nest in Congress—all for relatively little gain for the national interest.

Roosevelt made the initial, general decision that the United States should include Argentina among the nations with which trade treaties would be negotiated. In doing so he demonstrated the access enjoyed by Espil and Undersecretary of State Sumner Welles. Hull concurred, despite the fat file on trade difficulties between the two countries. Although Hull told Espil official talks couldn't begin until Congress had approved the president's policy, he sent experts in the department to consult with their fellows in the Department of Agriculture and the Tariff Commission on possible concessions to Argentina. Their findings, communicated by Secretary of Agriculture Henry Wallace in December 1933, were negative.[25] The State Department took the matter up in the Interdepartmental Advisory Board on Reciprocal Treaties, obviously a sympathetic forum more sensitive to stimuli from the international political system than most government agencies. By stressing the principles involved, the State Department forced a compromise that included cuts in the duty on goods, which Wallace admitted would not be hurt by Argentina's competition, and a token cut in the duty on flax, which the Argentines considered of primary importance. Later, Wallace simply refused to implement the board's decision. Pressed by the State Department, Roosevelt preferred to avoid a decision, to go "slowly and cautiously," to feel out members of Congress before pushing the Department of Agriculture into anything Wallace thought unwise. Resigned, the State Department turned its attention to preparations for other trade pacts.

The initial success of the Hull trade program further delayed talks with Argentina. The government thought it unwise to announce the inauguration of negotiations with too many agricultural countries at the same time. Meanwhile the experts would proceed with their appointed tasks. From the State Department viewpoint, the key to the talks would be flax. With Espil's help the Interdepartmental Committee continued its preparatory detail work and, by the end of 1934, had fixed the U.S. bargaining position as a 10 percent cut in duty on the "safe" items and a 50 percent cut in the duty on flax. The State Department wrenched this compromise out of Secretary Wallace only after throwing the matter back into Roosevelt's lap, virtually insisting on the president's support by calling for his decision in a "basic policy question," a matter "of vital and pressing importance to our whole trade agreements program because the contemplated plan [to increase flax production] seems . . . to run counter to the whole purpose upon which the program is based."[26] The department carried its point by forcing a confrontation between competing elements of the bureaucracy, exerting more pressure on behalf of Argentine interests than had ever been exerted in any previous commerical dispute between the two nations.

The victory showed the vulnerability of a liberal trade policy to domestic economic and political pressure. It turned out that the State Department won its point only at great political cost; it could not take every dispute with Wallace to the president. The constant bickering with Congress and the

Department of Agriculture was costly from a bureaucratic point of view. Inevitably, senior officers in the department questioned whether it was worth the effort. During the extensive, severe droughts of 1935 and 1936, Espil tried to sell some Argentine corn in the United States. It was a modest proposal, and the Department of Commerce joined the State Department in urging it on Secretary Wallace. Wallace resisted, and as the discussions progressed the liaison officer in the Department of Commerce became alarmed by the growing tension between Argentina and the officers in the Department of Agriculture and felt there was a "real danger" that Agriculture's hostility "may lead to reprisals and restrictions which will cripple our growing trade with Argentina." Herbert Feis, the economic adviser, and Hull decided in 1936 it was useless to press the issue without the active support of the Department of Agriculture. They feared the domestic repercussions of any price declines or possible labor troubles linked to agricutural imports.[27]

Rather than destroy all chances for an accord with Argentina, the Department of State retreated and told the Argentine government that it would be better to wait until the United States had concluded trade agreements with industrial countries that would show the American farmer the advantages of a liberal trade policy. Such a moment never arrived. The exchange issue continued to plague relations between the two countries, because the Argentines could see no reason to compromise what had become the keystone of their commercial policy without comparable concessions by the Americans.

As in their negotiations with the British, the Argentines came to the point where they saw the possible consequences of rigidity and failure as less onerous than the consessions they would have to make without being certain of a payoff that would compensate for their concessions. Meat was out, corn was out, even flax was out. In retrospect, we can see that Argentine needs would have been satisfied in the United States only by total, sustained commitment of presidential power in Congress and in the bureaucratic policy formulation process. Weighed against the danger to the entire farm program that such intervention entailed together with the possibility of salvaging the trade program by successes elsewhere and the other demands on the president's time, such a commitment was politically impossible.

The constant frustration of Argentina's foreign policy efforts had important consequences at home. The Roca-Runciman Pact never excited any enthusiasm in Argentina. Its onerous terms and the shoddy treatment of the Argentine negotiators provoked the government to seek new trading partners. Dissatisfaction with Great Britain intensified Argentine resentment with the protectionist policies of the United States, which closed off that alternative to dependence on the British market. Out of this resentment and frustration emerged a politically neutral form of Argentine nationalism that was thoroughly divorced from the old liberal democratic model and that set as its goal maximizing the nation's control over its destiny. In international affairs, that meant maintaining maximum independence of action, particularly in the uncertain international marketplace. It is significant that the Argentine government made a major issue of the provisions in the Roca Pact granting control of the meat quota to the meat packers and calling for an investigation of the packing industry. The government chose direct intervention in the economy as the means of breaking the foreign monopoly of an Argentine industry. This policy provided a variety of instruments for asserting the nation's sovereignty and neutralized the British techniques of informal imperial control.

The growing strength of Argentine industry resulting from the depression and fostered by government policy buttressed the nation's sense of self.[28] By 1936 there was a general coolness toward the revision of the Roca Pact.[29] One editorial writer noted that the British commitment to empire trade "is antagonistic to our interest in conserving our political and commercial national identity," while another said, "This interference of foreign capital in our destiny is getting every day more unbearable and it will be necessary for the country to prepare to rid itself as soon as possible of a submission which is incompatible with its national sovereignty."

No group vying for power at the time proposed a significantly different mode of insertion into the world economy. It is true that during the decade nationalist forces on the Right, favoring autarchy, grew stronger and increasingly radical in their demands. They would have their moment in the 1940s; but in the 1930s their program was not acceptable to most of the nation's leaders because it almost certainly would have entailed a period of economic decline as well as obvious dependence on the United States for the supplies an industrializing economy would require. Neither of these costs was acceptable, and so the governing elite fell back on a series of palliatives designed to deal with the crisis as best it could, hoping that, somehow, the world would be reconstructed along the lines of its traditional growth model and its power within the Argentine society would be sustained. The Left offered no significant option in the international role of the nation. Meanwhile, the elite held power through corruption and periodic repression of the political opposition. The coming world war would unseat them from power and precipitate the most serious crisis in the history of Argentine relations with the United States.

NOTES

1. Tulchin, *Aftermath of War* (New York: New York University Press, 1971); Ellis Hawley, *The New Deal and the Problem of Monopoly: A Study in Economic Ambivalence* (Princeton, N.J.: Princeton University Press, 1966); Joan Hoff Wilson, *Herbert Hoover* (Boston: Little, Brown, 1975); Frank Costigliola, "The Politics of Financial Stabilization: American Reconstruction Policy in Europe, 1924–1930," Ph.D. diss., Cornell University, 1972; Michael Hogan, *Informal Entente. The Private Structure of Cooperation in Anglo-American Economic Diplomacy, 1918–1928* (Columbia: University of

Missouri Press, 1977); Joseph S. Tulchin and David J. Danelski, *The Autobiographical Notes of Charles Evans Hughes* (Cambridge, Mass.: Harvard University Press, 1973), chapters 14–16.

2. For a fascinating discussion of national perceptions and their origins, see Stanley E. Hilton, "Brazil and the Post-Versailles World: Elite Images and Foreign Policy Strategy, 1919–1929," *Journal of Latin American Studies* 12, no. 2 (1980): 341–64.

3. Sara Caputo de Astelarra, "La Argentina y la rivalidad entre los Estados Unidos e Inglaterra," *Desarrollo Económico* 23, no. 92 (1984); Rosemary Thorp, Introduction to *Latin America in the 1930s*, ed. Rosemary Thorp (New York: St. Martin's Press, 1984).

4. The aftosa episode is in Manuel A. Machado, Jr., *Aftosa, a Historical Survey of Foot and Mouth Disease and Inter-American Relations* (Albany: State University of New York Press, 1969). The embarrassing correspondence is in RG 59, 710.35. The depth of Pueyrredón's outrage was relayed to me by his son, Carlos Alberto, in an interview, 15 June 1967, and by his successor, Felipe Espil, in an interview, 12 June 1970.

5. On these episodes see Walter M. High III, "The United States and the Mediterranean Fruit Fly: Restrictions on Argentine and Spanish Grapes in the 1920s," and "Neo-Colonialism and Argentine Foreign Trade: The Failure of Economic Nationalism, 1916–1933," unpublished papers in the possession of the author. An interesting case study of British decline and U.S. penetration of the Argentine market is the transportation industry. See Raúl García Heras, *Automotores Norteamericanos, Caminos, y Modernización Urbana en la Argentina* (Buenos Aires: Libros de Hispanoamerica, 1985).

6. Tulchin, *Aftermath;* Tulchin and Danelski, eds., *Autobiographical Notes;* Ministerio de Relaciones Exteriores, *Circular Mensual Informativo*, no. 129, February 1928.

7. Two useful essays on the Argentine economy during the 1920s are R. Cortés Conde, "La economía argentina," and Javier Villaneuva, "El comercio internacional," both in *Todo es Historia*, no. 180–81 (May–June 1982). On the D'Abernon pact, which never was ratified, see A. O'Connell, "Argentina in the Depression," in Thorp, ed., *Latin America in the 1930s.*

8. Dereck H. Aldcroft and Harry W. Richardson, *The British Economy, 1870–1939* (London: Macmillan, 1969); Frederic Benham, *Great Britain under Protection* (New York: Macmillan, 1941); Sidney Pollard, *The Development of the British Economy, 1914–1967* (London: Arnold, 1969); and A. J. Youngson, *Britain's Economic Growth, 1920–1966* (New York: Augustus Kelley, 1967).

9. RG 59, 835.00Revolutions/2; Bliss, 7 September 1930. British Ambassador Macleay, 10 September 1930, reported U.S. businessmen as "jubilant" at the revolution (FO A6008/666/2).

10. FO A5824/66/2, Minutes; RG 59, 835.00Revolutions/11.

11. The debate over economic policy was carried on in the press. For a good summary see the issues of *Revista de Economía Argentina* for 1929–31.

12. Carlos Tornquist, "El Balance del Año Comercial," *Revista de Economía Argentina*, xxviii.

13. A fascinating account of the technocratic team put together by Alejandro Bunge and led by Raúl Prebisch is in the Instituto Torcuato Di Tella Oral History Project, Interview with Enrique Malaccorto, 24 August 1971.

14. Virgil Salera, *Exchange Control and the Argentine Market* (New York: Columbia University Press, 1941).

15. Daniel Drosdoff, *El Gobierno de las Vacas (1933–1956). El Tratado Roca-Runciman* (Buenos Aires: Ediciones La Bastilla, 1972), 14–15.

16. *La Prensa,* 13 February 1932, 8:4.

17. FO A4565/1040/2.

18. Minutes on Macleay's 6 September 1932, FO A6262/1040/2.

19. Drosdoff, *Gobierno de las Vacas,* 24–36.

20. Roger Gravil, "State Intervention in Argentina's Export Trade between the Wars," *Journal of Latin American Studies* 2, no. 2 (1971).

21. Roger Gravil, "British Retail Trade in Argentina, 1900–1940," *Inter-American Economic Affairs* 24, no. 2 (1970).

22. Winthrop R. Wright, "Foreign Owned Railways in Argentina: A Case Study of Economic Nationalism," *Business History Review* 41, no. 3 (1967); Drosdoff, *Gobierno de las Vacas,* 94–116; Gravil, "British Retail Trade."

23. *Foreign Relations of the United States,* 1936, volume 5.

24. Michael J. Francis, *The Limits of Hegemony: United States Relations with Argentina and Chile during World War II* (South Bend, Ind.: University of Notre Dame Press, 1977), 49.

25. RG 59, 611.3531/221, Wallace to the secretary of state, 1 December 1933. File 611.353 contains relevant correspondence on these issues.

26. RG 59, 611.3531/304½ Memorandum, January 16, 1935; and 611.3531/319½ Memorandum, March 19, 1935.

27. RG 59, 611.353Corn/33, Memorandum, undated; and Hull's memorandum, April 14, 1936, RG 59, 611.353Corn/34.

28. Javier Villaneuva, "La gran depresión y la industrialización argentina," *Desarrollo Económico* 12, no. 47 (1972); Carlos Diaz Alejandro, *Essays on the Economic History of the Argentine Republic* (New Haven: Yale University Press, 1970); Aldo Ferrer, *The Argentine Economy* (Berkeley: University of California Press, 1967); Federico Pinedo, *En Tiempos de la República* (Buenos Aires: Editorial Mundo Forense, 1946); Alejandro Bunge, *Una Nueva Argentina* (Buenos Aires: Kraft, 1940).

29. Drosdoff, *Gobierno de las Vacas,* 60–61 and 80–92.

chapter 5

AN ARGENTINE DILEMMA:
BETWEEN EUROPE AND AMERICA

The growing tensions in Europe made Argentina's position in world affairs more and more precarious. As the major nations prepared for war each appeared to become more nationalistic and less interested in the sort of free-trading market in which Argentine felt most comfortable. The British, long Argentina's principal customer as well as its principal source of capital, grew less and less able or interested in doing business on terms that the Argentines considered acceptable. The Germans were interested in trade, but only on a barter basis. That, in and of itself, was not objectionable to the new administration after 1938 headed by President Roberto Ortiz, but it never was sufficiently appealing to warrant running the great risk of establishing trade links that such a barter deal entailed. As the the decade wore on, and Argentina's once and potential trading partners careened toward closed trading systems, those trading partners increased their pressure on the Argentine government to favor their cause. Because of the nature of the Nazi regime and because they were the latest to enter the market, the Germans exerted the greatest pressure. The explicit connections between commerce and international politics ran counter to Argentine tradition and served to raise the stakes in the domestic debate over policy.

As the battle lines were drawn ever tighter in Europe, the nations of the Western Hemisphere turned to one another and, especially, to the United States, for aid and comfort. Such a situation, in which the hemispheric system was given added prestige, was not congenial to Argentine leaders.

While the United States had become the most important source of manufactured goods and of machine tools for the budding industries in Argentina, creating a lobby of vocal supporters of closer relations with the United States, it was not sufficient to erase half a century of jealous rivalry or the deep-seated conviction that Argentine destiny, somehow, was linked more closely with Europe than with the Western Hemisphere.

From the North American perspective, the growing coherence of the hemispheric system under U.S. leadership was only logical and right, an appropriate response to the good neighbor policy. Argentine resistance to this trend was considered perverse, suspicious; it offered further proof, if such proof were needed, that Argentine leaders were out of touch with the rest of the hemisphere, with the realities of world politics, and even with their own people. Once the United States was attacked at Pearl Harbor and had entered the war, Argentine reluctance to fall in line behind the United States became intolerable. The conduct of relations with Argentina during the war literally tore the U.S. government apart and very nearly embarrassed relations among the Allies. The Argentine situation became an obsession with Secretary of State Cordell Hull and his followers, especially Spruille Braden, culminating in the publication of the famous State Department "Blue Book," conveniently prior to the Argentine general elections of 1946, spelling out the aid and comfort the Nazis had derived from Argentina's neutrality.[1] By the end of the war, Argentine policy had become a rock on which diplomatic and political careers foundered in the United States, while in Argentina the definition of a correct posture in response to U.S. pressure became the crucible in which nationalism was redefined, contributing to policies that were detrimental to the nation's prestige and harmful to its well-being.

In the peculiar, corrupt political system of Argentine politics at the end of the 1930s, the debate over Argentina's role in world affairs increasingly became central to the struggle for power. The struggle exacerbated differences within the elite and gave increasing strength to the nationalists. Over time, as the debate became more intense, there was an increasing tendency to identify the nationalists with opposition to democracy and the internationalists with support for democracy. To make the political groups more muddled, the supporters of democracy were split between those who favored strong ties to the British and those who advocated closer ties to the United States.[2]

The configuration of domestic political groups was reflected fairly in the composition of the Ortiz administration. His vice president, Ramón Castillo, was considered less open than he to a return to free elections and more sympathetic to the extreme nationalistic factions among the elite and their sympathizers in the military.[3] The return to fair pluralistic politics was bound to favor the Radical party. Since the Radicals were outspoken advocates of close relations with the British and hostile to the Axis, the opponents of a return to democracy, ably abetted by the German Embassy in Buenos Aires, used foreign policy as an excuse to oppose the Ortiz administration. As Ortiz continued his campaign to bring Argentina back to constitutional government, he was caught between the right wing of his own party, growing in size and power, and the formal or open opposition parties. His own power base began to erode. When illness forced him from office in mid-1940, he lost whatever control he possessed over events in Argentina.

The situation in the Foreign Ministry reflected the situation in the government generally and in the armed forces. Foreign Minister José Maria Cantilo shared the president's sympathy for the Allies and was correspondingly anti-Nazi. The same was true of the subsecretary of foreign relations. Further down the hierarchy in the Ministry, officials were either inclined toward Germany or indifferent.[4] Ortiz and Cantilo were restricted in the execution of their policies by pro-Nazi elements in or close to the government. The army was said to be 10 percent pro-Nazi, 20 percent simply admirers of Germany, 20 percent pro-Ally, and the rest indifferent and ready to join either side. This combination of a very active group that favored the Axis and a large group afraid or unwilling to commit itself undercut the power of the pro-Ally faction and neutralized the majority of the press and public opinion, said to be partial to the Allies. Other domestic and international issues made the definition of a policy in favor of the Allies increasingly difficult, among which the most signficant was the increasingly obvious linkage between support for the Allies and policies that recognized U.S. hegemony in the hemisphere. Even Argentine who favored the Allies moved in that direction with reluctance and grave misgivings.

Continuing economic difficulties with the United States embarrassed the government in its efforts to keep Argentina on the side of the Allies. When war began in Europe, the economic issues assumed crisis proportions for Argentina. As had happened at the outset of World War I, there was a financial panic and fear that Argentina would not be able to sell its staple crops or import the manufactured products it vitally needed. President Roosevelt had promised, on Pan-American Day, 14 April 1939, that the United States would not only repel any attempt to violate the integrity of the hemisphere, but that it would also provide whatever economic support might be necessary "so that no American nation need surrender any fraction of its sovereign freedom to maintain its economic welfare."[5] Now was the time for the United States to redeem its promise of economic aid. Argentina had large obligations in sterling and other European currencies that had to be repaid or refunded. Loans from Europe were unobtainable. Worse, Argentina was caught with large surpluses of corn, wheat, and meat. These were the nation's lifeblood. Unless Argentina could export these goods it could not earn the foreign exchange necessary to pay its debts, import materials for its budding industries, or run its government. All politically articulate Argentines, even those most sympathetic to the Allied cause and to inter-American cooperation, maintained that Argentina could not afford to cooperate with the

United States in a war against European powers unless the United States provided a market for Argentina's exportable surplus of agricultural products. The more nationalistic elements of society, which looked forward to an Axis victory, certainly were not going to do anything to hurt Argentina's markets after a European war.

These issues outlined, for all who cared to see, the limits of Argentine cooperation with the United States and the extent to which nationalism—in one form or another—had become part of the public policy of any Argentine government, and the extent to which the loud defense of the nation's strategic interests had become the condition for domestic political support.[6]

The U.S. Embassy in Buenos Aires tried to impress upon the State Department the importance of some initiative by the United States to relieve the economic crisis. Ambassador Norman Armour stressed the fact that "the most unbiased and mature thought" in Argentina was suspicious of the United States and critical of its commercial policy. Their criticism asserted that U.S. trade practices did not jibe with the government's official proclamations in favor of a liberal trade policy. One editorial stated, with evident references to the failures of the trade negotiations that had broken down in January 1940, "We are not unaware of the efforts of the present Administration of the United States to attenuate the effects of protectionism, but those efforts have been shattered by the intransigence of Congress, and they have recently lost their importance, due perhaps to political considerations."[7] This pessimism on the part of the pro-Ally or undecided groups gave the initiative to their opponents. Failure to have the United States bolster the Argentine economy would weaken dangerously their hold on political power. Their policies would be discredited. For this reason, through 1939 and into 1940 as the war in Europe spread, the Ortiz government became more and more desperate to arrange an economic settlement with the United States. Such a settlement would strengthen the economy and restore its political control over the anti-Ally elements.

To facilitate such a settlement the Ortiz government went out of its way to establish its credentials as a friend of the United States and loyal member of the inter-American community. The problem was that in the context of the relations between the two nations and their history, such efforts were extremely costly to Ortiz whereas the government in Washington remained insensitive to the internal situation in Argentina, skeptical of Argentine gestures of friendship, and quite unwilling to alter its broad policy goals to meet the needs of the Argentine government.

The Argentines participated in the general condemnation of German aggression against Poland and expressed their sympathy for the democratic powers. Immediately after the outbreak of hostilities on 1 September 1939, Foreign Minister Cantilo called for inter-American consultation and readily assented to the United States' plan for a meeting at Panama. His instructions to the Argentine delegation stressed the theme of cooperation and the need to tighten the bonds with the other American republics. Sumner Welles, who later had some harsh things to say about the Argentine Government, called attention to "the altogether co-operative, helpful, and able services rendered during the meeting at Panama by the Argentine delegation." With only minor exceptions, Argentina went along with the measures approved at Panama, the most noteworthy of which were the creation of the Inter-American Financial and Economic Advisory Committee and Resolution XIV, which set up a neutrality zone three hundred miles wide around the Americas.[8]

The Panama declaration was tested before the year was out and, once again, the Argentine government demonstrated its desire to support the Allies and cooperate with the other nations in the hemisphere. Early in the morning of 13 December the German pocket battleship *Graf Von Spee* came into contact with the British vessles *Achilles, Ajax,* and *Exeter.* The *Graf Von Spee* damaged the *Exeter* and made off. Later that same day, the *Achilles* and *Ajax* caught up with the German ship, inflicted heavy damaged upon it and forced it to seek shelter in Montevideo. The Uruguayan government was upset over this violation of the security zone, so recently put into effect, and asked the U.S. State Department to take the lead in framing a strong protest to the combatants. The State Department circulated a draft of a statement and was surprised to find that the Latin American nations considered it too mild. The Argentine foreign minister feared that the Panama declaration would become a dead letter unless the nations of the hemisphere acted rapidly and firmly. He proposed an amendment to the American draft making reference to the steps which the American republics might find it necessary to take to prevent a repetition of similar incidents. Later, he joined with the Brazilian foreign minister to insist that the protest include a reference to the scuttling of the *Graf Von Spee.*

The *Graf Von Spee* incident had brought home the fact that declarations alone would not protect the interests of the American nations. On the same day, in January 1940, representatives of the Argentine and Uruguayan governments spoke out against passive neutrality. The Uruguayan representative stated that it was absurd to think that Uruguay would violate its vital interests just to maintain neutrality. He implied that Uruguay might not consider as belligerents democratic nations defending their own rights or the rights of victims of aggression.[9] The Argentine spokesman criticized the British rebuttal to the protest against the *Graf Von Spee* incident. He stated that the neutral nations of America had the right to establish their own rules of neutrality which "are applicable only in the Americas." He was willing to see a Pan-American agreement barring all belligerent ships from American waters.[10]

The *Graf Von Spee* incident precipitated a full-dress discussion of the Panama declaration within the State Department. One policy paper argued for a basic change in U.S. neutrality policy and a move toward what Argentina later would call "nonbelligerency."[11] Any indication, however, vague or informal, that the United States was wavering on the policy of neutrality would have served to buttress the pro-Ally group within the Argentine government.

All the while, Argentina's economic woes intensified. By the beginning of 1940 the Argentine government was casting about frantically for financing to cover its short-term debt. By the end of March the government was so embarrassed that it had a top-level representative apprise the American ambassador of its difficulties and ask for aid. Armour endorsed the request. At the same time, two other developments combined to force the hand of the Ortiz government. The series of federal interventions in the provinces, designed to speed the democratization process, had created animosity and tension within the ruling coalition and in the nation. The intervention of the province of Buenos Aires on 7 March 1940 was the most important. It precipitated a cabinet crisis, and two ministers resigned. For a few days in March the situation was tense. It was clear that the return to nonfraudulent democracy was not going to be smooth. The intervention brought into the open the divisions within the ruling coalition and prompted Ortiz to attempt to consolidate his political power by means of a dramatic gesture that would strengthen his hand domestically and secure the international position of Argentina.[12] He proposed to the United States that the American nations declare their "nonbelligerency" in the European conflict.

Cantilo called Norman Armour to his office on the afternoon of 19 April 1940 to inform him that the Argentine government was "worried by the position in which the American Republics find themselves as a result of the evolution of the war in Europe." Neutrality, he declared, no longer existed in Europe, and a neutral status created duties but gave no rights. He suggested that the American republics agree to declare that they become "nonbelligerents."[13] Armour immediately cabled the results of this interview to Washington. Later the same day, Cantilo repeated his proposal to the Brazilian ambassador in Buenos Aires, José de Paula Rodrígues Alves. He also cabled the Argentine ambassador in Washington, Felipe A. Espil, apprising him of what had taken place that day and instructing him to bring the proposal to the attention of the State Department at the earliest opportunity. How the hemispheric declaration of "nonbelligerency" would be made would be determined by the response of the U.S. and Brazilian governments. Espil communicated this to Wells in an interview, 22 April 1940, as follows:

> The American countries are neutral and have even established a zone of security to protect that neutrality, a zone which the belligerents have not recognized and do not respect. Furthermore, in Europe neutral countries are either being invaded or else are on a war footing as a result of the threats of the great powers. . . . In a word, neutrality does not exist in reality. It creates obligations but it does not offer guarantees. The norms and conventions which we neutrals apply and which we invoke are a dead letter. Meanwhile the European war is assuming proportions and a threat which

must necessarily disquiet America. I propose that we Americans issue forth
from fiction and adapt ourselves to reality and that by common accord we
declare that we are ceasing to be neutrals in order to be "nonbelligerents."
This signifies, as the case of Italy demonstrates, not to enter into war and to
proceed according to one's own interest.[14]

During the period of political crisis, Nazi propaganda increased markedly. It
reached a crescendo of sorts when the nonbelligerency proposal was made
public in May. Cantilo was glad to have discussion of the proposal in the
open. He hoped to bring greater pressure to bear on the United States by
playing upon public sensitivity to the German invasion of the low countries.
There is reason to believe that word of the proposal reached the public by way
of a leak from Cantilo's office to an American correspondent.[15]

Public exposure, coming on the heels of the German invasion of the low
countries, produced a great deal of favorable publicity for the Argentine
government. Roosevelt addressed the Pan-American Scientific Congress,
then in progress, and intimated that neutrality might not be the best policy
for the hemisphere. Uruguay submitted to the government of Panama, representing the American nations under the Panama declaration, a proposal for a
joint declaration of solidarity with the Belgian and Dutch people. At many
points, the Uruguayan proposal matched the nonbelligerency proposal. Sympathy for the invaded nations dovetailed with the discussion of the Argentine
proposal to enhance the prestige of the Ortiz government. This period in May
seems to have been the high point for the Ortiz-Cantilo group in its fight to
maintain power.

The pro-Ally group soon came crashing down from this high point. The
United States refused to accept the nonbelligerency proposal, and the antidemocratic forces in Argentina stepped up their attacks on the government.
Their voices grew louder as Nazi successes in Europe continued. They hanged
Foreign Minister Cantilo in effigy; they demanded his resignation on the
grounds that he was selling out to the North Americans. Rumors circulated
that the antidemocratic forces were getting ready to make their move.[16] To
counteract the antidemocratic propaganda, Ortiz tried to clamp down on all
criticism of the government while reasserting his defense of Argentine national interests. He submitted a bill to the National Congress outlawing
unneutral behavior. Doubtless, Ortiz thought to take advantage of the powers
given the executive in this bill to squelch Nazi activity, although on the
surface, the bill looked like a concession to the conservative nationalists. The
bill precipitated a violent debate in the National Congress that strained the
fragile alliance between democratic elements of the Conservative party and
the leadership of the opposition parties.[17]

In the congressional debate over the bill to outlaw unneutral behavior,
widely different political groups adopted a pro-Argentine or moderate nationalistic line, revealing a very broad consensus on what the Argentine economy

needed and what Argentina should get from the United States or from the Allies. This broad consensus restricted the government's efforts to side with the United States and gave the anti-Allies an advantage because they could claim that complete neutrality was the traditional policy of Argentina and was in the nation's best interests.

The antidemocratic argument was disarmingly simple. It held that the government's policy of cooperation with the United States would fail because the United States would never offer the kind of help that Argentina needed. It was silly, therefore, gratuitously to alienate the Axis powers. Furthermore, taking advantage of widespread nationalism, they implied that the Ortiz policy was akin to a sellout to the Yankees. Aside from some miraculous solution to Argentina's problem, the only effective answer by the Ortiz government to this attack would be to produce some concrete demonstration of support from the United States. For a period of nearly four months, from April to July, President Ortiz sought to silence his enemies by clamping down on the rising political tension in the provinces, producing a commercial agreement with the United States, and seeking U.S. commitment to an active program of hemispheric defense (nonbelligerency) that would include Argentina in a position of prestige.

A commercial agreement with the United States that would protect Argentina's economic interests was the key because it would win support from the powerful, politically neutral commercial groups and rob Ortiz's opponents of their most potent argument. Formal bilateral negotiations had been suspended in January. Efforts to renew them had been frustrated by administrative confusion in the United States and by failure to agree on the basis for talks. Increasingly desperate, Argentina tried all manner of means to move the U.S. government. Beginning early in June, there was a series of leaks, first to U.S. diplomats by people close to the government, then to the press by minor officials in the government, and finally by major figures in the cabinet directly to the staff of the U.S. Embassy, to the effect that Argentina was under increasing pressure from Germany and from Nazi groups within Argentina; that the Argentine economy was weak and getting weaker; and that unless the United States responded with aid in some form, Argentina could not continue its policy of cooperation with the nations of the hemisphere, that Argentina would have to go to Germany for trade and aid, thus falling into the Nazi camp like a spent trout.

Armour was aware of the concerted effort to pressure the United States. He objected to the "crudely put" alternatives and the "unsavory features" of the pressures. And yet he felt that the issues at stake were important enough to urge the State Department to take "prompt and vigorous action" that would "place the friendly President in a strong position and enable him to make a definite decision in favor of American cooperation." Without such action, he warned, "it will be difficult to secure necessary cooperation by Argentina and its smaller neighbors and may even lead to a break in American solidarity."[18]

The balance of political forces in Argentina was very delicate. Ortiz had to strengthen his position. The democratic faction gambled on securing United States cooperation. It lost and fell from power.

The Argentine proposal for hemispheric nonbelligerency caught the State Department by surprise. Preoccupied with the slowly evolving, agonizing domestic debate over U.S. neutrality, the government was no prepared for such a proposal. It was surprised especially because the proposal came from Argentina—it was out of character, making it difficult to appreciate how it formed part of a desperate strategy by the Ortiz government to maintain power. The element of surprise may have been ample reason for turning aside the Argentine initiative. Another, and less flattering, reason may have been reluctance on the part of U.S. leaders to give Argentina too much influence in hemispheric councils—to give Argentina credit for determining the policy of the United States and the other nations of the hemisphere. This would weaken U.S. leadership.

While the element of surprise may or may not have been critical in formulating the U.S. response to the Argentine proposal, the question of timing definitely was of primary importance. The proposal came into the State Department at a bad moment. The department was being deluged with reports from Europe. Germany had taken the Scandinavian countries. The round of top-level discussions in the department seemed to go on without recess. The sheer quantity of material coming in from Europe made it difficult to give proper consideration to a proposal that had serious implications for the entire hemisphere. The fact that Sumner Welles was in charge of Latin American affairs did not ease the situation. He was burdened with the responsibility of coordinating U.S. relations with Europe. The fine details of hemispheric relations were obscured. A crucial telegram from Armour in June, discussing his talk with Finance Minister Pedro Groppo, took three months to reach the trade and economic advisors in charge of commercial negotiations with Argentina. By that time, the situation in Argentina was beyond repair.[19]

The proposal was embarrassing to the United States for yet another reason. It came at a time when the domestic debate over neutrality had as much influence over U.S. policy as did events in Europe themselves. Roosevelt had been involved for years in a running battle with Congress about control of foreign affairs. In 1940 the approach of the presidential election compounded his difficulties. Espil was convinced that the domestic political battle in the United States killed his government's proposal. He reported at the end of April that as long as the Republicans made use of the neutrality issue in their campaign,

> the present administration will look with little sympathy and even with alarm
> at any suggestion for a collective declaration, be it of "non-belligerency" or
> merely "the abandonment of neutrality," no matter how many explanations or
> reservations might accompany it. This and not a strict adherence to the

principles of international law . . . explains the position of the Department of State in its memorandum of April 24. This is true even though this country has an administration which, despite the label of neutrality, moves closer and closer to "non-belligerency" in the European sense of the term.[20]

Given the harried state of the department and the nature of the domestic political situation, it is not surprising that an unexpected Argentine proposal that had implications for the entire hemisphere would not receive a warm reception. The United States was trying to build hemispheric solidarity slowly and on its own terms. The basic U.S. strategy was to win specific military commitments from individual countries. Political declarations were kept vague, with the understanding that meaningful political cooperation would be built on a solid foundation of bilateral military agreements. In return for the military commitments, the State Department was offering the only aid it had to give, credits from the Export-Import Bank. Neither the proposal for nonbelligerency nor Argentina's demands for long-term financing and marketing agreements fit U.S. strategy.

This is not to say that the United States was unwilling to accommodate Argentina in 1940. While the State Department turned aside the non-belligernecy proposal without much ado, it pressed the commercial negotiations with goodwill. The department was not able to reach an agreement with Argentina in time to help the Ortiz administration, partly because it did not immediately connect the nonbelligerency proposal with the economic talks or appreciate the seriousness of the crisis in Argentina, partly because of the personalities involved, and partly because it had very little flexibility in its commercial negotiations with Argentina.

As late as April, the State Department went to great pains to draft a formal rebuttal to Argentine criticism of U.S. tariff policy. Such a strong, logical note no doubt pleased Secretary Hull. It only served to weaken the Ortiz government. While the Argentine proposal was still pending, the State Department used the German invasion of the low countries to divert attention to an innocuous Pan-American protest against the Nazi aggression. Over and over again, Ambassador Armour urged the department first "to consider sympathetically any suggestions that the Argentine Government might wish to make in the direction of American solidarity, even though we might not find it possible to accept time," and later to speed the financial and commercial agreements to forestall the expected political difficulties. Instead of expediting negotiations, the State Department entered into a maddening series of discussions within itself and with other departments of the executive over the details of each proposal. The discussions were maddening to anyone who wanted to see action because they analyzed abstractly each proposal without reference to the exigencies of the situation in Argentina. Sumner Welles made one attempt to tie U.S. economic policy to the objectives of U.S. foreign policy in Argentina. He urged the president and secretary of state to make certain commercial concessions to the Argentines in order to ensure Argentine cooperation in hemispheric defense. Nothing came of the suggestion, and economic negotiations languished in the hands of the technicians.[21]

The trouble with the technicians was that they were too busy being politicians. The Argentine negotiations were caught in the upheaval in Washington over the administrative reorganization for war. Every department wanted to carve out for itself the greatest possible sphere of responsibility. Department heads and bureau chiefs jockeyed for position, hoping that the president would favor them in the wartime reorganization. The commercial negotiations with Argentina involved the Treasury, Agriculture, and Commerce departments and the Export-Import Bank. Within the State Department they were subject to the scrutiny of the Treaty Division, economic advisor, trade advisor, Latin American Division, two assistant secretaries, and the undersecretary.[22]

At every turn Argentina was made to bend to the needs of U.S. policy. Prior to April 1940 the Export-Import Bank was the only agency able to be of help to the Latin American countries. Jesse Jones, administrator of the Federal Loan Agency, that controlled the bank, was opposed to any but the most conservative financial ventures.[23] In July and August the Argentine government wanted a top-level U.S. mission to visit Argentina to discuss all pending economic issues. Instead, Argentines had to come to Washington in October. Warren Lee Pierson, president of the Export-Import Bank, visited Argentina in September to discuss credits for Argentine imports from the United States. Pierson got a good look at the Argentine economy and seconded the Argentine requests for broad talks. These talks opened in Washington during October and, two months later, produced a Stabilization Agreement that involved a credit from the Export-Import Bank for $60 million, restricted to use in paying for imports from the United States, and a $50 million "contract" with the Treasury Department designed to stabilize the U.S. dollar–Argentine peso exchange rate. The agreement was a case of too little, too late.

The United States' summary rejection of the Argentine proposal for nonbelligerency stirred more profound responses throughout the hemisphere than did the proposal itself. The consequences of the rejection were most important in Argentina. They were significant also in Brazil, Uruguay, Chile, and the United States. The Argentine proposal forced the United States to speed up its program for hemispheric cooperation. Uruguay, Brazil, and Chile indicated that they were favorably disposed toward the proposal. They were willing to reject it only if the United States offered a specific alternate strategy for dealing with the problems arising out of the war in Europe. Chile was worried about its military weakness. It was fearful of an attack by Japan and of its inability to defend its long coastline. In 1939 the government of Chile had requested military aid from the United States. The State Department was aware of the importance of the aid, that it was needed to win Chilean cooperation; but U.S. military authorities were unable to provide the necessary *matérièl*. Chile's failure to get aid from the United States, together with its sense of military weakness, made it suspicious of bilateral arrangements and receptive to hemispheric or multilateral protective measures, even measures whose results clearly would not be favorable to the totalitarian powers. When the United States led the rejection of the Argentine proposal and intensified its own efforts to weave a network of bilateral relationships centered on itself, the Chilean government became less cooperative.[24]

The Uruguayan government faced the same constellation of political opponents as the Ortiz government in Argentina. The government of President Alfredo Baldomir feared a Nazi coup and seized upon the Argentine proposal for multilateral action as an ideal way to blunt the barbs of its domestic critics. It embarrassed the Uruguayan government, therefore, when the United States rejected the Argentine proposal and pressed for immediate bilateral military staff talks. Foreign Minister Alberto N. Guani received a fearsome roasting in the press and the Uruguayan congress for selling out to the Yankees. Guani's fear of a Nazi coup proved to be greater than his aversion to public criticism, and he persevered in his efforts to wrest from the United States more than promises of military support. At the height of the crisis, in June 1940, the United States cruiser *Quincy* arrived in Montevideo and had a most salutary effect. By the end of 1940 the United States and Uruguay had agreed to establish air bases on Uruguayan soil.[25]

Brazil was a special case. Foreign Minister Cantilo communicated the Argentine proposal to Brazilian Foreign Minister Osvaldo Aranha at the same time he sent it to Washington. He wanted Brazil to help Argentina convince the United States to cooperate in such a multilateral venture. Instead of siding with Argentina, the Brazilians turned over the proposal to the State Department and promised to be ruled by it in every particular. Aranha was reluctant to turn down the Argentines. He told Sumner Welles that he hoped the Americans would be able to keep the Argentines in the fold; otherwise they could become disagreeable. As a result, it was the United States that influenced Brazil in handling the Argentine proposal and not the other way around, as Ortiz had hoped. The Brazilian role and Aranha's close personal relationship with Welles were added fuel for the Argentine political fire. Nationalists since Zeballos and before had been jealous and disdainful of Brazil. That Cantilo had looked to Brazil for leadership only gave more ammunition to his domestic critics. As it turned out, the Argentines did become disagreeable, and Brazil benefited from its cooperative posture toward the United States during the war.[26]

The Argentine proposal, together with events in Europe, forced the United States to increase the pace of its preparations for hemisperhic defense. With new energy the State Department urged all the nations in the Americas to accept U.S. leadership in bilateral talks to determine the military requirements of defense and to establish strategic commodity agreements. The only multilateral agreements that the United States seemed to favor in 1940 were broad statements of purpose giving the United States the right or the responsibility for the defense of the hemisphere. Bilateral military agreements carried with them definite political commitments that were distasteful to several Latin American nations. Argentina was unwilling to commit itself in bilateral staff talks because it was not convinced that the United States could meet its ever-expanding commitments in the hemisphere. The breakdown of negotiations between the United States and Chile in 1939, and the frustrating postponement of the agreement with Uruguay, gave the Argentines further grounds for skepticism. Their talks with U.S. military representatives did not bear fruit until well into 1941, long after Ortiz and Cantilo had fallen from power.

To the Argentines, the United States seemed insensitive and unbending. Throughout 1940 the U.S. government refused to make any important compromise that might have given Ortiz a lever against his political opponents. The Argentine-United States trade agreement was not signed until October 1941, too late to help the democratic forces. The United States refused to consider the kinds of trade or commodity agreements the Argentines deemed vital to their well-being while persisting in promoting agreements that would not help and, in some cases, might even cause difficulties. The strategic commodity program, aimed as it was at products not produced in the River Plate, did not benefit Argentina and, as it gathered momentum, pushed the two nations still further apart. Argentina seemed irrelevant to the intensifying preparations for the defense of the hemisphere.

The most serious consequence of the rejection of the Argentine proposal was that it upset the delicate balance of political forces within Argentina and ended any effort for constructive cooperation with the United States. Ortiz and Cantilo sensed their defeat. Ortiz, almost immediately, began to cover himself and to retreat from the politically exposed position he had taken in making the proposal for nonbelligerency. He continued to speak against totalitarian government and to support democracy, but his criticisms of the Axis now were combined carefully with statements of Argentina's absolute neutrality. Ambassador Armour felt that Ortiz, having been rebuffed by the United States and realizing that he could not count on the support of the army in taking a strong line with respect to Germany, considered it prudent to modify the government's attitude. Ortiz was disheartened further by the failure of the United States to respond with alacrity to the Uruguayan crisis in June, and he lashed out bitterly at the United States during a public celebration of Argentine Independence Day, 9 July 1940. Neither the president nor his foreign minister had felt themselves involved personally in the Argentine proposal, but they were put off by the American response. Cantilo, a man of great pride, was insulted. He considered himself partially disgraced and retreated even more completely than Ortiz. Thereafter, he was not cooperative in his dealings with the United States, and left the cabinet in August.[27]

Disheartened, physically spent, and nearly blind from diabetes, Ortiz turned over the mandate to Vice President Castillo on 3 July. Many people believed that the president was too ill to return to office. Castillo's accession to power stimulated a trend to isolationism, a return to *principismo*. The Argentine representative to the Havana Conference, 21–30 July 1940, was not given specific instructions. He went to find out what the United States would do to solve Argentina's economic problems. He was told not to expect much because Argentine policy must be to keep in good relations with both sides. Only days before the conference opened the politically powerful cattlemen passed a resolution that the government should refrain from entering into any political or economic commitments that would limit the country's freedom of action in selling meat to Germany if and when that country should be in a position to take it. The cattlemen and their allies in the meat packing industry and in banking were convinced that the goodwill of Germany was of great importance to them and that in the event of the defeat of Great Britain, the Germans would be by far their most important customers. The United States, apparently, scarcely counted. The political tide in Argentina had turned. It was no longer a matter of siding with the Americans or with the Germans. A more rigid nationalistic attitude prevailed that refused to side with either.

Acting Foreign Minister Julio A. Roca resigned in January 1941 and was replaced in March by Enrique Ruiz Guiñazú, Argentine minister to the Vatican, outspoken critic of democracy in Argentina and of the Allies, and a warm sympathizer of the totalitarian nations. From the moment he took office in June 1941 cooperation with U.S. objectives in the hemisphere was impossible. The Argentines took no action to approve the loan agreements reached in Washington at the end of the 1940; they failed to renew the military staff conversations; they now opposed the establishment of U.S. bases in Uruguay; they refused to confiscate German ships in Argentine ports, even to prevent sabotage; and they argued loudly against an Uruguayan proposal to toughen the terms of American nonbelligerency.[28]

Sumner Welles felt that Ruiz Guiñazú was the villain of the episode and referred to him as "that calamitous figure." Ruiz Guiñazú influenced more and more of Argentine foreign policy as time went on. The lines of policy he followed were in great part determined for him by ultranationalist groups and by pro-Nazi elements in the Argentine army. Welles decried "his almost incredible lack of comprehension of the salient points in the field of foreign relations," and pointed out that

> he had a strong prejudice against the United States and a barely concealed belief that the civilization of this country was so decadent and inefficient because of its democratic institutions, that it would not conceivably be able to stand up against the power and might of the Axis nations. . . . he was obsessed with the belief that it was beneath the dignity of the Argentine Republic ever to follow the course upon which the United States had

embarked. . . . [He was dominated by a group of young men] representative of the retrograde ultranationalism which had recently been shaping in the Argentine Republic. Denouncing democracy as a failure, they were proclaiming that a purely nationalistic authoritarian regime was the only form of government that could save Argentina.[29]

Given this judgment of Ruiz Guiñazú and the strong pro-Ally tone of the Argentine press throughout the war, it is congenial to explain Argentine hostility as the result of malevolent leaders controlling the nation by means of the army and preventing the true feelings of the Argentine people from being expressed in the nation's foreign policy.

This was the opinion of many U.S. officials at the time and has been the opinion of many academic analysts since.[30] It ignores the linkages between domestic politics and foreign affairs; it ignores the deeply ingrained distrust of the United States across a broad spectrum of political groups; most important, it ignores the land-owning oligarchy and their financial allies who remained coldly neutral, focused on the national interest as defined by access to markets for the nation's exports and oblivious to questions of international power politics. Their neutralism only intensified as the United States insisted on bilateral defense measures and on a form of hemispheric cooperation that did not suit their concept of Argentina's prestige. This identified neutrality with nationalism and made Ruiz Guiñazú appear as a defender of Argentine sovereignty. It was a nationalism powerfully buttressed by the traditional view of Argentina's position in world affairs. Argentines who had clung to this view during the difficult days of the depression saw in the coming war an opportunity to reassert Argentine importance in the world—and at the expense of the United States.

It is tempting to speculate on what might have occurred had the United States accepted the Argentine proposal. Argentine Ambassador Espil was convinced it would have committed the Argentine government to an avowedly pro-Ally policy. This alone might have been sufficient to forestall the transfer of more than the formal trappings of power to Vice President Ramon S. Castillo or the sweeping changes within the government Castillo made soon after he assumed power in June 1940. Even had it not done that much, it would at the very least have inhibited Castillo and his pro-Axis friends from making Argentina the outcast of the inter-American community during the war and might have kept Perón from coming to power.[31] But this would be too romantic. It does not take into account that Ruiz Guiñazú accurately reflected a set of powerful, deeply rooted assumptions about Argentina's role in world affairs. That those assumptions had become painfully inappropriate ought not to blind us to the fact that they continued to exercise a curious power over many Argentines and virtually determined the boundaries of discourse concerning Argentine foreign policy.

NOTES

1. The actual title was *Consultation among the American Republics with Respect to the Argentine Situation. Memorandum of the United States Government* (Washington, D.C.: U.S. Government Printing Office, 1946).

2. Mario Rapoport, *Política y Diplomacia en la Argentina*, (Buenos Aires: Editorial Tesis, 1986), chapter 2.

3. Robert Potash, *The Army and Politics in Argentina, 1928–1945* (Stanford: Stanford University Press, 1969).

4. This estimate, by a high-ranking official in the Foreign Ministry, is included in Armour's dispatch of 14 June 1940, National Archives, RG 59, 835.00/866.

5. Quoted in William L. Langer and S. Everett Gleason, *The Challenge to Isolation, 1937–1940* (New York: Published for the Council on Foreign Relations by Harper & Brothers, 1952), 133.

6. On the imperative need for economic aid before Argentines would accept a policy of cooperation with the United States, see Armour's dispatch, 7 June 1940, 810.20 Defense/20 1/2; *La Prensa*, 13 June 1940, 11:5–7 and 12:1–2. On the foreign exchange problems see Armour's dispatches of 27 February and 11 March 1940, 835.51/1271 and 1274; *New York Times*, 1 February 1940, 35:3 and 12 April 1940, 35:1. On the commodity export problem see Armour's telegram, 22 May 1940, 641.1115/40. On the Bolivian petroleum problem, 1940, see file 724.35; for more general background see Bryce Wood, *The Making of the Good Neighbor Policy* (New York: Columbia University Press, 1961), 168–202.

7. Armour's dispatch of 11 March 1940, 611.0031/4925, enclosing an editorial from *La Prensa*. On Argentine nationalism at this time see Arthur P. Whitaker and David C. Jordan, *Nationalism in Contemporary Latin America* (New York: The Free Press, 1966), 53–66; and Potash, *Army and Politics*, 79–140.

8. Sumner Welles, *The Time for Decision* (New York: Harper & Brothers, 1944), 214. For the Argentine instructions and other information on Argentine activities at the Panama and Havana conference see *Reuniones de consulta entre ministros de relaciones exteriores de las Repúblicas Americanas, Panama . . . 1939, la Habana, . . . 1940. Participación Argentina* (Buenos Aires: Ministerio de Relaciones Exteriores y Culto, Division de Asuntos Jurídicos, 1941).

9. Statement in the government newspaper, *El Diario*, reported in Ambassador Wilson's dispatch, 19 January 1940, 740.00111A.R./952.

10. Quoted in the *New York Times*, 19 January 1940, 11:1. Cantilo disputed the British contention that nothing in international law gives neutrals the right to apply sanctions against belligerents who violate a safety zone. He said, "The very name 'safety zone' indicates that what is desired is that there be removed from American coasts all danger to all interference with navigation caused by the continuous presence of belligerent warships." The United States refused to respond publicly to the British note. See the *New York Times*, 17 January 1940, 2:2.

11. The memoranda were drafted between 29 January and 1 February 1940 and are filed in 740.00111A.R./915 and 960 1/2.

12. The political crisis can be followed in *La Prensa*, February–March 1940, and Mario Rapoport, *Gran Bretaña, Estados Unidos y las Clases Dirigentes Argentinas, 1940–1945* (Buenos Aires: Editorial Belgrano, 1981).

13. Armour's telegram to the secretary of state, 19 April 1940, printed in *Foreign Relations of the United States,* vol. 1, 1940 (Washington, D.C.: U.S. Government Printing Office, 1959–61), 743–44. This collection of documents is cited hereafter as *FRUS,* with the appropriate year and volume.

14. Memorandum of conversation by the under secretary of state (Welles), 22 April 1940, *FRUS,* 1940, 1:745–48. The sequence of events is reconstructed from the American documents and from Stanley E. Hilton, "Argentine Neutrality, September, 1939–June, 1940. A Re-Examination," *The Americas* 22, no. 3 (January 1966): 227–57, and Adolfo Scilingo, "Doctrina de la Neutralidad a la no Beligerancia: El Aislacionismo norteamericano y una iniciativa argentina en la Segunda Guerra Mundial," *Jurisprudencia Argentina* 28, no. 2590 (12 July 1966).

15. On the leak see the memorandum by Assistant Secretary Adolph A. Berle, 11 May 1940, 740.00111A.R./1079. For reports on the proposal see the *New York Times,* 13 May 1940, 1:3 and 4:8, and 14 May 1940, 12:3; *Boston Evening Transcript,* 13 May 1940, 11:4; *La Prensa,* 13 May 1940, 1:5–6; *Washington Post,* 13 May 1940, 1:6.

16. *New York Times,* 19 May 1940, 25:4. Late in May word reached the State Department from France that a pro-Nazi coup in Argentina was imminent. This was passed on to Armour. See Ambassador William Bullitt's telegram, 24 May 1940, 835.00N/48.

17. Socialists, labor unionists, student groups, National Democrats, ultra-nationalists, and Radicals spoke against the so-called Public Order Law. The Argentine press was hostile toward it. The minister of the interior defended it by pointing to the "evident" public unrest and confusion, to rumors rampant in the country. The president's secretary went on the radio 12 June to deny rumors of a cabinet crisis and arrests of military officials. These events are recounted in *La Prensa,* June 1940. Amour's dispatches are in RG59, 835.00N, and in Rapoport, *Política y Diplomacia en la Argentina.*

18. *FRUS,* 1940, 5:465–66 and 5:468–69.

19. The telegram in question is published in *FRUS,* 1940, 5:468–69. The office memoranda complaining of the delay in circulating the telegram are filed in 611.3531/1549. The files of the department attest to the bulk of material coming into Washington at this time. For a general statement on the situation see Langer and Gleason, *The Challenge to Isolation,* 419–29. In this context, Langer and Gleason refer to the Argentine proposal as "premature" (610). They allude to the discussion of hemispheric problems that went on at this time but say that that discussion was general and not connected with the specific problems bothering the Argentines (607–8).

20. Quoted in Scilingo, "Doctrina de la Neutralidad a la no Beligerancia," 3:2–3. This view is shared by two Argentine scholars, Alberto Conil Paz and Gustavo Ferrari, *La política exterior de Argentina, 1930–1960* (Buenos Aires: Huemul, 1965), 69–70. There is even some evidence for this view in the U.S. documents; see the undated inter-office memorandum (probably written at the end of September) by the economic advisor, 835.51/1342.

21. For a general discussion of distinguishing between irrelevant information (noise) and critical warnings (signals), see Roberta Wohlstetter, *Pearl Harbor: Warning and Decision* (Standford, Calif.: Stanford University Press, 1962). The department's justification of U.S. tariff policy is in Hull to Armour, 9 April 1940, 611.0031/42925. The use of empty rhetoric is shown in Langer and Gleason, *Challenge to Isolation,* 609,

and the *New York Times*, 14 May 1940, 12:3. Armour's warnings are in his dispatch of 26 April 1940, 740.00111 A.R./1028, and his telegram of 22 November 1940, 835.51/1371. On the department's attention to detail and its propensity for delay see the memoranda of 11 April 1940, 835.51/1282; 5 July 1940, 611.3531/1547 1/2; 28 September 1940, 835/51/1368; and 2 October 1940, 835.51/1342. Fear of interfering with the Havana conference slowed things up in July (*FRUS*, 1940, 5:470–74). Argentine impatience was reported with brutal clarity in the *New York Times*, 22 September 1940, 30:2, and 8 November 1940, 6:2. Welles's attempt to combine commercial and military considerations is in 810.20 Defense/20 1/2. General discussion of U.S. policy toward Argentina at this time is Randall Bennett Wood's *The Roosevelt Foreign Policy Establishment and the "Good Neighbor": The United States and Argentina, 1941–1945* (Lawrence: The Regents Press of Kansas, 1979).

22. On the administrative shuffling before the war see Eliot Janeway, *The Struggle for Survival*, 2d ed. (New York: Waybright and Talley, 1968); Welles, *The Time for Decision*, 217; and Langer and Gleason, *The Challenge to Isolation*, 278–79 and 630.

23. Janeway, *The Struggle for Survival*, 67. State Department officials were not more adventuresome. They opposed governmental loans to Argentina and, while they wanted to wean Argentina from dependence on Great Britain, they were unwilling to try any of the schemes put forward. See 835.51/1274, 1282, 1285.

24. On the Chilean situation see Langer and Gleason, *Challenge to Isolation*, 276; Ambassador Claude G. Bowers to the secretary of state, 15 May 1940, 740.00111 A.R./1104; *FRUS*, 1940, 5:52–57 and 5:670–94; and Michael J. Francis, *The Limits of Hegemony. United States Relations with Argentina and Chile during World War II* (West Bend, Ind.: University of Notre Dame Press, 1977).

25. Langer and Gleason, *Challenge to Isolation*, 611–14, and *The Undeclared War 1940–1941* (New York: Harper & Brothers, 1953), 153–56; *FRUS*, 1940, 5:162–74 and 5:1147–66; and the telegrams of Ambassador Edwin C. Wilson, 19 and 28 June 1940, 810.20 Defense 19 1/4 and 19 2/14.

26. *FRUS*, 1940, 5:757–68; Frank D. McCann, Jr., *The Brazilian–American Alliance, 1937–1945* (Princeton: Princeton University Press, 1973); Stanley E. Hilton, *Hitler's Secret War in South America* (Baton Rouge: Louisiana State University Press, 1981); and Joseph S. Tulchin, "Una perspectiva histórica de la política argentina frente al Brasil," *Estudios Internácionales* 13, no. 52 (October–December 1980).

27. *FRUS*, 1940, 1:769; Armour's dispatch of 24 May 1940, 740.00111 A.R./1178; Armour's 12 July 1940, 835.00/868; Scilingo, "Doctrina de la Neutralidad," 4:1. This was at a time when the Argentine press and public were outspoken in condemnation of German aggression. See Armour's 11 May 1940, 740.0011, European War 1939/2863. On Ortiz's reaction to Uruguayan crisis see Armour to the secretary of state, 12 July 1940, 835.001 Ortiz, Roberto M./105, and Langer and Gleason, *Challenge to Isolation*, 611–17 and 621–22. Cantilo's pride was discussed in the author's interview with Ambassador Adolfo Scilingo, 12 June 1968; Armour's dispatches of 26 April and 24 May 1940, 740.00111 A.R./1028, 1178, and 26 July 1940, 835.00/880.

28. Harold F. Peterson, *Argentine and the United States* (New York: State University of New York, 1964), 407–8 and 415; Tuck's telegrams of 24, 26, and 28 June 1941, 740.00111 A.R./1330, 1334, 1348. Ironically, at the time of his appointment, Ruiz Guiñazú was considered an antitotalitarian by the Germans. See Potash, *The Army and Politics in Argentina*, 152.

29. Welles, *Time For Decision*, 220, 225.

30. For this characterization of Argentine policy see Thomas F. McGann, *Argentina: The Divided Land* (Princeton, N.J.: D. Van Nostrand Co. 1966), 84; James R. Scobie, *Argentina: A City and a Nation* (New York: Oxford University Press, 1964), 185; Samuel Flagg Bemis, *The Latin American Policy of the United States* (New York: Harcourt, Brace & Co., 1943), 380; and, in a more guarded fashion, Arthur P. Whitaker, *The United States and Argentina* (Cambridge, Mass.: Harvard University Press, 1954), 112. For an extreme and critical description of Argentina's attitude see J. Lloyd Mecham, *The United States and Inter-American Security, 1889–1960* (Austin: University of Texas Press, 1961), 185–200.

31. Scilingo to the author, 5 February 1969; Conil Paz and Ferrari, *La política exterior de Argentina*, 70.

Estanislao Zeballos served as foreign minister under three presidents before World War I.
Courtesy Archivo General de la Nación

Honorio Pueyrredón, foreign minister under Hipólito Yrigoyen and ambassador to the United States. *Courtesy Archivo General de la Nación*

Carlos Saavedra Lamas, foreign minister under Augustín P. Justo and winner of the 1937 Nobel Peace Prize. *Courtesy Archivo General de la Nación*

José María Cantilo, foreign minister under Roberto Ortíz. *Courtesy Archivo General de la Nación*

Diplomatic rivals Spruille Braden and Carlos Saavedra Lamas meet at the Buenos Aires Peace Conference in 1936. *Courtesy Archivo General de la Nación*

Enrique Ruíz Guiñazú, Ramón Castillo's foreign minister who earned Sumner Welles's ire at the 1942 hemispheric meeting in Rio de Janeiro. *Courtesy Archivo General de la Nación*

Orlando Peluffo, member of the military junta that took power in 1942. *Courtesy Archivo General de la Nación*

Juan Carlos Bramuglia, Perón's chief foreign affairs advisor. *Courtesy Archivo General de la Nación*

Hipólito Jesus Paz, one of Perón's foreign ministers.
Courtesy Archivo General de la Nación

Mario Amadeo, one of Perón's foreign ministers, explaining the Third Position to reporters in 1955. *Courtesy Archivo General de la Nación*

Carlos Florit, foreign minister under Arturo Frondizi. *Courtesy Archivo General de la Nación*

Clifford Berryman in the 27 January 1944 *Washington Star* comments on Argentina's policy of neutrality during World War II. Copyright 1944 by the *Washington Post. Reprinted by permission.*

chapter 6

WORLD WAR II AND
U.S. PERSECUTION OF ARGENTINA

Ruiz Guiñazú went to the hemispheric meeting in Rio in February 1942, called to discuss the Japanese attack on the United States, with instructions to avoid being bulldozed by the United States. The dominant factions in the Argentine government certainly would accept no course of action that made it appear as if the nation were subjected to United States leadership. In addition, the Argentine military were nervous about making commitments at Rio because they didn't have the equipment and weren't capable of defending any portion of the coastline. On the other hand, they were anxious to get their hands on some of the lend-lease equipment the United States was making available to the British and would soon make available to the Brazilians. Senior United States military officers were attempting to moderate FDR's bold assertions and to curb the enthusiasm of the State Department for hemispheric defense because they fully realized that none of the countries in the region was capable of fulfilling its commitments and that the United States was not in a position to provide them with the equipment necessary to carry out their task. The negotiations with the Chileans, conducted just prior to the Rio meeting, showed very clearly the relationship between a Chilean promise to join a hemispheric defense effort and United States shipments of critical material, although the Americans never were able to ship everything the Chileans required. The negotiations with the Argentine military had not progressed as far as those with the Chileans, but the outcome was as obvious to the Argentines as it was to the Americans.[1]

The meeting at Rio brought to a head a conflict within the United States government that had been simmering for several years and precipitated a process of confrontation and antagonism between the United States and Argentina that can only be characterized as severely detrimental to the national interests of both nations as well as to long-term relations between them. It was a process marked by irrational behavior by several senior figures in both governments, it ruined the diplomatic and political careers of not a few participants on both sides, and it caused serious irritation in the wartime relationship between the United States and Great Britain.[2]

In one sense, Argentina got caught up in a bitter bureaucratic political struggle that had less to do with its behavior than it did with control over the foreign policy process in the United States. From the very beginning of the Roosevelt administration, there had been tension between Under Secretary of State Welles and Secretary of State Hull. The two men were vastly different in personality. Hull always resented the close friendship between Welles and the president and felt himself excluded from the East Coast foreign policy establishment of which Welles was a prominent member. This tension and the personal animosity were exacerbated by their policy disagreements. Welles led the faction within the department bent on preserving hemispheric unity, which they believed fervently was the direct result of the good neighbor policy and the reciprocity it had earned from the Latin American nations. Hull was supported by a group of internationalists, who saw Latin America as part of a larger problem and who felt that Latin America should follow the United States' lead because of the principles at stake and because of the economic benefits that would accrue to all if they did. At the same time, other figures within the Roosevelt administration, notably Morgenthau and Henry Wallace, contested Hull's preeminence in the foreign policy process, although they did not necessarily side with Welles.[3]

Hull was determined to win hemispheric support for the United States at Rio. Welles led the United States delegation. Skillfully using the Brazilians and other Latin American delegations to exert pressure on the Argentines and the Chileans, he got Ruiz Guiñazú and Chilean Foreign Minister Rossetti to agree to the basic conditions of joint action against the Axis. But while the Chilean government acquiesced in the agreement and then sacked Rossetti on his return to Santiago, Castillo refused to go along and forced Ruiz Guiñazú to go back to Welles and renege on the commitment he had made. The Brazilians were unwilling to coerce the Argentines for fear of creating a serious problem on their southern flank. Welles appealed to Hull for permission to be more flexible in the negotiations. Hull refused. Welles finally invoked his friendship with the president and, in a famous telephone conversation among the three, got the president to support his approach in dealing with the Argentines, preserving hemispheric unity.

But the under secretary won the battle only to lose the war. It is often forgotten that the Latin Americanists did not disagree with their bureaucratic rivals over the basic goals of United States policy, only over the appropriate means to achieve them. It was Welles who told Ruiz Guiñazú at Rio that unless the Argentines broke relations with the Axis they should not even think about getting military aid from the United States, a condition the Argentine military command had imposed upon Castillo for cooperation with the Allies. Welles had convinced the president not to force the Argentines out of the hemispheric family, but he had assumed the implicit obligation of moving them to change their behavior by other means. The Latin Americanists turned to a policy of propaganda and economic pressure against the Argentine government. By mid-1943 the policy of selective coercion was considered a failure. Welles had lost.

One of the reasons he lost was the dissension within the government. Powerful members of the Roosevelt government, sensitive to the split within the State Department, became bold in asserting their own influence over the policy process. Roosevelt's administrative style of encouraging or not discouraging competition among his advisers only contributed to the confusion. There were so many channels for conducting policy during the war that a government in the position of Argentina could play one actor off another with relative ease. So many different instruments were used in the effort to bring Argentina into line that none of them proved effective, and the result was the confusion on the face of policy.[4]

All members of the government in Washington saw the war as a struggle of democracy against fascism. Anyone who refused to support the Allies was probably sympathetic to the Axis cause, and they saw Argentines in this light. But as we have seen, the situation in Argentina was more complex. The central objective of Argentine policy was to avoid domination by the United States. Pro-British tendencies among the traditional elite in Argentina served to strengthen the political disposition against the United States and to buttress the neutrality policy adopted by successive governments. Such a policy, Welles argued, showed an inability to measure power realities in the world with any degree of accuracy. And, indeed, there is evidence that Argentine leaders often made their wishes the basis for foreign policy. Traditionalists among the Argentine elite could hope fervently that the British empire would be restored at the end of the war and that they might return to the privileged position in world affairs they had enjoyed prior to the Great Depression, with its built-in influence and prestige, a position from which they were relatively immune from U.S. pressures and ambitions. With equal fervor and equal illusion, the nationalists could hope to build a position of regional hegemony based on the value of the nation's exports, its military capacity, and its leadership in denying U.S. predominence in the hemisphere.

The British, or at least some officials in the government, were not above hoping this Argentine vision of the world would prove to be true. Ambassador Ovey, reporting from Buenos Aires, considered Ruiz Guiñazú's policy at Rio "very intelligent." The Board of Trade never lost sight of the possibility of restoring British influence in the River Plate, and it was British policy to put as much distance as possible between themselves and their American allies on all matters having to do with neutrality policy. Indeed, at one point in 1940, one Foreign Office official mused that it might be useful to have Argentina enter the war in order to protect its trade with Great Britain and prevent the United States from creating a Pan-American front during the war. The same official admitted that the weakness of the British economy might make such a project difficult to carry out.

After Pearl Harbor, the British were convinced that it was not necessary for the Argentines to declare war. The movement of foodstuffs could be maintained as easily or more easily as long as Argentina remained neutral. While the British never were happy with Argentine actions that clearly benefited the Axis—for example, they protested as vehemently as the United States against use of Argentine radio transmissions to divulge the movements of shipping in the South Atlantic—on balance, they opposed the harsh policy the United States adopted toward Argentina and went along with the restrictions on neutrals adopted at the Rio meeting only "reluctantly and by obligations." While the British never went as far as to undermine their relationship with the United States on which their very survival depended,[5] their oppositon to U.S. pressure enabled the Argentines to create political space for themselves by utilizing a triangle in which they played one ally off against the other. British ambiguity contributed to the confusion among the progressive opponents of Castillo. It made it hard for them to exploit a simple formula of pro-democracy and pro-Allies against totalitarian and pro-Axis.

Hull and most of the U.S. government could not understand why Argentina (and Chile) did not automatically fall in line behind the United States and join the war effort. Independence of action simply was not considered a legitimate option. U.S. policy had become myopically Wilsonian in the belief that the definition of U.S. interests and the U.S. definition of good and bad in the wartime situation was appropriate to all rightminded people and nations. U.S. leaders literally could not understand how anyone would not see the situation as they did. They expected compliance from allies in the hemisphere. Anything short of total support was seen as hostility and would be dealt with in an appropriate manner.

Of course, the Argentines saw the situation in very different terms. Pressure from the United States was considered unacceptable, and any government that even appeared to bow to that pressure was vulnerable to immediate and excruciating internal political pressure. After the Rio meeting, the U.S. government became a crucial player in the domestic power struggle in Argentina, but never understood the nature of the struggle well enough to exert pressure in a productive manner. Angry with the U.S. refusal to provide lend-lease equipment, Castillo instructed his government's representative in Berlin to open discussions with the Germans for the purchase of the military equipment the Argentine chiefs of staff considered indispensable for the nation's security. They were growing restive in the face of Brazil's increasing power and the Castillo's regime apparent inability to deal with the situation. Scathingly critical of the civilian regime's corruption and inefficiency, the military was convinced that preservation of the nation's security required more assertive leadership. Between 1943 and 1945 the military budget tripled and the number of men under arms increased by more than 100 percent.

Castillo tapped Robustiano Patrón Costas to be his successor, considered as a compromise among the hostile factions of the Argentine political elite. However, the military thought him too pro-Ally and overthrew the government in 1943 to prevent him from assuming power. The State Department saw in the coup confirmation of its darkest estimates of the Argentines' political predilections. Even the British were made nervous by the coup and by the political leanings of some of the officers involved. Nevertheless, they felt that Argentina could not hurt the Allies in any significant way except by curtailing shipments of food, and the only sufferer in such circumstances would be the British. In fact, the Argentines were not about to interrupt food shipments to the Allies. They had no other customers. U.S. officials saw this but never could convince their British counterparts that this was the case. The need to maintain the Allied market would serve as a brake on the behavior of the Argentine government.

The junta that ousted Castillo gave early indications that they would be more cooperative with the Allies than had their predecessors. Their primary goal was the reassertion of Argentine military preeminence in the region. For that, they needed modern arms. A rapprochement with the United States might be the only way to get the necessary equipment, but it had to be done without loss of face. The junta was not in agreement as to how their goal should be achieved, except that they knew the civilians couldn't do it. A cabinet shuffle replaced several members having Axis sympathies with others who were notoriously pro-Ally, most notably Admiral Segundo N. Storni, as foreign minister. Upon assuming office, Storni declared: "Bit by bit, the actions of the Argentine government will continue the policy of American solidarity. . . . Argentina will arrive where it must be in international relations. The foreign policy of Argentina will imply a meticulous fulfillment of her obligations with the American countries." Storni told Armour privately that this would include severing relations with the Axis.[6]

Instead of nurturing this sign of cooperation, Hull reacted with scorn, demanding some proof of the meticulous fulfillment to which Storni had referred. Hull wanted a quick decision by the Argentine government to break relations with the Axis and he wanted no strings attached. Such a clearcut decision was politically impossible in Argentina, and there was evidence that it would not be in Argentina's best interests to do so. General Ramírez, the head of the junta, tried to place himself between the two extreme groups that were fighting among themselves, but he was gradually losing control of the situation. The initial commitment to break with the Axis was becoming more and more difficult to carry out without some tangible evidence that the step would benefit the nation. This, Hull refused to give. As Welles told Armour, who virtually begged the department to make some tangible concession to the Argentines, severing relations was not as important as it had been a year earlier. Thus, at a time when the pro-Ally faction within the Argentine government had less political space than it ever had, the United States made greater demands; at a time the pro-Ally faction needed the greatest response, the United States was losing its will to make any concessions.

Eventually, at Hull's insistence, Storni agreed to put in writing the Argentine commitment to rupture relations with the Axis. The text of the letter, which was the cause of considerable debate within the government, tried to explain why Argentina could not break relations at that time without cause. He denied that the Argentine regime sympathized with the Axis. He insisted that his government would spare no efforts to comply with the obligations assumed. But he could not do so without a cause that would justify it. To act otherwise would be to provide arguments for those who might think that he was operating under pressure or threat from foreign agents. And this would be tolerated neither by the people nor by the armed forces of the country. He concluded:

> I can affirm to you . . . that the Axis countries have nothing to hope for from our government and that public opinion is daily more unfavorable to them. But this evolution would be more rapid and effective for the American cause if President Roosevelt should make a gesture of genuine friendship toward our people; such a gesture might be the urgent provision of airplanes, spare parts and machinery to restore Argentina to the position of equilibrium to which it is entitled with respect to other South American countries.[7]

Storni's letter closed with a plea for understanding and friendship on the part of the United States toward the Ramírez government during its difficult initial period.

Hull answered Storni's note in a most scathing manner. He went on at great length excoriating the Argentine government for its failure to carry out its obligations. He expressed surprise that fulfillment of contracted obligations could be a motive for considering such action to have been taken under the pressure of foreign agencies, especially when the obligations had all been freely subscribed to by the American republics and had been fulfilled by all except Argentina. He specifically rejected the appeal for arms and stated his belief that the questions of a South American equilibrium were inconsistent with the inter-American doctrine of peaceful solution of international disputes, a doctrine to which, he added, Argentine statesmen had made so many contributions.

The publication of the Hull letter in the Argentine newspapers inflamed nationalist sentiments across a broad political spectrum. Storni's position was untenable, and he had to resign the next day. The chief of state was also compromised, so Storni sent him a letter assuming full responsibility for the document. That very day, Ramírez issued a statement in which he declared, "the historical tradition of a nation . . . cannot be weakened by the confidential expressions of a functionary." When Ramírez finally ruptured relations with the Axis a few months later, following a scandal involving shady arms dealings with the Germans, Hull, instead of supporting the move and thereby strengthening Ramírez's position, pushed for further concessions. This only precipitated the fall of the government by strengthening the hand of the more nationalist faction. The nationalists, who were dominated by a group of junior officers banded together in a secret lodge known as the GOU, *Grupo de Oficiales Unidos* or United Officers' Group, promoted General Edelmiro Farrell, a military hardliner, from minister of war to the vice presidency, projecting into the forefront of political struggle his aide, Colonel Juan D. Perón. In response to U.S. pressure, Ramírez increased his government's efforts to secure arms from the Axis. When an Argentine agent was picked up by the British in the West Indies on his way to Spain to buy arms, the United States threatened to cut off all trade with Argentina unless relations with the Axis were cut. Ramírez capitulated and broke relations in January. Within weeks, the nationalists forced Ramírez to retire and installed Farrell as president. Perón, now considered by many diplomats to be the most powerful individual in the group, was made vice president and minister of labor. He made a personal appeal to Ambassador Armour for U.S. aid. Hull refused and insisted that the new government give evidence of its sympathies before it could be recognized.

The British thought Hull's reaction to the Argentine situation was simply irrational. Sumner Welles said as much in a newspaper column he wrote after leaving the government. Senior officials in the State Department complained that Argentina had become the Department's "bogeyman." Ambassador Kelly and the Foreign Office were in agreement that the new Perón junta was not fascist but nationalist, and that Argentina was doing a fairly good job of supplying the Allies with foodstuffs. Aside from that, although no one in the British government found the Argentine government sympathetic, the British understood that from the Argentine point of view the war really was none of their business. Nothing, said the British, moved Hull, so to protect their position they hammered on the need for Argentine beef in the war effort. At one point Hull, in desperation, begged Churchill not to renew the contract for the purchase of Argentine beef, but to buy meat as he needed it. Churchill asked what Allied soldiers were supposed to eat. Hull, totally in earnest, offered the prime minister special shipments of U.S. pork in the event that the Argentines held up shipments of their beef. Churchill erupted and demanded that Roosevelt call off his secretary of state.

The entire debate over the meat contracts is suffused with irony. Here, at the end of the war, the British were fighting with their closest ally in order to maintain their special meat supplies through long-term bilateral contracts with Argentina. Less than a decade earlier, it was the Argentines who were begging the British to maintain the link, and the British indicating that they were hardly interested. British dependence on Argentine beef during the war reached 40 percent of their beef supply. It was a general conviction within the British government during the war that without Argentine foodstuffs maintaining the standard of living of the British civilian population would be impossible and the war effort would be seriously compromised.

This dependence and the sense of urgency continued for several years following the war, as the Argentine foodstuffs were needed to maintain basic supplies for large areas of Europe in which normal food production was not resumed immediately. And yet within five years of the war the British again turned their back on their Argentine suppliers, this time as part of the negotiations for their entry into the growing European Economic Community. From 1950 to 1954 Argentine exports of beef fell 50 percent from their wartime levels. The "old, traditional" British link was anything but faithful after 1930. The British wanted Argentine beef when they needed it and spurned it when they didn't. The Argentines did not appear to learn this lesson in twenty years of negotiations. After the war the governing elite, although it had added several new elements to its ranks, continued to believe in the traditional view of Argentine influence in world affairs through the export of foodstuffs vital to the well-being of the European nations.

Hull's influence declined rapidly as the war drew to a close and his health deteriorated. He resigned from the department in November 1944. His departure and a series of other factors led to an end of the policy of pressure against Argentina, at least for a time. There was a constellation of forces opposing Hull's pressure tactics. The private sector in the United States was increasingly irate with the economic sanctions imposed on Argentina because they saw the sanctions opening the door to the Argentine market to the British. That market was considered one of the greatest postwar opportunities in the world. The American military also was opposed to the policy. It argued, as it had from the very beginning of the war, that U.S. security interests would be protected better within the framework of hemispheric unity than with open splits among members of the region. As the war drew to an end and strategic planning turned increasingly to postwar planning, military leaders became more adamant in the expression of this view.

There was a new generation of specialists in the State Department, notably Nelson Rockefeller, who believed, as Welles had earlier, that the best way to influence the Argentines was through accommodation, not through pressure. Another factor undermining Hull's policy was the growing opposition of the Latin American nations to the pressure on Argentina. They were especially upset with Hull's effort to get them to join the United States in prolonged nonrecognition of the Farrell regime that had replaced Ramírez in February 1944. Only the Uruguayans seemed to welcome an interventionist policy in support of democratic regimes. The majority of states in the hemisphere wanted to include Argentina in the planning for the postwar world, especially in their efforts to get the United States to support their plans for economic development.

Argentine economic success and the huge profits from the sale of foodstuffs to the Allies allowed the Argentine government to take and hold a tough stance in their dealings with the United States in 1945. They were perfectly aware of the British position in opposition to U.S. pressure, and they played it for all it was worth. But the war also provoked considerable dislocation in Argentina. While the nation made money from the sale of beef and grains, import restrictions hurt the development of the country. The result was an imposed industrialization that did not necessarily respond to the developmental needs of the country.

The final factor undermining Hull's policy was a shift in the political forces within Argentina. After rising to power with his patron Farrell in February 1944, Perón had built his own power base within organized labor and among the most nationalist groups within the traditional political parties. Perón was a consummate politician and shrewd pragmatist. He set himself up as a moderate between the ultra-nationalists, led by General Luis Perlinger, and the Communists. He sensed the coming change in U.S. policy when Edward Stettinius was appointed to replace Hull as secretary of state, and he immediately sought closer contacts with the U.S. embassy, calling for negotiations with the United States on trade and investment.

In matters of international trade, Perón was a traditionalist. He wanted an economic treaty with Great Britain after the war. He told Montague Eddy in July 1945 that the Argentines didn't want to take over the British railways. He preferred a comprehensive economic treaty under which the British would provide Argentina with basic machine goods and industrial equipment in return for Argentine foodstuffs. This was the sort of proposal built into the Roca-Runciman Pact. It was not realistic in 1945. First, the British were not capable of providing the goods Argentina wanted. Second, the British were no longer interested in protecting their investments in the transportation sector, long considered hostages to Argentine pressure. The British saw the profitability of the railways declining and, with the impending expiration of the Mitre Law in 1947, which protected their interests, they were increasingly anxious to get rid of the properties. Sale to the Argentine government in return for blocked sterling deposits accumulated during the war seemed to the British to be a very good deal indeed.

Perón was a traditionalist also in his search for a way to assert some influence in world affairs. U.S. policy condemned Argentina to a position of obvious subordination. National pride, however misplaced from the U.S. perspective, insisted on some policy that would provide the nation with a visible impact on world affairs. U.S. officials seemed unwilling to understand what was happening in Argentina. All they could see was the undemocratic nature of the government, together with its neutrality. These two characteristics, taken together, were enough to condemn anything the government did. Ambassador Kelly was a far more realistic observer than Armour, although in fairness to Armour, he certainly passed on adequate information to his superiors in Washington. The information in the U.S. press did not help government leaders to make balanced judgments. Correspondents for the principal liberal dailies, the *New York Times* and *Washington Post,* were unremittingly hostile to Perón. Arnold Cortesi a columnist of the *Times* virtually went on a crusade against Perón. That created a climate of public opinion in the United States that made compromise with the Argentines more difficult.

Ironically, Argentina's readmission into the hemispheric community was initiated by the Argentine government's very uncharacteristic call for a meeting of the Pan-American Union to discuss tensions in the hemisphere. Historically, Argentina never had been an advocate of the PAU, viewing it from the very first meeting in 1889 as an instrument of U.S. hegemony. In this instance, of course, the Argentines were using the PAU against the United States. Their argument was that, since the PAU was an organization of nations, not governments, Argentina still was a party to it. The U.S. government succeeded in blocking the move, but compromised with its allies in the hemisphere by agreeing to attend a meeting of foreign ministers at which the economic issues of the postwar world would be discussed along with the Argentine question.

The hemispheric meeting at Chapultepec castle in Mexico City from 15 February to 6 March 1945 was one to which the United States government dispatched its delegation with considerable trepidation. It could see little good emerging from the gathering. The Argentine issue was the least of its problems. The central preoccupation was to preserve the necessary measure of hemispheric support to guarantee the success of the forthcoming meeting at San Francisco, in April, to organize the United Nations. The representatives of the Latin American nations had made it plain throughout 1944 and the early months of 1945 that they expected a considerable measure of economic aid from the United States following the cessation of hostilities. Their positions, held with unusual consistence by a large majority of the countries, was that they had subordinated their economic interests to the war effort, specifically accepting controlled prices fixed by Allied commissions, and forgoing the importation of vital manufacturing goods. They wanted to catch up with the economic development that had been postponed during the war. The most popular view was that these economic programs should come through the regional organization as multilateral programs and under no circumstances were they willing to sacrifice the interests of the regional organization to the control of any universal organization, such as the United Nations.[8]

Treasury Secretary Wil Clayton led the U.S. delegation to Chapultepec. He and his principal aides spent most of their time fopping off the urgent requests of the Latin American delegates. Essentially, Clayton told his Latin

American colleagues that the United States recognized the sacrifices they had made during the war, but that it was too early for them to calculate accurately what money or goods would be available for the purposes defined by the Latin Americans. The first priority, argued Clayton, was the establishment of the postwar order and, more specifically, assuring the reconstruction of Europe, both to prevent widespread hunger and to blunt the threat of social upheaval that many people were suggesting would be a greater threat to the hemisphere than the Axis had been during the war. He committed the United States to attending a hemispheric conference after the war to deal with the economic issues raised at Chapultepec. In return, he secured the Latin Americans' agreement to a conference on hemispheric security.

To ensure Latin American cooperation at San Francisco, it was necessary to provide a means by which Argentina could be readmitted into the hemispheric community. The Latin Americans simply would not accept continued nonrecognition of the Farrell regime, nor would they allow their hemispheric organization to be undermined by the isolation of one of their members precisely at the moment when the new international organization threatened the legitimacy of all regional organizations. Clayton was forced to compromise on this issue in order to preserve some measure of confidence in the San Francisco conference. He agreed that the United States would preserve the identity and independence of action of regional organizations, and he negotiated a series of steps by which Argentina would earn recognition from the United States and the other nations of the hemisphere that had followed the U.S. lead, and would be seated at the San Francisco conference. Before the end of March the Argentine government declared war on the Axis. Two weeks later the United States recognized the Argentine government and immediately dispatched a joint State Department–military mission to Buenos Aires. On 30 April Argentina was seated at San Francisco, scarcely two weeks after Spruille Braden had been named the new ambassador to Argentina.

The shift in U.S. policy toward Argentina reflected an alliance between two groups within the government. The new Latin Americanists in the State Department, led by Nelson Rockefeller, with the support of Secretary of State Stettinius, a pragmatist, believed that the best way to maintain U.S. security in the hemisphere was through the cooperation of all the nations, and that the best instrument to secure that cooperation was U.S. trade and investment. Isolating Argentina, as Hull had done, only ensured the continued dominance of British interests there and, worse, threatened to create conditions propitious for communist infiltration and influence.

The other element in the alliance was the coterie of powerful senators who saw in the new United Nations the only effective way to curb Soviet expansion. Men like Arthur Vandenberg and Tom Connolly were the outspoken hardliners on dealings with the Russians, and in their view Hull's policy in Argentina gave the Communists an advantage. While the military leadership did not play a prominent role in the debate at this time, it did side with the pragmatic or compromise position. The U.S. public was less forgiving. Press comment on the overtures to Argentina at Chapultepec and San Francisco were almost unanimous in their hostility. This strong, widespread feeling in the press, together with the residual elements of support for Hull's position within the government, explains the appointment of Braden as the new ambassador to Argentina. His anticommunist credentials were impeccable, and he had established a reputation for himself as an outspoken, blunt advocate of democracy in the hemisphere. The appointment was a disaster.

Braden arrived in Buenos Aires on 19 May 1945 and immediately set to work to undermine Farrell and Perón. In a series of public statements, grossly in violation of normal diplomatic etiquette, he rallied the civilian opposition to the military government that had been demoralized by Rockefeller's policy of accommodation and demanded in the strongest possible language that the government fulfill the commitments it had made at the Chapultepec meetings. Specifically, Braden demanded that the Argentine government expel the Nazi agents alleged to be in the country, confiscate property belonging to Nazis, and ratify the resolutions made at both Chapultepec and San Francisco. The Argentine government claimed that it could not do the last until there was a congress, which there would be after the presidential elections anticipated for some time early in 1946. Meanwhile, Perón pointed out that his government was doing everything it could. He professed his government was anxious to cooperate with the effort to feed the people of Europe and would make their foodstuffs available on the most advantageous terms.

The British were furious with Braden but could do nothing to stop him. Neither could Rockefeller, although he was appalled at the activities of the new ambassador. With Roosevelt's death in April 1945, both Rockefeller and Stettinius were exposed politically, and neither had much support within the administration. Braden, on the other hand, had the strong support within the State Department of veterans like Spaeth, Briggs, and Mann, all former subordinates of Hull. Outside the government he enjoyed the support of hardliners in the Hull tradition, especially in the press—liberals who were concerned about the nature of the Argentine government and labor leaders who were extremely nervous about Perón's dealings with organized labor. Sensing that Rockefeller could not curb Braden, Perón did not force a confrontation with the ambassador, despite almost constant provocation, and dealt with the United States' demands in a cynical manner.[9] That Braden was appointed assistant secretary of state in August 1945, even though his policy in Argentina ran counter to Secretary of State James Byrnes's central concern with the Soviet threat, can be explained only as an anomaly created by the lack of attention the bureaucracy paid to Latin America in the months following Roosevelt's death.[10]

Braden returned to Washington determined to continue and intensify his efforts to oust Perón. He used his new influence to stop all British efforts to reinforce their economic links with Argentina and pushed through the reclassification of Argentina as an ex-enemy country. This meant that Argentina could not be considered for aid of any kind, especially arms shipments, and that it could not possibly participate in the projected hemispheric defense conference at Rio de Janeiro. The British were furious but impotent. As the head of the South American Department, J. V. Perowne, put it:

> The fascism of Colonel Perón is only a pretext for the present policies of Mr. Braden and his supporters in the State Department; their real aim is to humiliate the one Latin American country which has dared to brave the lightning. If Argentina can be cowed and brought into patent submission, State Department control over the Western Hemisphere . . . will be established beyond a peradventure. This will contribute at one and the same time to mitigate the possible dangers of Russian and European influence in Latin America and remove Argentina from what is considered our orbit.[10]

Braden's obsession with Perón was nothing short of pathological. He directed all of his energies to the campaign to bring down the military government. But from Washington he didn't have the same effect on Argentine politics as he had had in Buenos Aires. Without their spiritual leader, the opposition to Perón self-destructed. General Ramírez tried to eliminate Perón's influence from the government in September, but was outsmarted. For nearly three weeks there were constant rumors of golpes, counter-golpes, alliances, and attempts to control the situation by different factions within the military and among civilians allied with the military. Then, on 17 October, Perón emerged from his internal exile in a dramatic public uprising organized by his consort Eva Duarte and their labor allies. From the balcony of the government house, the Casa Rosada, Perón addressed a multitude of supporters and promised them a stirring campaign for the presidency.[11]

Braden now decided the only way to keep the Nazi menace from maintaining its foothold in the River Plate was to reveal Perón's links to the Germans and the Nazis during the war. In so doing, he expected that the Argentine public would repudiate so nefarious a leader and elect his democratic opponent. Braden set his staff to work in a frenzy collecting all the evidence they could find of Argentine links with the Nazis. The result, the so-called Blue Book, was supposed to be a multilateral effort, in consultation with the nations of the hemisphere, but none of them would become involved. To more than a few, Braden's public statements about Perón and other leaders were the rantings of a madman. The Blue Book was published on 12 February, scant days before the elections in Argentina. Perón immediately seized upon the book and hinged the remainder of his campaign around the slogan "Braden or Perón." Without question, the maladroit actions of the U.S. government and of Braden especially had contributed to Perón's electoral victory.

Even as his staff prepared the material for the Blue Book, the balance of forces in Washington and Buenos Aires was shifting against Braden. His claims that the Fourth Reich was in preparation in Argentina found fewer and fewer adherents. Chargé d'affaires John Moors Cabot warned his chief that Perón was firmly in control, that he had a broad base of popular support, and that the civilian opposition was in disarray. Unless the material was dramatic, Cabot recommended that it not be made public. Later in the year Cabot repeatedly made it clear that he sided with the anti-Soviets in the government and disapproved of Braden's policy.[12] Latin American response to the Blue Book was uniformly hostile. At the same time, the concerns in the U.S. Senate and Pentagon about hemispheric defense in the face of the Communist menace was growing by leaps and bounds. The State Department's cancellation of the Rio de Janeiro conference was a particularly galling blow to those who saw as the primary objective of U.S. foreign policy the creation of a means of defending the United States against the possibility of Soviet subversion and incursions in the West. The British were adamant by this time that Braden's policy must not jeopardize their plans for economic recovery. They recognized Perón almost immediately after the elections and announced that they would no longer be bound by the gentleman's agreement under which they had withheld arms from the Argentine government.

But the persecution of Argentina by the United States was not over. Braden's influence was on the decline, but it did not disappear overnight. President Truman and Secretary of State Byrnes did not wish to appear to be capitulating to the Soviet baiters in the Senate who howled for Braden's scalp. They agreed to appoint a new ambassador to Argentina, which was a concession to Perón, and in a private conversation the new appointee, George Messersmith, came away with the distinct impression that he was being sent to Buenos Aires to restore normal relations. But in announcing Messersmith's appointment Byrnes issued a supremely ambiguous public statement that appeared to support Braden's position that the Argentines had to comply with their international commitments before any arms or economic aid would flow in their direction.

During the next year occurred one of the strangest episodes in U.S. diplomatic history. Messersmith fell under Perón's spell almost as soon as he had landed in Buenos Aires. Within a month he was sending lengthy memoranda to Washington justifying Perón's slow compliance with the Chapultepec undertakings and explaining the new government's policies. Braden was appalled. Communication between the two became strained. The press, still dominated by the same correspondents who had expressed their opposition to Perón on many occasions, were quick to point out that such measures as the five-year plan, which the New York Post called "Hitler-style," the severe controls on the university, and the abusive treatment of opposition groups were hardly the exemplary acts of a reborn democrat. Messersmith began to leak stories to the press and to send private letters to Braden's superiors in Washington in an effort to force his government to take a more flexible approach toward the situation in Argentina. The debate became acrimonius and intensely personal. At one point Messersmith told the secretary of state that continuing the hardline policy "served the interests of only one country, and that is Soviet Russia." Messersmith showed himself to be as maladroit as Braden in his dealings with the department. George Marshall, who replaced Byrnes in January 1947, decided that both men would have to go, and that the relations with Argentina had to be placed on a normal footing. Within a few days, early in June, the president announced that Braden and Messersmith had resigned and that the "way had been cleared" for the defense conference at Rio de Janeiro.

Although formal relations between the two countries were restored to something approximating a normal basis, the persecution of Argentina was continued on an informal basis with considerable effect by the U.S. Economic Cooperation Administration. Unbeknownst to the State Department, the agency charged with organizing the massive program of aid to the former combatants in Europe, known as the Marshall Plan, systematically discriminated against Argentina in the allocation of contracts and hard currency and in the distribution of shipping for trade in manufactured goods that the Argentines considered vital to their development. Only after repeated complaints by the Argentines and by U.S. diplomatic representatives in Buenos Aires did the State Department learn the details of this curious informal diplomacy. And despite considerable effort, it took nearly a year to put together enough influence within the government to force the ECA to end its policy of discrimination.[14]

World War II left a bitter legacy on the relations between Argentina and the United States. Much has been made of the divisions within the U.S. government, the confusion and vacillation in U.S. policy-making. But from the Argentine perspective, all variations of U.S. policy during the period had as their primary objective the assertion of U.S. hegemony in the hemisphere. All of those policies were considered to be threatening to Argentine national interests by all of the governments that held power in Argentina during that period. Certainly, to the Castillo regime and the three military juntas that followed from 1943 to 1945, there was little to choose between the policy defined by Hull and the policy urged by Sumner Welles. Both insisted that Argentina toe the line drawn by the United States. Later the differences between the hardline defined by Braden and the more accommodating policy advocated by Nelson Rockefeller also covered the common objective of creating what the British called a "private hemisphere" free of external influences.

None of these policies could be considered congenial to an Argentine government, civilian or military, that wanted to assert a position of independence for the nation in world affairs. The capacity to assert such a position, challenged during World War I and weakened by the changes in the world economy during the depression, was diminished dramatically by the events of the war, even though Argentina profited handsomely from the sale of its primary products. Not only did the United States, Argentina's chief rival for influence in the region, increase its power relative to all other nations in the world; not only did the British, who had been something of a protector of Argentina in its struggle for independence from the growing power of the United States, lose their economic power and their empire; but the worst possible result had occurred: the Brazilians had used their special relationship with the United States to accumulate vast quantities of military material and to build their industrial and military capacity to the point where, in hindsight, it is easy to see why the balance of power in the region was permanently shifted in Brazil's favor. That may have been the cruelest blow of all. Not only had it become inconceivable that Argentina could challenge for hemispheric supremacy, but it was now highly doubtful that it could pretend to enjoy regional supremacy. The traditional sources of the nation's international prestige, its foodstuffs, continued to earn hard currency, but they no longer brought influence in world affairs. It was the challenge for the new Perón regime to devise a mode of reinsertion into the international system that would either counteract these unfavorable developments or adjust to them. The context in which that challenge would be met was the unfolding drama of the cold war.

NOTES

1. Michael J. Francis, *Limits of Hegemony. United States Relations with Argentina and Chile during World War II* (South Bend, Ind.: University of Notre Dame Press, 1977), chapters 4, and 5; and Gary Frank, The *Struggle for Hegemony in South America* (Coral Gables, Fla.: University of Miami, 1979), chapters 1 and 2.

2. It also has stimulated an extraordinary amount of scholarly activity in all three countries. In addition to the works already cited we might add Carlos Escudé, *La declinación Argentina* (Buenos Aires: Editorial Belgrano, 1983); Gary Frank, *Juan Perón vs Spruille Braden: The Story behind the Blue Book* (Lanham, Md.: University Press of America, 1980); Albert P. Vannucci, "United States–Argentine Relations, 1943–1948: A Case Study in Confused Policy Making," Ph.D. diss., New School for Social Research, 1977; Bryce Wood, *The Dismantling of the Good Neighbor Policy* (New York: Columbia University Press, 1985); Randall Bennett Woods, *The Roosevelt Foreign Policy Establishment and the "Good Neighbor": The United States and Argentina, 1941–1945* (Lawrence: Kansas Regents Press, 1979); R. A. Humphreys, *Latin America and the Second World War, 1939–1942* and *Latin America and the Second World War, 1942–1945* (London: Athlone Press, 1981–82); and Guido DiTella and D. C. Watt, *Between the Powers: Argentina, The United States, and Great Britain* (London: Macmillan, 1989). Humphreys takes strong exception to Wood's interpretation of the events, referring to the assertion that the British worked to widen the split between the United States and Argentina as a "myth." It is interesting to note that Rapoport, reading the same sources, comes very close to Wood's argument (*Gran Bretaña, Estados Unidos y las clases dirigentes argentinas, 1940–45* (Buenos Aires: Editorial Belgrano, 1981).

3. Woods, *The Foreign Policy Establishment and the "Good Neighbor,"* is the most detailed description of this split. While it is important to understand the fighting that went on within the State Department, Woods tends to forget the role of other actors in the formulation of U.S. policy and to underestimate the impact of events in Argentina on U.S. policy.

4. For an interesting discussion of the significance of the bureaucratic infighting and the importance of shared, general goals and values in the government, see E. R. May. "The Bureaucratic Politics Approach: U.S.–Argentine Relations 1942–47," and Guilliermo O'Donnell, "Reply to May," in *Latin America and the United States* ed. Julio Cotler and Richard Fagen (Stanford: Stanford University Press, 1974). Perhaps it is only natural that under the pressure of the constant bickering among the senior officials within the department, representatives in the field began to tailor their reports to the categories of debate in Washington rather than to reality in Argentina. The quality of reporting by U.S. professional diplomats in Argentina deteriorated seriously after 1942. The unreliable or simply inaccurate character of that information must be included as one of the factors in the inability of the U.S. government to deal effectively with the military junta that took power in 1943 or with any of the juntas that held power until the election of 1946.

5. Mario Rapoport, *Gran Bretaña, Estados Unidos y las clases dirigentes argentinas: 1940–1945,* 108; Warren F. Kimball, "Anglo-American Rivalry and Cooperation in World War II," in DiTella and Watt, *Between the Powers.*

6. For an account of this episode see Joseph S. Tulchin, "Two to Tango," *Foreign Service Journal* (October 1982).

7. Cited in ibid.

8. For a detailed account of the conference, see Rita Ana Giacalone, "From Bad Neighbors to Reluctant Partners: Argentina and the United States, 1945–1950," Ph.D. diss., Indiana University, 1977.

9. For detailed discussions of this episode see the papers by Newton and Macdonald in DiTella and Watt, eds., *Argentina between the Great Powers;* Roger R. Trask, "Spruille Braden versus George Messersmith: World War II, the Cold War, and Argentine Policy, 1945–1947," *Journal of Inter-American Studies* 26, no. 1 (February 1984); Frank, *Juan Perón vs Spruille Braden;* and Jesse H. Stiller, *George S. Messersmith: Diplomat of Democracy* (Chapel Hill: University of North Carolina Press, 1987).

10. See E. R. May, "Bureaucratic Politics Approach." Daniel J. Greenberg in "From Confrontation to Alliance: Peronist Argentina's Diplomacy with the United States, 1945–1951," *Canadian Journal of Latin American Studies* 7, no. 24 (1987), argues that Byrnes was a hardliner like Braden, but that interpretation does not jibe with the archival evidence.

11. Quoted in MacDonald, in DiTella and Watt, eds., *Argentina between the Great Powers.* Most of the Argentine students of the period agree with the British view. See, among others, Juan A. Lanus, *De Chapultepec al Beagle* (Buenos Aires: Emecé Editores, 1984); Marta Panaia et al., *Estudios sobre los orígenes del peronismo* (Buenos Aires: Siglo Veintiuno Editores, 1973); and Gonzalo Cárdenas et al., *El Peronismo* (Buenos Aires: Carlos Perez Editores, 1969).

12. The literature on this episode in voluminous. Three good sources are Robert Potash, *The Army and Politics in Argentina, 1928–1945.* (Stanford: Stanford University Press, 1969.) Mario Rapoport, "Foreign and Domestic Policy in Argentina during the

Second World War," in DiTella and Watt, eds., *Argentina between the Great Powers;* and Felix Luna, *El 45* (Buenos Aires: Editorial Jorge Alvarez, 1969).

13. Many of Cabot's dispatches and cables are printed in *Foreign Relations of the United States,* 1946, 2:220–35. For a discussion of German economic activity in Argentina, see Luis V. Sommi, *Los capitales alemanes en la argentina: historia de su expansión* (Buenos Aires: Editorial Claridad, 1945) and R. Newton, "Indifferent Sanctuary: German-Speaking Refugees and Exiles in Argentina," *Journal of Interamerican Studies and World Affairs* 34, no. 4 (1982).

14. Escudé, *La declinación Argentina,* is a detailed discussion of this episode. For a summary and more extensive analysis of the consequences of the episode for Argentine development, see his paper in DiTella and Watt, eds., *Argentina between the Great Powers.*

chapter 7

COLD WAR RELATIONS

The United States' obsession with Argentina and its government's behavior in world affairs played into the hands of General Perón and the Argentine leadership by providing them with a perfect foil for their nationalism. The 1946 election slogan "Braden or Perón" identified the general in the minds of Argentine voters as the candidate who opposed domination by the United States and who promised to assert Argentina's personality in world affairs. But if resistance to Yankee imperialism was a surefire way to win votes, by itself it was not a sound basis for Argentine foreign policy in the early years of the cold war. It had the effect of reinforcing anachronistic views of Argentine influence in world affairs and equally outmoded estimates of the extent of U.S. power.

In defense of Perón and his advisers, many observers, both in Argentina as well as abroad, considered Argentina to be in an ideal position to profit from the postwar situation. It had emerged from the war with its productive capacity intact and with enormous reserves of hard currency. It was ready and able to provide food for nations in Europe that had all but lost their capacity to produce foodstuffs for their populations. To many, it looked as if the nation were poised to resume the vertigious growth that had characterized its first burst of economic expansion at the end of the nineteenth century. Perón and his advisers assumed this privileged position would allow him to use the accumulated surplus to carry out his ambitious programs of social justice and industrialization and to restore the nation's prestige in the world arena that had been lost by its policy of neutrality in the war. As it turned out, Argentina could not profit from its postwar position. In fact, Perón's policies resulted in serious deterioration in the nation's productive capacity. By the time he was forced from power in 1955, the country was in sad shape, torn by dissent and well launched on a prolonged period of political division and a cycle of inflation and economic stagnation that continues to this day.

To the extent that Argentine foreign policy after the war was based on the optimistic views of the restoration of the nation's influence in the world, it made realistic and effective judgment of world affairs extremely difficult. At the same time, rhetorical expressions of anti-Americanism, so much a part of the nostalgic approach to foreign affairs, either in international gatherings or for purely domestic purposes, antagonized people in the United States who were reminded of Argentine behavior during the war, which many considered unfriendly. This was the case even when divorced from hostile actions or contradicted by policies of cooperation with the United States and carefully explained by U.S. ambassadors who saw Perón as a pragmatist. In retrospect, it appears that Perón's focus on the United States and on anti-Americanism in his public statements actually undermined his efforts to create a truly independent foreign policy for Argentina, made it difficult for him and his advisers to appreciate the extent to which the United States dominated the international economy in the years following the war, and prevented them from appreciating the impact of a bipolar conception of world power on U.S. policy. These failures of perception created severe difficulties for Perón during his second administration in the 1950s, when his economic policies failed and he was forced to turn to the United States for economic aid. The legacy of Perón's rhetorical nationalism made it difficult for any regime to cooperate with the United States in any manner without exciting rabid opposition from domestic forces on the Right and Left, seriously reducing the nation's flexibility in its international relations.

Once Messersmith and Braden had been removed in the spring of 1947, Argentina virtually disappeared as an issue among the senior leaders of the executive branch of the U.S. government. President Truman and Secretary of State Marshall were concerned with the reconstruction of Europe and the formulation of a policy that would contain the threat from the Soviet Union. Fear of communism as a doctrine and fear of the Soviet Union as an expansionist, ideologically hostile state were the underlying forces molding the United States' approach to world affairs in the years following the war. The dispute between Messersmith and Braden had been an annoying distraction. It drew attention from more important matters; it divided the State Department; it divided the Congress and the public at a time when the president considered it imperative to win the support of both for what amounted to a renewal of wartime effort in the face of a strong desire by the American people to return to peacetime activities.

Truman and Marshall wanted to end the Argentine episode in order to convene the hemispheric defense conference at Rio de Janeiro.[1] There, the United States succeeded in drafting the Inter-American Treaty of Reciprocal

Assistance, which essentially allowed the United States to protect the hemisphere from any external threat. Leaders of the United States believed the treaty protected their flank from attack so that they could concentrate their energies, economic and military, on confronting the Soviet menace as far from their borders as possible. They did not consider the Soviet Union a direct threat in the hemisphere. Neither the political analysts in the CIA or the State Department nor the military strategists in the defense establishment considered Latin America a vulnerable or endangered area. Virtually all policy planning in Washington at the time was Euro-centric. The nations of Western Europe were considered the primary risk, and the nations in the Eastern Mediterranean, the second line of defense, were under direct, immediate attack from Communist guerrillas. Ironically, the increasing preoccupation with events in the Balkans and the increasing concern more generally with the Communist threat had the effect of actually curtailing military aid to Latin America. Through 1945 and 1946 the U.S. military had insisted upon a program of standardization in the hemisphere so that defense efforts would be more effective. As the focus of concern became more specific to Europe and the cost of dealing with the threat escalated, it became clear that the United States was never going to be able to provide the material the Latin American nations might need.[2]

Realistic appraisals of the limitations on U.S. capabilities to meet their expanding commitments were buttressed by optimistic appraisals by policymakers that Latin American discontent, either on the part of the underprivileged against their rulers or on the part of the rulers against the United States, would not lead to advantage for the Soviet Union. The primary objectives of U.S. policy in the region, therefore, were stability and making sure the nations in the hemisphere would accept U.S. leadership in defense and would provide access to their primary products and markets on behalf of the international capitalist system. In the years immediately following the war, that meant encouraging Latin America nations to increase production of their primary products to relieve shortages in war-torn Europe and to curb the prices they charged for their exports. In keeping with such a view, it was important to accommodate Argentina and to assure steady flows of its foodstuffs. Ironically, in just a few years the terms of trade for Latin American products deteriorated so badly that in 1949 the United States switched its policy and encouraged Latin Americans to curb production, only to switch yet again with regard to certain strategic commodities once the war in Korea began. In this series of about-faces Washington revealed the limits on its belief in an unfettered international economy.[3]

Given the nature of the debate in later years over the causes of communism in developing nations and as to whether subversion of existing governments is sustained primarily by internal or external forces, it is interesting to note that during the immediate postwar years there was a broad consensus among policymakers in the United States that the conditions of poverty and misery in developing countries were the breeding ground for revolutionary doctrines. In Africa and Asia colonialism also was a factor. No one doubted that eliminating misery and poverty—what soon came to be known as the conditions of underdevelopment—was the surest way to stiffle the spread of communism. The only subject of discussion was the best way to make available to the poorer nations of the world the resources they needed to achieve developed status.[4]

Most observers in the United States did not consider Latin America as a whole among the poorest regions of the world, and Argentina was seen, correctly, as among the most developed, if not the most developed nation in the region. Consequently, even among those for whom economic development was part and parcel of their thinking about world peace, Latin America was not an area of great concern. The key to postwar reconstruction and to the development so earnestly sought by the Latin Americans, as understood in Washington, was to loosen restrictions on trade and to create the conditions in each country that would attract foreign investment, especially investment from the United States. According to this view, development problems in Latin American countries would be solved, over time, by the market, not by the U.S. Treasury. U.S. officials seemed never to tire of lecturing their counterparts from Latin America, or delegations of businesspeople from the region, that they must not expect the United States to solve their problems for them, that they must make the reforms necessary to use existing resources more efficiently rather than expect more aid from the United States. They should begin by creating the proper conditions for foreign investment to liberate the productive forces of their societies. Nationalist or statist policies were considered undesirable.

The reconstruction of Europe was considered vital to the United States' security, and, to a lesser degree, so was the poverty of South and East Asia. An overwhelming portion of U.S. economic aid to areas outside of Europe went there—more than ten times as much as was directed to Latin America during the Truman administration. (See Table 1 on U.S. Aid to Latin America in the years immediately following the war.) As early as the Chapultepec conference, Assistant Secretary of State Wil Clayton had told the Latin American delegates that they should not expect U.S. aid after the war, although he voted to hold an economic conference later the same year in order to win Latin American support for his resolutions on free trade and investment. George Kennan, chief of the State Department's Policy Planning Office, expressed the thinking behind this position. There was, he said, "a very sharp line that was drawn between the problem of European recovery and the problems of economic growth that existed elsewhere in the world. . . . In Europe, it was a case of releasing capacities for self-help that were already present. This was a short-term problem. Elsewhere, it was a matter not of releasing existing energies but of creating new ones. This was a long-term problem."[5]

The Latin Americans did not give up and insisted that the meeting at Rio

Table 1. Total U.S. Aid to Latin America
(in Millions of Constant 1989 Dollars)*

Year	Military	Nonmilitary	Total
1946	——	212.275	212.275
1947	——	166.711	166.711
1948	——	223.463	223.463
1949	——	138.867	138.867
1950	——	148.471	148.471
1951	——	87.791	87.791
1952	231.503	129.963	361.466
1953	452.154	179.934	631.088
1954	106.224	211.442	317.666
1955	120.714	429.288	550.002
1956	149.495	983.082	1132.577
1957	257.195	1154.243	1411.438
1958	193.249	694.507	887.756
1959	252.400	685.910	938.310
1960	282.437	623.781	906.218
1961	466.517	1604.880	2071.397
1962	603.844	3221.310	3816.154
1963	359.076	3053.770	3412.846
1964	401.158	3596.356	3997.514
1965	352.446	2625.777	2978.223
1966	463.233	2832.830	3296.063
1967	308.153	2052.937	2361.090
1968	256.481	1888.519	2614.469
1969	139.921	1216.872	1356.793
1970	73.737	1622.415	1696.152
1971	228.886	1186.806	1415.692
1972	261.713	1183.705	1445.418
1973	222.373	907.528	1129.901
1974	340.098	960.444	1100.542
1975	340.736	873.478	1214.217
1976	289.789	750.194	1039.983
1976 THIRD QUARTER	70.582	161.744	232.326
1977	90.745	549.475	640.220
1978	138.930	580.263	719.193
1979	48.674	572.117	620.791
1980	26.446	562.567	589.013
1981	74.174	624.053	698.227
1982	180.490	680.213	860.703
1983	183.466	1112.197	1295.663
1984	401.356	1038.274	1439.630
1985	281.239	1585.309	1866.548
1986	241.336	1264.101	1505.437
1987	215.646	1521.016	1736.662
1988	143.712	1053.637	1197.349
1989	183.020	1048.437	1231.475

*These data reflect total commitments on the year in which they were committed for aid, not on the year on which they were disbursed. From Congressional Research Service prepared data on 1989.

de Janeiro deal with economic issues as well as military ones. Truman told a press conference just before the meeting that there had been a Marshall Plan for the Western Hemisphere for a century and a half, known as the Monroe Doctrine. He said in his speech to the delegates:

> The problems of countries in this Hemisphere are different in nature and cannot be relieved by the same means and the same approaches which are in contemplation in Europe. Here [in Latin America] the need is for long-term economic collaboration. This is a type of collaboration in which a much greater role falls to private citizens and groups than is the case in the program designed to aid European countries to recover from the destruction of war.[6]

In the same speech he assured the delegates that the United States was "not oblivious to the needs of increased economic collaboration and promised to deal with them "in the coming period."

A year later, at the Ninth International Conference of American States in Bogotá, Colombia, 30 March–2 May 1948, Secretary of State Marshall told the delegations essentially the same thing. He said, "It is beyond the capacity of the United States Government itself to finance more than a small portion of the vast development needed. The capital required through the years must come from private sources, both domestic and foreign. As the experience of the United States has shown, progress can be achieved best through individual effort and the use of private resources."[7]

To appreciate the gap between Europe and Latin American in the priorities of U.S. aid programs, it is interesting to note that Belgium and Luxembourg received more economic aid from the United States during the Truman administration than did all of Latin America. The fact that Brazil received more than half of the $1.3 billion in economic and military aid to Latin America during these years did not make relations between the United States and Argentina any better. Nor did the fact that Argentina's official request in December 1947 to purchase surplus military equipment was rejected because the stocks of such equipment had been depleted by emergency shipments to Greece and Turkey. The rejection reinforced Argentina's natural disposition to delay ratifying the Rio de Janeiro treaty.[8]

Throughout the Truman administration U.S. policy toward Argentina was characterized by its lack of saliency within the government and by relative independence of action on the part of different units of the government. Truman dispatched a series of businessmen to Buenos Aires in the effort to come to terms with Perón. The State Department exercised less than perfect control over the policy process. Norman Armour replaced Braden as assistant secretary of state for Latin American affairs. As an old Latin American hand and a protégé of Sumner Welles, he favored correct dealings with the Argentine government and adherence to the principles of the good neighbor policy.

However, he had no special relationship to either the president or the secretary of state and frequently ran into difficulties in imposing his policy or the State Department's policy on other units of the government. He soon was replaced by Edward G. Miller, a Wall Street lawyer.[9]

In the immediate postwar years, many officials in Washington remembered with bitterness Argentina's posture during the conflict and joined willingly with private interests to reestablish U.S. presence in the Latin American Market, at Argentina's expense if that were necessary. In one episode Argentina and Chile agreed that coastal trade between them would be restricted to ships flying the flag of one nation or the other. The United States protested the agreement, and Latin American attempts to purchase ships in the United States were thwarted, undermining the Argentine scheme.[10]

Perón's basic foreign policy was to make Argentina less vulnerable in the postwar world. In the most grandiloquent fashion, on the anniversary of the nation's independence, 9 July 1947, he travelled to Tucumán to declare the "economic independence" of the nation. Just over a year earlier, in a radio address he had broadcast around the world, he had defined his government's foreign policy as the "Third Position," halfway between communism and capitalism. He invited the nations of Latin America to join Argentina in their quest for peace in the cold war. The Third Position was the logical corollary of his evolving political platform, *Justicialismo,* which he called his philosophy and the ideology of his movement. *Justicialismo* was a combination of Catholic and Aristotelian notions of justice and harmony clothed in a rhetoric of class harmony that singled out the oligarchy as the enemy of the people and the *descamisados,* or workers, as the beneficiaries of the new day.[11] Perón would make the nation less dependent upon its trading partners by industrialization fostered by mass consumption.

There were powerful domestic reasons to pursue such a foreign policy. The expansion of light industries, especially textiles, during the war as a response to the suspension of international trade, a process known as import substitution industrialization, had stimulated a massive movement from the land to the cities. In agriculture there had been a significant shift from farming to cattle raising, so there was no place for the recent migrant to return. Furthermore, those migrants and the older unionized workers in the cities were the foundation, "*la columna vertebral,*" of Perón's political support. He had to keep them on his side. At the same time, they were a necessary domestic market for the goods produced by Argentine industry, since the reentry of the United States into the Latin American market had reduced Argentine industrial exports to a tiny fraction of the wartime total.[12]

Making a virtue of the international illiquidity of the postwar financial system, and the inconvertibility of sterling, Perón pushed for the nationalization of foreign-owned utilities and railroads and for the elimination of the nation's foreign debt. Although critics argued that Perón had paid too much for a decaying infrastructure, there were few alternatives open to the government and the purchase fit its domestic political and economic plans perfectly. Taking into account the fact that Argentina had already expropriated German and Italian investments in the country as part of its declaration of war against the Axis, the United States was virtually alone as the source of foreign capital by the end of the decade.[13]

The creation of an industrial capability was the central feature of Perón's effort to make Argentina a powerful nation precisely at a time when its future was very much in question. In addition to the nationalization of foreign-owned infrastructure, his government raised tariffs to protect industry and stimulated domestic consumption by raising real wages almost 50 percent from 1946 to 1948. He set out to make the state the manager of the economy, responsible for public welfare. In the state marketing enterprise *Instituto Argentino para la Promoción del Intercambio* (Argentine Institute for the Promotion of Trade), established to buy agricultural products from the rural producers and sell them on the world market, Perón found a mechanism for draining profits from the rural sector and using them to finance the cost of import substitution industrialization. He also found that he had fashioned a powerful foreign policy weapon because with it the state was placed squarely in the middle of the international market and into any disputes with buyers. He actually was doing quite well until 1948–49, when, within a twelve-month period, the United States began to flood the European market with grains under the cover of the Marshall Plan and Argentina was hit by a drought.[14]

When President Truman spoke with James Bruce prior to his departure for Buenos Aires in 1947, he told the ambassador-designate to be as friendly as he could to the Argentines and to improve relations between the two countries. Bruce tried hard to do that. Except for the extraordinary behavior of the Economic Cooperation Administration, he was supported in his efforts by the U.S. government. But even under a policy of friendship the State Department was not entirely pleased with Argentine foreign policy. The Third Position was upsetting, even if it was largely rhetoric. U.S. diplomats in Buenos Aires sent countless cables to Washington attempting to explain that Perón's anti-Americanism was for domestic consumption only and that it did not reflect his true policy.[15] No one in official Washington liked the nationalism and statism of Perón's government, and it was hard to ignore the way in which he manipulated latent anti-Americanism. His control over the press and his ability to move goon squads around Buenos Aires for specific activities made it easy for him to manipulate public passion in this manner—the burning of the Jockey Club in April 1953 and the bombing of the Lincoln Library on the Calle Florida on Independence Day 1952 were calculated gestures.[16] His first ambassador to Washington, his personal physician Dr. Oscar Ivanissevich, was one of the most reactionary of the advisers surrounding him when he assumed office, and he never won more than formal respect during his tour. He did not help the Argentine cause.

Officials in the State Department perceived a split within the Peronist regime, between those they considered extremists, such as economic czar Miguel Miranda and Evita Perón, and those they termed moderates, such as Foreign Minister Juan Bramuglia. They attempted to use economic leverage to strengthen the hand of the moderates at the expense of the extremists, but they could never bring the instruments of policy together. The ECA wanted to push Perón to the wall. As with Braden's clumsy efforts earlier, the crude discrimination against Argentina enforced by the ECA, in cooperation with the British, only served to buttress the position of the extreme nationalists within the Argentine administration and their counterparts among domestic political groups.

The discriminatory actions of the British and the United States did have their effect.[17] The British decision in August 1947 to deny Argentina convertibility of sterling rendered all but useless nearly half of the reserves that Miranda had counted on to carry out his ambitious policies. Then, in the first months of 1948, over State Department objections, the U.S. government declared that Marshall Plan dollars could not be used to purchase Argentine goods. Perón personally asked Bruce to intervene, but he was not able to reverse the decision. Miranda was forced to resign over these episodes. Foreign Minister Bramuglia, who reached the apogee of his power in September 1948, when he presided over the United Nations Security Council during the Berlin crisis, was forced out shortly after he returned to Buenos Aires. He was replaced by Hipólito Jesús Paz, who had no following of his own and had not distinguished himself in the foreign service. Perón didn't like ambitious colleagues and did not let them stay around long.

Perón attempted to build Argentine prestige in the hemisphere through an active diplomacy. He used his links in the military to establish close relations with General Manuel Odría in Peru, General Ibañez in Chile, and the military rulers of Venezuela. In addition, the labor unions were an instrument of Argentine foreign policy. The Confederación General de Trabajo (CGT) established a hemispheric organ, Asociación de Trabajadores Latinoamericanos (ATLAS), in February 1952. Patterned on the Third Position, it called on labor organizations in all of the nations of the hemisphere to join in opposition to both forms of imperialism—capitalism and communism—for the betterment of working people everywhere.[18] Because of its proximity and the absence of control there, Uruguay was a special case. Many Argentine exiles sought refuge across the river. In fact, one of the most popular bars in downtown Montevideo was named the El Refugio. Uruguayan newspapers printed articles critical of the Argentine government and local radio stations broadcast frequent programs in which exiles and opponents of Perón discussed their differences with the Argentine regime. As repression increased and open opposition became more of a quixotic gesture, Montevideo increased in importance as a focal point of opposition to the regime.

Using the Third Position as a platform, Perón attempted to organize Latin American nations in some form of Bolivarian alliance without the United

States. These efforts are best understood in terms of the long tradition of Argentine opposition to U.S. hegemony. We can understand Perón's hemispheric policy as a repeat or effort to repeat the policies of Yrigoyen, and as an unceasing struggle to reduce U.S. hegemony. For example, at the United Nations Conference on World Trade in Havana at the end of 1947 and the beginning days of 1948, Perón cast Argentina in the role of champion of Latin America against Yankee imperialism. The Argentine representative announced that his government was prepared to provide $5 billion for the economic development of the rest of the hemisphere, whereas the United States was not only refusing to extend the Marshall Plan to Latin America, but was trying to cripple the region's infant industries by urging on them a general reduction of protective tariffs.

Just a few months later, at the Organization of American States meeting in Bogotá, Foreign Minister Bramuglia touted the Argentine credit to Spanish dictator Francisco Franco as proof both of the health of the nation's economy and its independence from the United States, which was leading the effort to isolate the Spanish dictatorship. But these were empty gestures. Argentina did not have the resources to play an independent role, and it was no longer able to use its economic links with Great Britain as a buttress or justification for its anti–United States policy. Great Britain no longer played the role in the hemisphere it once did. By assuming a public anti-American stance precisely at the time when the United States was so dominant in world affairs, and when Great Britain no longer would or could serve as Argentina's lawyer to blunt the edge of U.S. policy in the region, Argentine leaders revealed how ensnared they had become by the traditional methods of asserting the nation's influence and how blind they were to the potential consequences of such position or attitudes.[19]

Of course, as Ambassador Bruce realized, both Peronists and their opponents "express a certain pride in what Perón has done to make Argentina better known and given her a more important role in hemispheric and world affairs. 'You must hand it to him,' they say in effect. 'He has made the others sit up and take notice.' "[20] Perón recognized the widespread feeling in Argentina that the nation was not getting the recognition and respect that it deserved in world affairs and that most of the blame for this lay at the feet of the United States. The nation's own merchant marine and airline were sources of great pride to the Argentine people. They also made strategic sense and contributed to the creation of a more autonomous future. Similarly, the assertive position taken over Argentine rights in the Malvinas and in the Antarctic, through the reorganization of the National Commission on the Antarctic in 1946, served internal and external purposes.[21] Sometimes Perón's gestures backfired, as when he attempted to lure several German atomic scientists to Argentina to establish the nation's atomic energy capability. The so-called Huemul Project was a great hoax and produced only profound embarrassment for Perón.[22]

Although he attempted to play the United States and the Soviet Union off one another, the latter never was a viable alternative, in either geopolitical, ideological, or economic terms. Contacts between the two began even as Soviet Foreign Minister Molotov was excoriating the Argentine military regime at the San Francisco conference. Luiz Carlos Prestes, chief of the Brazilian Communist party, served as the principal intermediary. He also attempted to convince his counterpart in the Argentine Communist party, Victorio Codovilla, that "There was no fascism in Argentina. . . . Perón is a caudillo but he is not a fascist boss."[23] A Soviet trade mission arrived in Buenos Aires in April 1946, making much of Argentine–Soviet complementarity. The visit threw both the United States and Great Britain into a tizzy. This was followed on 6 June 1946, just two days after Perón was inaugurated, by the announcement that formal relations were being established between the two countries. Nothing much came of this initiative, however, as the Argentines and the Soviets could not agree on the terms of a treaty and the Soviets could not deliver the light machinery that the Argentines so desperately wanted.

Relations with the Soviets improved during Perón's second administration, culminating in the historic meeting between Argentine Ambassador Leopoldo Bravo and Josef Stalin in 1952—the first Soviet meeting with a representative of a Latin American nation—and the signing of a treaty on 5 August of the same year, again a first for Latin American nations. The Soviets placed great political significance on these steps, as did U.S. intelligence officers. But trade during the period never exceeded 3 percent of Argentine exports, although Argentina did take nearly two-thirds of Soviet exports to Latin America. A pattern was set that would reemerge thirty years later with much greater significance for both parties.[24] At this time, however, it was impossible for Perón to rely on the USSR, even if he wanted to, as Fidel Castro would fifteen years later. Thus the tradition of friction with the United States, the desire to avoid or to balance U.S. hegemony, the sincere (if misguided) belief that Argentina still had a future as a world power, and Perón's fervent anticommunism led to the formulation of a neutralist foreign policy in the cold war. Secretly, Perón assured U.S. representatives that in a true crisis he would be on the side of the United States, while publicly, he confronted the United States on all economic questions. It was a foreign policy that fit perfectly with the domestic situation in which Perón found himself.

From the early years of his first administration, even before he had declared his Third Position in foreign policy, Perón publicly declared that Argentina would not take a position in the emerging cold war. Indeed, in articles published in the newspaper *Democracia*, he argued that World War III already had begun. He called on the other nations of the hemisphere to join Argentina in a neutral front to preserve their civilization. This policy included a much-publicized series of economic treaties with Chile, Paraguay, Bolivia, and other Latin American nations.[25] These agreements were to abolish customs barriers, provide trade, and bring about investment of considerable Argentine funds for the development of mineral and other resources required for their country's new industrial program. They sounded good, but nothing ever came of them. After 1950 Argentina couldn't even produce the quantities of foodstuffs for exports that were the foundation on which Perón, like other leaders before him, intended to build Argentine influence in world affairs. With the decline in agricultural productivity and the dramatic decline in food exports, expecially meat, after 1950, Perón was forced to change both the tone and substance of his foreign policies.

Over half a century earlier, at the first Pan-American Conference in Washington, Roque Saenz Peña's defiance of U.S. hegemony was based on realistic calculation of U.S. power and hardheaded commercial calculation. Had Perón used the same approach he might have been more selective in donning his nationalist trappings. By 1950 the United States had become Argentina's best customer, taking about one-fourth of its exports, twice the prewar average. At the same time, U.S. exports to Argentina soared to nearly ten times their prewar levels. Argentine dependence on the United States was clear and becoming more profound. Because of declining productivity and the massive migration to the cities, Argentines were eating more and more of their meat and grains. They even failed to meet the quota set in the new treaty with the British, which had been signed to guarantee supplies of fuel oil from the Middle East. On top of all this, Argentine terms of trade fell 30 percent during Perón's first administration.[26]

By 1949 Perón's wages and financial policies were in shambles, and he was desperate for U.S. aid. His government never had ratified the Rio de Janeiro treaty, so the State Department tried to use the carrot of an EXIM Bank loan in the amount of $125 million to get the Argentines to honor the commitment they had made at Rio. Negotiations dragged on for over a year, and finally, in May 1950, Assistant Secretary of State Edward Miller signed the loan in Buenos Aires, and Perón got the Argentine National Congress to ratify the defense treaties. Negotiations had been delayed for months by Perón's insistence that the agreement could not be called a loan. He had sworn publicly that he would cut off his hand before asking the United States for a loan. It had to be a credit. The amount granted by the EXIM Bank barely covered the arrears in the Argentine current account with the United States. No new capital entered Argentina.[27]

Just a few months later, when the North Koreans burst over the 38th parallel and attacked the forces of the United States and South Korea, Argentina supported U.S. efforts to create a U.N. peace-keeping force, a move that stirred the Radicals and the civilian nationalists to vocal complaint. The honeymoon ended almost as soon as it had begun. Perón changed his position on the conflict in Korea and never contributed the support he had promised. In his May Day address, 1952, he accused the U.S. press of spreading lies about him. He suspended news from U.S. agencies and banned several prominent publications. The State Department was disappointed, though not surprised, by this turn and reverted to its policy of "masterly inaction" as one official put it, using the small amounts of financial credit and arms transfers available under Point Four and other legislation to encourage more cooperation from the government in Buenos Aires. These pressures, together with the collapse of Perón's economic policies, were having their effect by 1953, and the external pressure certainly contributed to the end of his regime. In 1954, at the Caracas conference, the Argentine representative abstained in the vote on Secretary of State John Foster Dulles's controversial motion condemning Guatemala for introducing communism to the hemisphere. The next year, the persistent fuel deficit forced Perón to invite Standard Oil of California to participate in the exploitation of the nation's petroleum reserves, a move that alienated many of his own supporters. The State Department never trusted Perón and was relieved to see him go in September 1955.[28]

The military regimes that replaced Perón explicitly rejected the Third Position as their foreign policy, although General Eduardo Lonardi, the leader of the coup against the government, insisted on an independent foreign posture in the United Nations and the Organization of American States, while calling publicly for friendship with the United States. The dominant mood among the military, after ten years of Perón's populism, was that stability, order, and anticommunism required a more positive relationship with the acknowledged leader of the Western world. From their perspective, the policies followed by Perón had served to weaken Argentina's position relative to Brazil. The legacy of policy of defiance and ostentatious independence was increasingly clear regional dominance by Brazil and the gradual erosion of Argentina's position, as well as an ambiguity in the campaign against communism that made them nervous.[29] The military now had come to identify national security with closer alignment with the United States. Among domestic groups, those calling themselves realists and liberals also advocated strengthening ties with Washington. Outspoken anti-Americanism was restricted increasingly to groups on the extreme Right and on the extreme Left, together with remnants of the traditional elite who longed nostalgically for an era in which their nation had greater influence in world affairs, and Peronist loyalists who were faithful to the rhetoric of hostility to Yankee imperialism.[30]

The United States responded to the new government in a constructive manner, if not with unbounded generosity. During the interim government, from 1955 to 1958, when Argentina ratified the OAS charter and joined the World Bank and the International Monetary Fund, the United States provided $100 million through the EXIM Bank, $50 million in loans through private banks, a $75 million credit line from the IMF, and $30 million in credit from Standard Oil of California. The balance of payments bottleneck appeared to be relieved, at least for the moment.

During the decade following the end of World War II, the United States

Table 2. Total U.S. Aid to Argentina
(in Millions of Constant 1989 Dollars)*

Year	Military	Nonmilitary	Total
1946	——	0.007	0.007
1947	——	0.006	0.006
1948	——	0.005	0.005
1949	——	——	——
1950	——	——	——
1951	——	——	——
1952	——	——	——
1953	——	——	——
1954	——	——	——
1955	——	10.815	10.815
1956	——	72.754	72.754
1957	——	——	——
1958	——	0.427	0.427
1959	——	105.138	105.138
1960	1.123	3.266	4.389
1961	15.774	27.872	43.646
1962	115.510	107.157	222.667
1963	83.642	427.621	511.263
1964	38.726	36.890	75.616
1965	62.213	19.937	82.150
1966	100.288	24.494	124.782
1967	56.035	5.655	61.690
1968	39.042	9.562	48.604
1969	37.799	6.156	43.955
1970	1.809	3.062	4.871
1971	47.647	1.454	49.101
1972	56.836	——	56.836
1973	31.638	——	31.638
1974	55.905	0.002	55.952
1975	66.459	0.221	66.670
1976	70.366	0.002	70.368
1976 THIRD QUARTER	0.198	——	0.198
1977	1.374	0.212	1.586
1978	——	——	——
1979	——	0.029	0.029
1980	——	——	——
1981	——	——	——
1982	——	0.076	0.076
1983	——	0.055	0.055
1984	——	0.101	0.101
1985	——	——	——
1986	——	0.006	0.006
1987	——	——	——
1988	0.052	——	0.052
1989	0.130	——	0.130

*These data reflect total commitments on the year in which they were committed for aid, not on the year on which they were disbursed. From Congressional Research Service prepared data on 1989.

gradually came to define its national security requirements in terms of the bipolar competition and nuclear confrontation with the USSR. The concept of containment gave the global reach of the nation's security interests both military and political components. How Latin America fit into these global concerns was a question to which the answer or answers always were ambiguous. By focusing its attention elsewhere, Soviet policy facilitated U.S. efforts to take Latin American acquiescence or support for granted and to fit the region into its own scheme of priorities where it rested painfully near the bottom.

The United States' policy, so preoccupied with the cold war in its bipolar formulation, considered as an adequate policy goal in Latin America the achievement of a condition in which subversion was either absent or at least modulated. As long as the area was considered stable, the U.S. government was more or less content. During the 1950s the achievement of stability was accomplished in a wide variety of political forms. Many of them were non- or antidemocratic. By the mid-1950s a number of governments throughout the hemisphere had come to power through nondemocratic means or governed in nondemocratic ways. That was nothing new. What was new in the early part of the 1950s was that Washington did not see this as a problem. In fact, the use of U.S. force, through the manipulation of a military puppet to oust the reformist democratic government of Guatemala in 1954, was considered one of the greatest successes of the administration. Lamentably, it was held up as a model for future operations in Latin America and elsewhere. It was considered the ultimate success in counter-insurgency.[31] At the time, Latin American outrage, expressed at the Caracas meeting of the Organization of America States and after, was either ignored or not heard.

During the decade, when as many as thirteen out of twenty Latin American states were ruled by dictators, the Eisenhower administration changed its view and came to see the lack of democratic governments in Latin America as a serious policy problem. Anti- or nondemocratic regimes were considered to be unsympathetic to the problems of underdevelopment, to the misery of the populations in the area. They were therefore, considered to be inherently unpopular and hence potentially unstable. And since it was believed that instability, along with misery, was what provoked subversion, policymakers concerned with Latin America in the second Eisenhower administration were increasingly convinced that antidemocratic regimes in the hemisphere were a liability and that the United States should do something about them.[32]

The thinking within the U.S. government came to focus on the linkage between development and democracy through a series of events and the concurrent public debate over them. First, the president's brother, Milton Eisenhower, made several trips through Latin America reporting directly to the president concerning conditions in the hemisphere. He spoke to Perón in 1953, and the two hit it off immediately. It was Milton Eisenhower's belief, from the first trip through the last, that development and democracy were

Table 3. Trade between the United States and Argentina

Year	U.S. Exports to Argentina	Argentine Exports to U.S.
1829	0.626050	0.912110
1830	0.629885	1.431880
1831	0.659780	0.928100
1832	0.923040	1.560170
1833	0.699725	1.377115
1834	0.971835	1.430115
1835	0.708915	0.878615
1836	0.384930	1.053500[1]
1870	2.9	3.8
1871	2.1	3.7
1872	3.2	4.3
1873	5.2	3.0
1874	3.9	3.7
1875	—	
1876	1.9	2.5[2]
1877	1.226782	3.449309
1878	2.152109	4.948016
1879	2.127123	3.518105
1880	1.882841	6.214575
1881	3.427863	5.669240
1882	2.964253	5.234914
1883	3.543196	6.192111
1884	5.074593	4.110038
1885	4.676501	4.328510
1886	4.725646	5.022346
1887	6.364545	4.100192
1888	6.643553	5.902159
1889	9.293856	5.454618
1890	8.887477	5.401697
1891	2.820035	5.976544[3]
1892	2.927488	5.343798
1893	4.979696	5.239095
1894	4.862746	3.497030
1895	4.456163	7.675270
1896	5.979046	9.313385
1897	6.384984	10.772627
1898	6.429070	51.915879
1899	9.563510	5.112561
1900	11.558237	8.114304

1. Casimir Prieto Costa, *Intercambio comercial argentino 1810–1915* (Buenos Aires: n.p., 1916), 32. Value in millions of current dollars.
2. B.R. Mitchell, *International Historical Statistics: the Americas and Australasia* (London: Macmillan, 1983), Official values in millions of pesos. Includes only import for domestic consumption and export of domestic produce.
3. *Statistical Abstract of the United States* (Washington, D.C.: Bureau of the Census, 1891), 69. Value in millions of current dollars. All figures for the following years are from this source, published each year.

1901	11.537668	8.065318
1902	9.801804	11.120721
1903	11.437570	9.430278
1904	16.902017	9.835161
1905	23.564056	15.354901
1906	32.673359	18.379063
1907	32.163336	16.715325
1908	31.858155	11.024098
1909	33.712505	22.230182
1910	40.694941	33.463264[4]
1911	50.140438	28.487431
1912	51.170397	34.007864
1913	54.980415	25.575667
1914	27.147958	56.274246
1915	52.840965	94.677644
1916	76.874258	116.292647
1917	107.098895	178.260648
1918	105.104548	228.388215
1919	155.899390	199.158401
1920	213.725984	207.776868[5]
1921	110.836	59.926[6]
1922	95.542	85.678
1923	112.782	115.276[7]
1924	117.093	75.298
1925	148.759	80.170
1926	143.575	88.058
1927	163.485	97.240
1928	178.899	99.438
1929	210.288	117.581[8]
1930	129.862	71.891
1931	52.652	35.980
1932	31.133	15.779
1933	36.927	33.841
1934	42.688	29.487[9]
1935	49.374	65.408
1936	56.910	65.882
1937	94.183	138.940
1938	86.793	40.709
1939	70.945	61.914[10]
1940	106.874	83.301
1941	109.314	166.618
1942	71.866	149.853
1943	31.818	144.864
1944	29.091	176.965[11]
1945	38.719	168.698
1946	191.144	194.380

4. P. 351, 1910, millions of current dollars.
5. P. 411, 1920, millions of current dollars.
6. Starting 1921, exports are noted to include reexports.
7. Pp. 450–51, 1925, millions of current dollars.
8. Pp. 492–93, 1930, millions of current dollars.
9. Pp. 438–39, 1935, millions of current dollars.
10. Pp. 508–9, 1940, millions of current dollars.
11. Pp. 913–17, 1946, millions of current dollars.

1947	679.851	154.637
1948	380.866	179.765
1949	130.843	97.523[12]
1950	141.996	206.060
1951	233.083	219.754
1952	148.028	158.669
1953	404.265	181.896
1954	122.638	103.043[13]
1955	149.028	125.995
1956	211.586	133.980
1957	284.373	129.331
1958	249.124	160.741
1959	230.561	126.265[14]
1960	349.994	98.216
1961	424.192	101.914
1962	379.526	106.229[15]
1963	189.140	164.929
1964	261.591	111.326[16]
1965	268	122[17]
1966	244	149
1967	230	140[18]
1968	281	190
1969	378	155[19]
1970	441	172[20]
1971	391	176
1972	396	201
1973	451	274[21]
1974	597	38
1975	628	215
1976	544	308
1977	731	392
1978	842	563[22]
1979	1890	587[23]
1980	2625	741
1981	2192	1124[24]
1982	1299	1128[25]
1983	965	853
1984	900	954
1985	721	1069[26]
1986	944	856

12. Table no. 994, 1951, millions of current dollars.
13. Pp. 914–15, 1956, millions of current dollars.
14. Pp. 896–97, 1960, millions of current dollars.
15. Pp. 876–77, 1964, millions of current dollars.
16. Pp. 868–69, 1966, millions of current dollars.
17. Starting in 1965, trade includes uranium, thorium, and related products in millions of current dollars.
18. Graph no. 1220, 1969, millions of current dollars.
19. Graph no. 1241, 1971, millions of current dollars.
20. Starting in 1970, includes silver ore and bullion.
21. Graph no. 1326, 1974, millions of current dollars.
22. Beginning in 1978, includes monetary gold.
23. Graph no. 1541, 1980 millions of current dollars.
24. Beginning in 1981, includes trade of Virgin Islands with foreign countries.
25. Graph no. 1473, 1984, millions of current dollars.
26. Graph no. 1406, 1987, millions of current dollars.

inextricably linked and that the absence of both was a liability for U.S. national security. His first report, in 1954, was filed without comment. By 1957 and 1958, however, successive reports were having increasing echo within the foreign policy establishment and among the informed public. They were having more echo because of events contemporaneous with them, and because a growing consensus among academics and policy advisers confirmed their conclusions.[33]

Perhaps the most influential academic argument for the use of public funds to aid general societal development in underdeveloped countries was that put forth by Walt W. Rostow and Max Millikan, professors at MIT.[34] Echoing many of the apocalyptic sentiments of George Kennan, they called on the United States to rededicate itself to its "sense of world mission." Rostow's arguments were grounded in a thoroughly optimistic view of U.S. society. His prescription was for the United States to look beyond its borders to problems in the Third World, the nations of which shared the priorities and values of American liberalism. It remained for U.S. foreign policy to "increase the awareness elsewhere in the world that the goals, aspirations, and values of the American people are in large part the same as those of the people in other countries." These arguments would influence the Eisenhower administration, but would have a much more profound impact on Kennedy and his circle.

A most important event occurred in May 1958 when Vice President Richard Nixon visited Latin America. During his trip, in Caracas, Venezuela, Nixon was stoned, spat upon, and very nearly hurt seriously. Some think his life was in danger. The first reaction in Washington was shock. Why was there such anti-Americanism in Latin America? What started this fear and hatred in Latin America? It no longer could be attributed to irresponsible demagogues, as had been the attitude toward Perón, or to isolated agents of the Soviet Union. A month later, in June 1958, a formal proposal in which the linkage between underdevelopment and democracy on the one hand and hemispheric security on the other was made in the strongest possible terms was sent to President Eisenhower by the presidents of Colombia (Alberto Lleras Camargo) and Brazil (Juscelino Kubitschek). Kubitschek's letter accompanying the memorandum referred to the unpleasant episode the previous month in Caracas indicating to President Eisenhower that it was time for the United States to act. The president responded by sending a task force to Brazil to have conversations with the two Latin American leaders. The resulting memorandum, known as Operation Pan-America proposed a hemispheric program of public aid to alleviate the conditions of underdevelopment and instability.

It was no coincidence that during the months in which these memoranda were drafted, a movement of guerrillas in the Cuban hills was gathering force, so that by mid-1958 most people who bothered to look, including those in Washington, were convinced that the rebel movement led by Fidel Castro was bound to win. On 31 December 1958 Castro marched into Havana in triumph. He immediately called for massive reform throughout Latin America and began to campaign against U.S. influence.

It is important to remember that the Latin Americans had been clamoring for public funds to aid them in the quest for development ever since the end of the war. Their frustration with U.S. disdain for their concerns led them to consider ways to solve their problems without depending on the United States. That was why Perón's proposals, empty as they were, had such an echo elsewhere in the region. Given the global reach of the struggle with the Soviet Union, tendencies toward independence or neutralism were not looked on with favor from Washington, but they did not prompt a constructive response until the end of the 1950s.

The Latin American approach consisted of theoretical and practical dimensions, just as the policy process did in the United States. The theoretical dimension began with a series of formulations explaining international economic relations in terms of unequal exchange between the developed nations, at the center of the world economy, and the underdeveloped, at the periphery. Of great significance was the fact that these theoretical formulations did not spring from an academic source. They began in the research arm of the United Nations Economic Commission for Latin America, under the fertile, energetic leadership of Raul Prebisch, a conservative Argentine economist and banker forced into exile by Perón. An entire generation of Latin American social scientists and policymakers learned the principles of international economics according to Prebisch, and they refined them. Dependency theory is an intellectual descendant of the work of the Prebisch group in ECLA (or CEPAL as it is known in Spanish) during the 1950s. The *CEPALinos* argued strenuously that the structural rigidities in the international economy could only be overcome with state intervention and with international state-to-state aid. Private investment could not accomplish the task. As if to strengthen their argument, Soviet Premier Nikita Khrushchev offered in 1956 to help the Latin Americans develop their economies with Soviet aid. Officials in Washington watched closely. Catching the mood of the times, Fidel Castro at the Inter-American Economic Conference in Buenos Aires in July 1959, boldly called on the U.S. government to provide $30 billion in aid to the Latin American nations.[35]

All these events, coming in a crescendo, convinced the administration that the policy toward Latin America that had been in effect since World War II was no longer adequate. A hands-off policy focused on private enterprise and investment would not work. It was time for a concession to the Latin American demand for economic cooperation. In the next formal meeting of the Organization of American States, in Bogotá in September 1960, the United States, for the first time, signed a multilateral convention calling for or agreeing to *multilateral* measures for economic and social development of the nations of the hemisphere. The Inter-American Development Bank, which had been created a few months earlier, had been designated as the vehicle for such multilateral efforts, and the U.S. administration made a commitment called the Social Progress Trust Fund, which the United States would make as a contribution to the hemispheric effort to alleviate the conditions of underdevelopment. Those monies, in fact, would not be committed formally until the new administration entered office in 1961.

Although the creation of the Inter-American Development Bank represents a significant innovation in U.S. policy toward Latin America, there is evidence that, like the policy it supplanted, it was authorized because it fit the general assumptions underlying global policy. Plans were being made for a similar institution in the Middle East, leading Under Secretary of State Douglas Dillon to argue that, under such circumstances, continued resistance to a bank in Latin America would be untenable.[36] Despite its recurrent crises, Latin America remained a relatively minor strategic priority for U.S. policymakers. Competing against the ferment in Latin America in the late 1950s were conflicts in other areas of the world deemed to be of far greater importance to U.S. interests: Europe, Southeast Asia, and the Middle East. Faced with a choice between spending time to devise a set of policies tailored specifically to Latin America and relying on general approaches formulated on the basis of experiences in other regions and tested in other regions, officials often chose the latter course.

Ironically, U.S. intervention in support of democracy was being urged publicly by a number of Latin American leaders at the end of the 1950s, especially José Figueres of Costa Rica and Rómulo Betancourt of Venezuela. And what they were advocating in Operation Pan-America explicitly was multilateral efforts in favor of good government. They wanted the United States to join them through the Organization of American States to get rid of dictatorship, to oust bad governments so that democratically elected popular governments could lead the movement toward development. Because it seemed to fit into the global policy of containment and because continuing to refuse carried increasing risks, the United States—reluctantly at first and then, once Kennedy assumed office, with more conviction and energy— seized upon this policy and made it its own. In doing so, the U.S. government deliberately manipulated its Wilsonian past and combined promises to act in concert with Latin American allies in ousting dictators like Rafael Trujillo in the Dominican Republic in return for support in the campaign to neutralize Castro's influence in the hemisphere. It was a policy that never sat easily among Argentine leaders.

Arturo Frondizi, leader of the Intransigent Radical party, won Argentina's presidential election of 1958, from which the Peronists were barred. The end of the populist, semi-authoritarian regime fit neatly with the evolution of Eisenhower's attitude toward pluralistic democratic regimes. Frondizi was the beneficiary of this change, winning strong support from both the Eisenhower and Kennedy administrations, although the support was not without reservations. The U.S. ambassadors in Buenos Aires were instructed to inform

General Pedro E. Aramburu, who replaced Eduardo Lonardi, and then Frondizi, that the price of U.S. support would be unequivocal adherence to free enterprise and anticommunism.[37] Frondizi tried to stimulate economic growth by massive investments in infrastructure, much of it with foreign capital. His foreign policy emphasized hemispheric affairs in a manner that seemed a throwback to Ortiz and Cantilo prior to World War II. He cultivated the friendship of the United States (he was the first Argentine president to visit the United States while in office); he was one of the strongest supporters of the Alliance for Progress; he supported the United States at the OAS meetings on democracy, most notably at the San José, Costa Rica, meeting in August 1959; he made shrewd use of the personal ties between his foreign minister, Miguel Angel Cárcano, and the family of John F. Kennedy.[38] At the same time, he tried to balance these overtures to the United States and demonstrate his independence by maintaining relations with Castro's Cuba. This displeased the U.S. government and upset the Argentine military, who were ideologically opposed to Castro's doctrines.[39]

Frondizi's domestic economic policy, known as developmentalism, sought to control foreign investment in the country while attracting it in order to free Argentina from its dependence on primary-product exports. This policy called for mild doses of nationalistic rhetoric, which prompted fits of anxiety in Washington. State Department officials appeared not to understand that Frondizi was a moderate compared to some of his nationalistic critics who opposed all foreign investment and who were skeptical of the virtues of democratic government. Although he tried to win the support of the Peronist masses, his austerity program after 1959 and his invitations to major multinationals solidified the opposition of a nationalist coalition among sectors of the military and the unions, which used as their slogan "Peronism without Perón." His policy also antagonized those among conservative civilian groups who opposed his willingness to cooperate with the OAS and those who were rigidly opposed to any dealings with Communists.[40]

In April 1961 Frondizi signed a treaty of friendship and consultation with the president of Brazil, Janio Quadros, in the border city of Uruguayana. This rapprochement with Brazil was part of Frondizi's efforts to build a bloc of underdeveloped countries and use foreign policy to further economic development, as explained by his undersecretary for foreign relations, Oscar H. Camilión:

> Argentina is a Latin American country, that is to say, it is made up of a geographical area belonging to the underdeveloped continents of the world, but she has conditions of negotiations that are very inferior to those of the other areas by virtue of her lesser strategic significance. . . . Our present solidarity with Latin America rises not only from the obvious traditional sympathy by reason of blood and language, but also from conscience that only action can call attention to our necessities, as was demonstrated,

through limited measure, by the partial success achieved with Operation Pan-America.

The key to Frondizi's hemispheric policy was to be in his attempt to arbitrate the growing differences between Cuba and the United States. The role of mediator would demonstrate Argentina's independence of action and its influence in world affairs. This would calm nationalists within the military who were nervous about Castro's politics and calm those within the military, Frondizi's own party, and the Peronist labor movement who considered his efforts to attract U.S. investment a mark of subservience and who were uncomfortable with his association of Argentina with the underdeveloped nations of the world. In rebuffing the Argentine initiative and increasing the pressure on Frondizi to break relations with Cuba, the United States did coerce a rupture in relations; but, as in World War II, the U.S. government achieved its narrow objective at the cost of playing into the hands of the more extreme nationalists contending for power in Argentina, in this case the antidemocratic military looking for an excuse to be rid of Frondizi.

The parallels with earlier events are striking. Frondizi publicized his efforts to mediate between Cuba and the United States, just as he publicized his support for the Alliance for Progress. Washington acknowledged only the first. In September 1961 the U.S. government made public a batch of documents purloined from the Cuban embassy in Buenos Aires that purported to show the links between Cuban and Argentine officials. The military publicly declared that it would not accept any compromise with communism: "starting from the premise that the struggle against communism involves a principle of national defense and not of politics, and that international communism constitutes today the gravest threat to liberty and democracy, we reaffirm our position as western and our solidarity with those countries that have assumed the defense of the free world, and we will not tolerate any threat to our way of life."[41] Frondizi reacted strongly, characterizing the documents as forgeries, denouncing a Cuban exile group for their interference in Argentine affairs, and complaining to the U.S. government about unfriendly pressure to influence normal relations with another sovereign nation. Then, in a public speech in Paraná early in February, he attacked his domestic critics in language reminiscent of Perón. This firm defense of Argentine sovereignty helped Frondizi for a little while, but it did not win him any new permanent allies. The combination of pressure from the United States and from his own military forced him to break relations with Cuba in February 1962 and led, in the space of little more than a month, to his ouster.

Despite their dislike of Frondizi's maneuvers with Castro, officials in the State Department reacted in anger to the military golpe. They called upon President Kennedy to make a public statement condemning the coup. DeLesseps Morrison, ambassador to the OAS, opposed such a move. He considered Frondizi an unstable troublemaker. With support from key senators, he prevented a public condemnation of the Argentine military. Democratic regimes were important, but only if they were sound on the Cuban question. To make the point clearer, just four months later, in 1962, the administration took a vigorous unequivocal stand against the military golpe that overthrew Peruvian President Manuel Prado. Kennedy announced that the Alliance for Progress had sustained a "serious set-back." The military's action, had "contravened" the common purposes of the inter-American system. Prado was considered a team player on the Cuban issue, Frondizi wasn't. Morrison again played an important role a year later defining the severe stance Washington assumed in dealing with Jango Goulart in Brazil. Goulart was overthrown by the military in 1964, who held power nearly twenty years. Kennedy and his advisers did not like instability.

By mid-1963 the Kennedy administration had lost patience with the policy of intervention to support democracies in Latin America. The president was convinced that the Latins were not with him. He was supposed to be the leader of a multilateral effort to defend democracy but he found that most of the Latin Leaders who had encouraged his activism would not back U.S. actions in the hemisphere designed to support democracy. The United States, through its policies of nonrecognition and political intervention in support of democracy, found itself isolated in the hemisphere and subject to increasing criticism. Furthermore, Kennedy was not convinced, nor were his advisors, that the activist policy in support of democracy contributed to stability in the hemisphere. There was a rising tide of comment that suggested that the policy was undermining stability, and stability, he was convinced, was the root cause of subversion. The belief in pluralism and diversity had all but disappeared.

At the same time, events elsewhere were throwing Kennedy's hemispheric policy into doubt. There were the quickening events in Southeast Asia, particularly Vietnam and Laos. The Soviet Union took a hard line in its confrontations with the United States in 1961 and 1962, as if to test the new president. The high point of this pressure came in October in the Cuban missile crisis. There was a significant and wide national debate concerning national security doctrine, which had its echo in hemispheric policy in the increased concern over political stability. And there was, in Congress, an ever more insistent questioning of public aid as an instrument of foreign policy.

The commitment to democracy, ambivalent from the start, was undermined fatally by the profound and persistent faith in Washington in counterinsurgency. This faith was part of the broad rejection of the strategy of nuclear deterrence dominant during the Eisenhower administration. Kennedy, as a member of the Senate Foreign Relations Committee, had cited the limitations of massive retaliation for dealing with "brush-fire wars" that were "nibbling away at the fringe of the Free World's territory and strength, until our security has been steadily eroded in piecemeal fashion." He adopted with enthusiasm the flexible response approach of Maxwell Taylor, designed to shift part of the burden of defending the country away from nuclear weapons and onto conventional forces. An important component of Taylor's formula for defense was the concept of counter-insurgency, which provided new methods of fighting the brush-fire wars that concerned Kennedy. The major appeal of the flexible response to the New Frontiersmen was that it purported to be an innovation in strategic thinking while not jeopardizing their credibility with the U.S. public as tough-minded realists. After winning the closest presidential election in history, Kennedy always was sensitive to the composition of public opinion, and he almost certainly kept in mind Henry Luce's warning, passed on to him by his father, "if he shows any weakness in defending the cause of the free world [i.e., anticommunism], we'll turn on him . . . we'll have to tear him apart."[42]

Counter-insurgency was considered a response to Khrushchev's boasts that the Soviet Union would win the war for the Third World and to Castro's strategy of world revolution. The United States countered with a multifaceted approach involving the CIA, the FBI, police training, and use of the Agency for International Development (AID) public safety program.[43]

According to Walt Rostow, counter-insurgency was an essential ingredient in the strategy of nation-building. As he told a graduating class of Green Berets at Fort Bragg in 1961, "Your job is to work with your fellow citizens in the whole creative process of modernization. From our perspective in Washington, you take your place side by side with those others who are committed to help fashion independent, modern societies out of the revolutionary process now going forward. I salute you as I would a group of doctors, teachers, economic planners, agricultural experts, civil servants, or those who are now leading the way in fashioning new nations and societies."[44]

The result was a painful confusion within the government as to the priorities of its Latin American policy. For example, in country after country the military advisory group was poised to defend the free world while the State Department and the executive attempted to coax reformist regimes into constructive channels of cooperation. The result, in El Salvador and the Dominican Republic, was civil war, in which the United States was implicated on the side of reaction, seriously undermining the U.S. claim to support democracy and social justice in the hemisphere.[45] And, after 1963, when Thomas Mann became the dominant force in the formulation of the nation's policy toward Latin America, his severe doctrine of official nonintervention had the effect of giving even greater prominence or influence to the security forces operating in each country.

Kennedy's assassination in November 1963 seems to have triggered a shift in U.S. policy. The timing of the changes suggests the influence of personality in the direction policy takes. Where Kennedy was dynamic and charismatic and operated with a high degree of rhetorical flourish, Lyndon B. Johnson was none of those things. His political strength always had been quiet manipulation or massaging groups—the brilliant orchestration of political forces, particularly in Congress. Johnson had little interest in the concerns that underlay the Alliance for Progress and, in a series of very swift personnel changes, removed all of the warriors that had fought with Kennedy in the quixotic episode of the Alliance. He replaced them with professionals who adopted a more formalistic, cautious approach to the region. Thereafter, he left policy-making to those advisers, much the way Eisenhower had. He never attempted to achieve the same command of detail as he did on domestic issues nor did he evidence the same intellectual interest Kennedy did in the foreign policy issues themselves.[46] Argentina, per se, virtually never came to his attention.

While it is tempting to explain the changes in U.S. policy during the 1960s in terms of presidential personality and leadership, there is an accumulation of evidence that suggests that the Alliance for Progress would never have worked and that Kennedy himself had become disillusioned with the Wilsonian policy of intervention on the side of democracy. The basic concerns of the cold war were as high on his agenda as they were on Johnson's. Would Kennedy have intervened in the Dominican Republic in 1965? We cannot say with any certainty. We can say, however, that the episode was a spasmodic response to domestic political concerns over "another Cuba."[47] Kennedy was at least as vulnerable as Johnson to such domestic pressures. The advisers who might have had a different view of reformers in the Caribbean than the military advisers, Thomas Mann and the others around Johnson, had been cowed and chastened by the Bay of Pigs. Kennedy gave no more evidence than Johnson of his ability to use the nation's power in a restrained manner. His disposition to cooperate with Latin American nations, the most distinguishing feature of his policy, had begun to weaken by 1963. And, if anything, he was more in thrall to the paradigm of counter-insurgency and stability than was Johnson. On balance, the Kennedy supporters who would have us believe things would have been different, make an unconvincing case. The Kennedy administration made no move to intervene in Argentina to speed the return to democracy after Frondizi was ousted.

In any event, the episode in the Dominican Republic effectively brought to an end any effort during the decade for multilateral cooperation. Following the intervention, the nations of Latin America were no longer willing to deal with the United States within the framework of the OAS. The OAS was considered a tool of U.S. policy, even though, ironically, President Johnson had the lowest opinion of the organization. He is reported to have said that the OAS was so ineffective it couldn't "pour piss out of a boot if the instructions were written on the heel." The Dominican intervention marked a great break in hemispheric relations. It marked an end to efforts on the part of the United States to cooperate within multilateral agencies in an effort to bring about social change. It marks a break also, on the Latin American side, in the willingness to cooperate with the United States. The lack of confidence in the United States is a legacy with which we live today.

Of course, as the decade wore on, events outside the hemisphere came to assume transcendent importance in U.S. policy-planning, so that Johnson, having once broken away from Kennedy's lead, was content to leave the hemisphere to its own devices. He maintained the high levels of direct public aid, but in effect, Latin America returned to the low priority in U.S. policy where it had been before 1958. Events in Asia, beginning with the Gulf of Tonkin episode, quickly took the administration's attention away from the Western Hemisphere and skewed U.S. policy so as to redefine national security in terms of our experience in Southeast Asia. After 1966 the foreign policy debate became so obsessively focused on events in Asia that it changed totally the perspective on national security that had shaped policy since World War II. That obsession so haunted President Johnson that it finally drove him from office. It continued to haunt his successor, Richard Nixon, and his principal adviser, Henry Kissinger. Kissinger believed the war in Vietnam threatened the delicate world balance of power, and he sought to restore the normal balance by bringing an abrupt end to the war, almost at any price. The balance Kissinger had in mind and toward which he worked during his years in Washington was a traditional view of global power, one in which Latin America continued as an insignificant region as far as U.S. strategic thinking was concerned.

The military that overthrew Arturo Frondizi was seriously divided on how to deal with the political situation in which the nation was mired. One group, the Blues (Azules), preferred a rapid return to constitutional government and assimilation of the Peronist mass into the political process. The other group, the Reds, or *gorillas*, were adamantly opposed to accommodation with the Peronists and preferred to eliminate the Peronist cancer by remaining in power indefinitely. For a short while, the two factions joined in turning the government over to José María Guido, president of the Chamber of Deputies under Frondizi, while they conducted their own form of political dialogue. For more than six months, the two factions jockeyed for support, literally counting their backers in terms of tanks and troop contingents. To test their calculations they would call out their supporters from the various units and installations around the capital. The *porteños* watched in amusement and embarrassment as their military leaders engaged in an elaborate, public game of chicken, the details of which were recounted in the newsweeklies that had proliferated since Frondizi's election. Finally, General Juan Carlos Onganía, army chief of staff and leader of the Azules, won the day. Elections were held in July 1963, with the Peronists still proscribed.

Without the Peronists and with the Radicals severely split, Arturo Illia, who headed the People's Radical party, won the election with only 25 percent of the popular vote. As the avowed heir of Yrigoyenist policies, Illia set out to put into effect the military's policy of winning the Peronists away from Perón. For a while the Radicals had things going for them. Thanks mainly to a three-year series of bumper harvests and dramatic increases in

sales to the Soviet Union and the People's Republic of China, export earn-
ings soared, solving the chronic balance-of-payments difficulties and stimulating the economy. Through wages and prices policies, the Illia government
managed to increase real wages significantly without fueling inflation. He
also appealed to labor with his strong nationalism. This, too, was part of the
Yrigoyenist legacy.

As soon as he entered office, Illia announced that he was cancelling the
contracts with U.S. oil companies that Frondizi has signed. The United
States took a very heavy-handed approach in dealing with the new government over this issue, and the tension in relations with Washington did not
lower the anxieties of the military watching over the process. The Kennedy
administration showed no disposition to display sympathy for the political
necessities of the newly restored democracy. Congress reacted to the episode
by adding the Hickenlooper amendment to the pending foreign aid bill,
stating that aid would be cut off to a country annulling contracts with U.S.
investors unless significant progress was made toward compensation within
sixty days.[48]

In the last analysis, Illia was undone by the same combination of internal and
external factors that had doomed Frondizi. He couldn't win an election against
the Peronists and he couldn't get any important segment of the mass away from
Peronist leaders so that he could win an election without Peronist parties. The
crisis in foreign affairs occurred in 1965 over the U.S. intervention in the
Dominican Republic. Foreign Minister Zavala Ortiz initially supported the
United States' efforts to involve the OAS, but President Illia opposed.
Onganía, now head of the joint chiefs, was furious at Illia's stance. He called
publicly for the creation of an ideological alliance with Brazil to fight communism in the hemisphere.[49] The prominent role of the Brazilians in the OAS
peace-keeping force emphasized the growing dominance of that country in the
region. This particular stance contributed to the demise of the Illia regime a
year later. Cooperation with the military regime in Brazil was one of Onganía's
principal objectives when he took power. It worked reasonably well until 1968,
when a change in Brazilian leaders brought a shift to an independent foreign
policy with emphasis on Brazil's Third World and African aspirations. This
change forced Onganía to abandon his ideological alliance.

By the beginning of the Onganía regime, the anticommunism and national
security doctrine of the military had become a double-edged sword in Argentina's foreign and domestic politics.[50] On the surface, it argued for close
cooperation with the United States, but it was espoused as well by antidemocratic military and civilian groups and by nationalists who were bitterly
hostile to the United States. This was yet another instance of asymmetry
between U.S. and Argentine attitudes, which appeared similar but which led
to different goals or different objectives in foreign policy. The difference
would become apparent a decade later when an internal threat would be
mounted against the Argentine government and the national security doc-

trine would be used to confront and defeat the internal threat, with the totally unexpected result that the nation would become an international pariah, shunned by the United States, the nations of the Western alliance, and by the nations of Latin America and the entire Third World.

NOTES

1. Inter-American Conference for the Maintenance of Continental Peace, Rio de Janeiro, 15 August to 12 September 1947. For a convenient summary of the proceedings, see J. Lloyd Mecham, *The United States and the Inter-American System* (Austin: University of Texas Press, 1960).

2. On the gradual hardening of U.S. attitudes toward the Soviet Union see John Lewis Gaddis, *The United States and the Origins of the Cold War, 1941–1947* (New York: Columbia University Press, 1972); on the Eurocentric nature of official thinking in Washington at the time see George Kennan, *Memoirs, 1925–1950* (Boston: Atlantic, Little Brown, 1967); on the estimates of Soviet military threat in the region see C. J. Pach, Jr., "The Containment of U.S. Military Aid to Latin America, 1944–1949," *Diplomatic History* 6, no. 3 (Summer 1982): 225–44; and Roger R. Trask, "The Impact of the Cold War on United States–Latin American Relations, 1945–1949," *Diplomatic History* 1, no. 3 (Summer 1977): 271–84; David Green, "The Cold War Comes to Latin America," in *Politics and Policies of the Eisenhower Administration*, ed. Barton Bernstein (Chicago: Quadrangle Press, 1970).

3. For general discussions of U.S. policy in the early cold war see R. Harrison Wagner, *United States Policy toward Latin America* (Stanford, Calif.: Stanford University Press, 1970); David Green, *The Containment of Latin America* (Chicago: University of Chicago Press, 1971); Herbert Agar, *The Price of Power: America since 1945* (Chicago: University of Chicago Press, 1957); and James C. Tillapaugh, "From War to Cold War: United States Policies toward Latin America, 1943–1948," Ph.D. diss., Northwestern University, 1973.

4. On the discussion of eliminating poverty in the developing world at this time see Wagner, *United States Policy*; Samuel L. Baily, *The United States and the Development of South America, 1945–1975* (New York: Franklin Watts, 1976); Terry H. Anderson, *The United States, Great Britain, and the Cold War, 1944–1947* (Columbia: University of Missouri Press, 1981); James M. Jones, *The Fifteen Weeks* (New York: Harcourt Brace, 1955); Robert A. Pollard, *Economic Security and the Origins of the Cold War* (New York: Columbia University Press, 1985).

5. Kennan, *Memoirs*, 352–53.

6. News conference in the *New York Times*, 15 August 1947, 8; speech in Robert N. Burr, ed., *Latin America*, vol. 3 of Arthur M. Schlesinger, Jr., *The Dynamics of World Power: A Documentary History of United States Foreign Policy, 1945–1973* (New York: Chelsea House Publishers, 1973), 36–40.

7. Burr, *Latin America*, 42–45; trade figures from the Agency for International Development, *U.S. Overseas Loans and Grants* (Washington, D.C.: U.S. Government Printing Office, various years). Wagner argues persuasively that even if there had been no Marshall Plan and even had the United States disposed of great resources in the years following the war, it is unlikely that there would have been higher levels of aid to

Latin America or that the U.S. government would have embarked on development programs involving significant participation by the public sector.

8. Pach, "Containment of U.S. Military Aid," 242–43. During Perón's first administration Brazil received $148 million in aid from the United States while Argentina received less that $1 million. Amounts, in constant 1989 dolllars, are taken from the Congressional Research Service's report for Congress, "An Overview of U.S. Foreign Aid Programs," March 1988. I am indebted to Leona Pallansch for sharing these data with me.

9. Bryce Wood, *Dismantling the Good Neighbor Policy*; Stanton Griffis, *Lying in State* (New York: Doubleday, 1953).

10. Carlos Escudé, *La Declinación Argentina*; Rita Ana Giacalone, "From Bad Neighbors to Reluctant Partners," Ph.D. diss., University of Indiana, 1979.

11. The literature on Peronism is vast. For a quick introduction see Alberto Ciria, *Perón y el justicialismo* (Buenos Aires: Siglo XXI, 1973); Miguel Murmis and Juan Carlos Portantiero, *Estudios sobre los orígenes del peronismo* (Buenos Aires: Siglo XXI, 1973); David Rock, ed., *Argentina in the Twentieth Century* (London: Duckworth, 1975); and Peter Waldmann, *El peronismo, 1943–1955* (Buenos Aires: Sudamericana, 1955).

12. Perón's economic policies are discussed in Carlos F. Díaz Alejandro, *Essays on the Economic History of the Argentine Republic* (New Haven, Conn.: Yale University Press, 1970); David Felix, "Industrial Structure, Industrial Exporting, and Economic Policy: An Analysis of Recent Argentine Experience," in *Fiscal Policy for Industrialization and Development in Latin America*, ed. David T. Geithman (Gainesville: University of Florida Press, 1971).

13. The debate over Perón's macroeconomic policies is summarized in Díaz Alejandro, *Essays on the Economic History*; Jorge Fodor, "Perón's Policies for Agricultural Exports, 1946–1948: Dogmatism or Common Sense?" in Rock, ed., *Argentina in the Twentieth Century*; and Thomas Skidmore, "The Politics of Economic Stabilization in Post-War Latin America," in *Authoritarianism and Corporatism in Latin America*, ed. James M. Malloy (Pittsburgh: University of Pittsburgh Press, 1977).

14. It is important to understand that this kind of policy planning and this thinking about the state's role in national development was part of a broad trend in the region, a trend that would be known in retrospect as Cepalismo, and that it had its strong analogue in the social welfare programs of the European democracies. See Leslie Bethell and Ian Roxborough, "Latin America between the Second World War and the Cold War: Some Reflections on the 1945–48 Conjuncture," *Journal of Latin American Studies* 8, no. 22 (May 1988).

15. These cables are reprinted annually in *Foreign Relations of the United States* (*FRUS*) for the years in question, 1946, 1947, and 1949. Daniel J. Greenberg ("From Confrontation to Alliance: Peronist Argentina's Diplomacy with the United States, 1945–1951," *Canadian Journal of Latin American and Caribbean Studies* 12, no. 24 [1987]) also argues that Perón was a pragmatist and a conciliator between extreme Argentine nationalists and State Department advocates of U.S. capital.

16. These events are described in graphic detail in Joseph A. Page, *Perón: A Biography* (New York: Random House, 1983) and Robert D. Crassweller, *Perón and the Enigmas of Argentina* (New York: Norton, 1987).

17. Juan Archibaldo Lanús, *De Chapultepec al Beagle: Política Exterior Argentina,*

1945–1980 (Buenos Aires: Emecé, 1984), 25–26, considers the economic discrimination the most significant external factor confronting Argentina at this time.

18. Lanús, *De Chapultepec al Beagle,* 72–80, sees Perón as the precursor of nonalignment. For a very different view see Alberto Ciria, *Política y Cultura Popular: la Argentina peronista, 1945–1955* (Buenos Aires: Ediciones de la Flor, 1983), 106–13 and Carlos J. Moneta, "Argentine Foreign Policy in the Cold War," in *The Impact of the Cold War,* ed. J. M. Siracusa and Glen St. John Barclay (Port Washington, N.Y.: Kennikat Press, 1977).

19. Bethell and Roxborough, "Latin America between the Second World War"; Carlos Escudé, "United States Political Destabilization and Economic Boycott of Argentina During the 1940s," in *Between the Powers: Argentina, the United States, and Great Britain,* ed. Guido DiTella and D. C. Watt (London: Macmillan, 1989).

20. James Bruce, *Those Perplexing Argentines* (London: Eyre & Spottiswoode, 1954), 37; Lanús, *De Chapultepec al Beagle,* 33, in what amounts to an apology for Perón, says the Lider "never wanted to be anti-American, he maintained a great prudent posture toward the government in Washington." Greenberg, in "From Confrontation to Alliance," takes a similar position.

21. Moneta, "Argentina Foreign Policy in the Cold War," 108–9.

22. Mario Mariscotti, *El secreto atómico de Huemul* (Buenos Aires: Sudamericana, 1985).

23. Pablo Neruda, *Confieso que he vivido,* quoted in Mario Rapoport, "Argentina and the Soviet Union: History of Political and Commercial Relations (1917–1955)," *Hispanic-American Historical Review* 66, no. 2 (1986): 251. Much of the information in this paragraph is drawn from Rapoport's article. See also Aldo César Vacs, *Discreet Partners: Argentina and the USSR since 1917* (Pittsburgh: University of Pittsburgh Press, 1984).

24. Rapoport, "Argentina and the Soviet Union," 278–84.

25. This is documented, for Chile, in Heraldo Muñoz and Carlos Portales, *Una Amistad Esquiva: Las relaciones de Estados Unidos y Chile* (Santiago: Pehuén, 1987).

26. Data from Díaz Alejandro, *Essays;* Jorge Fodor and Colin Lewis, in Rock ed., *Argentina in the Twentieth Century,* and Guido Di Tella and Miguel Zymelman, *Etapas en el desarrollo argentino* (Buenos Aires: Editorial de la Universidad de Buenos Aires, 1964).

27. Lanús, *De Chapultepec al Beagle,* 46–53, argues that Perón's foreign policy was global in perspective and, as a consequence, conflicted with U.S. efforts to consolidate its regional hegemony. But Argentina, in traditional fashion, never joined any of the global organizations getting started after the war and focused its economic and commercial efforts on bilateralism.

28. These events are recounted in C. MacDonald, "The United States, the Cold War and Perón," in *Latin American Economic Imperialism and the State,* ed. Christopher Abel and Colin M. Lewis (London: University of London by the Althone Press, 1985), and, with more attention to Argentine domestic politics, Gary W. Wynia, *Argentina in the Postwar Era* (Albuquerque: University of New Mexico Press, 1978), and Tulio Harperin Donghi, *Argentina en el callejón* (Montevideo; Editorial Arca, 1964).

29. Gary Frank, *The Struggle for Hegemony in South America* (Coral Gables, Fla.: University of Miami, 1970).

30. Carlos Escudé, *Patología del nacionalismo. El caso argentino* (Buenos Aires:

Editorial Tesis, 1987), has the most penetrating analysis of the domestic groups with positions in the foreign policy debate. Edward S. Milenky in *Argentina's Foreign Policies* (Boulder, Colo.: Westview, 1978) argues that there were two separate tendencies in Argentine foreign policy, classic-liberal and statist-nationalist. This misses the historical imperative of Argentine nationalism and the powerful impact of independent foreign policy stances on domestic political groups of the Left, Center, and Right.

31. On the Guatemala episode see the summary discussion in Stephen G. Rabe, *Eisenhower and Latin America: The Foreign Policy of Anti-Communism* (Chapel Hill: University of North Carolina Press, 1988), and the sources cited there.

32. For a general discussion of these issues see Robert Packenham, *Liberal America and the Third World: Political Development Ideas in Foreign Aid and Social Science* (Princeton, N.J.: Princeton University Press, 1971).

33. In an early review of policy, in NSC 144/1, March 1953, a listing of U.S. objectives in Latin America indicates that all of these were of concern, but at that point, the precise relationship among them was not specified.

34. W. W. Rostow and Max Millikan, *A Proposal: Key to an Effective Foreign Policy* (New York: Greenwood Press, 1957).

35. These initiatives are recounted in F. Parkinson, *Latin America, the Cold War, and the World Powers* (Beverly Hills, Calif.: Sage Publications, 1974). For another perspective, see Baily, *The United States and the Development of South America.*

36. Arthur M. Schlesinger, Jr., *A Thousand Days: John F. Kennedy in the White House* (Boston: Houghton Mifflin, 1965). For Dillon's position see Dillon and Mike Mansfield, "What Kind of U.S. Aid for Latin America?" *Foreign Policy Bulletin* 40 (15 October 1960).

37. MacDonald, "The United States, the Cold War, and, Perón, 411–13.

38. See Miguel Angel Cárcano, *Churchill and Kennedy* (Buenos Aires: Ediciones Pampa y Cielo, 1966). Cárcano told me in an interview that his social contacts with the Kennedys were used on more than one occasion to win special favors for Argentina, and to postpone or to soften criticisms of Frondizi's foreign policy emanating from Washington. Jacqueline Kennedy enjoyed riding horses on Cárcano's ranch (interview, 23 July 1967). For Frondizi's policies see the collection of his speeches, *Discursos en los EE. UU. de Norteamerica* (Buenos Aires: Presidencia de la Nación, 1959), and *Introducción a los Problemas Nacionales* (Buenos Aires: Centro de Estudios Nacionales, 1964), which includes a chapter on foreign policy.

39. Alberto Conil Paz and Gustavo Ferrari, *Política Exterior Argentina, 1930–1962* (Buenos Aires: Huemul, 1964), chapter 7.

40. Ibid, 247; Clarence V. Zuvekas, Jr., "Argentine Economic Policies under the Frondizi Government," *Inter-American Economic Affairs* 22 (1968): 45–74.

41. These speeches are cited in Conil Paz and and Ferrari, *Politica Exterior* 255–57.

42. John F. Kennedy, *The Strategy of Peace* (New York: Harper & Row, 1960), 184; Maxwell Taylor, *The Uncertain Trumpet* (New York: Greenwood Press, 1960). The Luce quote is from David Halberstam, *The Best and the Brightest* (New York: Random House, 1972), 18. See also Edwin Lieuwin, *Generals vs Presidents: Neomilitarism in Latin America* (New York: Praeger, 1964) 124.

43. Cole Blasier, *The Hovering Giant: U.S. Responses to Revolutionary Change in Latin America* (Pittsburgh: University of Pittsburgh Press, 1976), 246. As Michael

Shafer has shown recently (*Deadly Paradigms* [Princeton: Princeton University Press, 1988]) the policy was a misapplication of a paradigm aimed at the Soviet Union, based on the misperception of reality in the Third World, and even the deliberate distortion of the analysis of the results of the policy's application. Critical to an understanding of this paradigm is the evolving view of the military in the Third World, from predatory ally of the oligarchy to agents of change and development. But, at least until 1967, when Che Guevara was hunted down, and killed in Bolivia, it was hard to deny the paradigm. Everyone appeared to live according to its rules—the Cubans, the Soviets, the Chinese, and, of course, the Vietnamese.

44. W. W. Rostow, "Guerrilla Warfare in Underdeveloped Areas," in *The Viet Nam Reader*, ed. Marcus G. Raskin and Bernard B. Fall (New York: Vintage Books, 1965), 115–16.

45. On El Salvador see T. S. Montgomery, *Revolution in El Salvador* (Boulder, Colo.: Westview, 1983). For a good summary of the episode in the Dominican Republic, and citation of the standard sources, see Lester Langley, *The United States and the Caribbean* (Athens: University of Georgia Press, 1982). Blasier, *Hovering Giant*, suggests that the threat to U.S. private investments has played too large a role in shaping U.S. response to reformist regimes in the hemisphere. His examples include the expropriation of IPC in Peru and the sugar companies in the Dominican Republic. Blasier also says that our fear of great power rivals' action motivates the response of the United States, even though Soviet help to the regimes in question, other than Cuba, has been minor. In several cases we have forced reformers to turn to Eastern Europe for aid or arms because the United States refuses to provide one or the other or both.

46. For an introduction to the rapidly growing literature on the Johnson administration see G. L. Sigelmann, "LBJ and His Interpreters," *Social Science Quarterly* (September 1986); Alan Matusow, *The Unraveling of America* (New York: Harper & Row, 1985); Robert Divine, ed., *Exploring the Johnson Years* (Austin: University of Texas Press, 1981); and Paul Conkin, *Big Daddy from the Pedernales* (Boston: Twayne Publishers, 1987).

47. On this theme see Langley, *The United States and the Caribbean*, and my article "Inhibitions Affecting the Formulation and Execution of the Latin American Policy of the United States," *Ventures* 7, no. 2 (1967).

48. The episode is recounted in Baily, *The United States and the Development of South America*, 101–10.

49. This episode is in Parkinson, *Latin America, the Cold War, and the World Powers*, 208–9.

50. For a summary of policies and objectives of the Onganía regime, see Circulo Militar, *Política Internacional Argentina* (Buenos Aires: Círculo Militar, 1966) and Raul Puigbó et al., *La "Revolución Argentina": analysis y prospectiva* (Buenos Aires: Galerna, 1966).

chapter 8

ARGENTINA AS PARIAH
IN THE INTERNATIONAL COMMUNITY

Politics in Argentina from 1955 to 1973 have been characterized as an "impossible game."[1] Hardliners in the military kept Peronists from voting, which meant that any regime governed without the approval of that numerous portion of the electorate. Once in office, minority governments tried to effect social and economic policies to stimulate the economy and realized that they needed the cooperation of the highly organized labor movement. To win labor support, they held out the carrot of political participation and promised to temper economic policies that might hurt labor. As the government and Peronists drew closer, the military grew more wary until they would stand by no longer and ousted the elected leaders, starting the process all over again. This cycle was repeated even in situations of military rule, where factions of the military out of power constantly took more rigid positions than the faction in power. The economy went through a series of "stop-go cycles" characterized by high levels of inflation and vulnerability to fluctuating international prices for the export staples accompanied by alternating periods of stagnation and expansion.

The tense instability precipitated terrorist violence, which increased steadily at the end of the 1960s. In 1973 the Peronists were allowed to participate in the political process and won successive presidential elections, the second of which returned Juan D. Perón to power. But not even Perón could contain the violence, which escalated out of control after his death in June 1974. The military returned to power in March 1976, determined to extirpate the virus of subversion from the body politic. It embarked on a campaign of state terror that claimed at least 10,000 lives, most of them "disappeared" without due process. Once again, the military was unable to effect the restructuring of the society or politics they had made their stated goal. And, again, the economy foundered after a brief period of success at the end of the 1970s. The regime collapsed in 1982, following the disastrous war with Great Britain over the Malvinas Islands, and stepped aside for the resumption of constitutional democracy in 1983.

Foreign policy during this period was without clear focus. Concern grew for geopolitical questions, and there were moments in which the government took a position in opposition to the United States. But on balance, Argentina remained firmly committed to the Western side in the cold war.[2] The reign of terror that began during Perón's brief rule attracted unfavorable international attention. This became a major issue after 1976, when the Carter administration made Argentina the primary focus of its human rights policy. Conflict between the two governments reached levels not seen since Braden had attempted to influence the election of 1946. The military government sternly rejected U.S. pressure to soften its campaign against subversion. It was obsessed with the national security doctrine, which was the driving force behind the campaign. The same doctrine led them in 1978 to the brink of war with Chile over the Beagle Channel, to reject an arbitral award in the dispute, and to an arms buildup that culminated in the occupation of the Malvinas Islands and a war with Great Britain. These episodes marked Argentina as an international outcast, a pariah.[3] From the U.S. perspective, Argentina was not a major issue, scarcely coming to the attention of senior figures in the Nixon administration. As former Secretary of State Henry Kissinger told the weekly *Siete Días* during his visit to Argentina to attend the World Cup in soccer in 1978, "Argentina is a fascinating country. It is a pity that I didn't pay any attention to it while I was Secretary of State."[4]

The situation changed dramatically when Jimmy Carter became president in January 1977. He made the defense of human rights around the world the centerpiece of his foreign policy and, within months of taking office, had made Argentina the principal target of his policy. For the next three years, affairs in Argentina were a matter of daily concern in the policymaking circles of the State Department and in the White House, and none of the attention was favorable.

When Ronald Reagan assumed office early in 1981, U.S. policy returned to its normal pattern as, in keeping with arguments put forward by U.N. Ambassador Jeane Kirkpatrick, military authoritarian regimes on the Right were considered less menacing than communist, authoritarian regimes of the Left. In such a scheme, members of the Argentine military were potential friends and allies, not pariahs. The Reagan administration sought the international rehabilitation of the Argentine military by incorporating it into the campaign against communist subversion in Central America. The effort was cut short when Argentine troops occupied the Malvinas. The United States supported its old ally Great Britain, contributing to the Argentine defeat in the war that ensued and adding yet another chapter to the bitter relations between the two countries.

The military junta that removed Illia from office in 1966 was held together by a firm dedication to the doctrine of national security. From the military's perspective, the civilian regime that they had ousted was incapable of ending the internal discord that was tearing Argentine society apart. Unless and until that discord was ended, the nation was at risk. It was at risk from the danger of internal subversion either in the form of a revival of demagogic populism, or in the form of communism, and it was at risk from the continuing encroachment of Brazil into the River Plate delta. The political discord that had characterized Argentina for nearly a generation severely inhibited the influence of the nation in international affairs and made it impossible for the nation to exercise its power in an effective manner.[5] The civilians were faulted as well for their inefficiency in the drive for national development. In their quest for votes, minority governments were unable or unwilling to make the difficult decisions that were required if the nation was to accumulate the capital it needed to take its place among the major nations of the world.[6] As far as the military was concerned, national security was nearly synonymous with prestige and influence.

Onganía and his colleagues were determined to remain in power as long as it took to achieve their objectives. They were determined to impose discipline on Argentine society and restructure the economy and politics; they would create a bureaucratic-authoritarian state.[7] Onganía was a believer in the methods of Francisco Franco. In cabinet discussions of policy issues he often would refer to advice "my good friend Franco" had given him. He wanted Argentina to have a "disciplined democracy" or an "organic democracy."[8] Onganía and his colleagues would begin with the economy. They brought in Adalberto Krieger Vasena, who had extensive experience with U.S. multinationals, as a superminister, a pattern that would be repeated ten years later by another military junta. He had more power over the nation's foreign policy than did the series of ministers of foreign relations.

For a while, he enjoyed considerable success. There was a surge of foreign investment in the country, although much of it went to purchasing existing economic enterprises and not to creating new capacity; there was a series of good export years and relief from the chronic balance-of-payments difficulties.[9] For a short while there was temporary relief from the interminable social tension precipitated by truculent unions. Prices and wages were controlled, with considerable attention paid to maintaining real wages. Dissent was stifled, beginning with a tragic invasion of the Universidad de Buenos Aires, one of the world's great universities, which was reduced to an empty shell. Laboratories were smashed and closed, and faculty by the hundreds were hounded from their positions, many fleeing into exile. Discussion of public issues during the regime was restricted to a few minor magazines and the halls of small, private universities. Those social scientists and publicists who did not go into exile—a phenomenon that came to be known as "brain drain"— retreated to one of a growing number of small, discreet research centers that, from 1966 to the present, are the site of nearly all the serious social science research done in the country.[10]

The threat to the nation's security was a cause of great concern to the new military regime, and the focus of its concern was Brazil. While Onganía hoped to join his military colleagues in Brasilia in an alliance based on shared ideology with reference to international communism and internal subversion, he was concerned primarily with stopping what he and his fellow leaders saw as the threatening advance of the Brazilians into the heartland of America. The principal source of concern was the coherent geopolitical policy articu-lated by the leaders of the Brazilian regime, which relegated Argentina to a subordinate position in the region, and the concrete steps already taken by the Brazilians to join the Paraguayans and the Uruguayans in hydroelectric projects along the river system, and the projected continental road linking Bolivia to the Brazilian coast.

The lack of energy and energy dependence was Brazil's major strategic weakness. The series of ambitious hydroelectric projects would end that de-pendence. To make matters worse for Argentina, the dams Brazil intended to build were upriver from projects that Argentina had considered building ever since the first administration of Hipólito Yrigoyen. Frondizi and Quadros had discussed joint exploitation of the river system during their meeting in 1961. Nothing ever had come of the Argentine projects, and now Brazil actually had signed agreements with Paraguay to build two huge dams. If the dams were above a certain level, they would rob the Argentine projects of the water necessary to drive turbines. Brazil held the key to Argentine's hydroelectric future. A nation in chaos could not negotiate to good effect. In addition, the Brazilians were flexing their political muscles in Uruguay, which the Argen-tines considered their sphere of influence.[11]

The focus on national security and geopolitical concerns dictated two tendencies in the foreign policy of the military regime. First, it was imperative to be closely allied with the hegemonic power, and, if possible, to be allied in such a manner that Brazil would not benefit from its relationship with the United States more than did Argentina. The traditional policy of hostility toward and rivalry with the United States was no longer viable. The Nixon administration had indicated its satisfaction with Brazilian subparamountcy— geopolitical dominance over its neighbors—in the region and was effusively supporting the military regime in Brasilia. The Argentines had to regain U.S. confidence and offset the Brazilian advantage before it was too late.[12] The second tendency was to reinforce Argentine ties to the nations of Latin America and the region, which now came to include the entire South Atlantic. For the first time, serious consideration was given to a military alliance among Argentina, Brazil, and South Africa, to contain communism and prevent communist influences from taking over any of the vital sea lanes in the area. Of course, such an alliance would have strengthened Argentina's position in its dispute with the British. Through such an alliance, it would establish its position among the Western nations defending against international communism and earn the right to take over the islands in dispute.[13]

But Onganía's foreign policy collapsed because the Brazilians decided to shift to an independent foreign policy line, with strong appeals to Africa and the Third World, and simply ignored Argentina's repeated efforts to reach an accommodation on the dams. It collapsed also because his regime could not contain the social conflict and turned all of its attention inward. In 1968 a series of violent labor conflicts, beginning in the provincial capital of Córdoba (known as the Cordobazo), set off a period of conflict that quickly resulted in the outbreak of urban terrorist violence, led by small groups of young leftists, some of whom acted in the name of the exiled Perón.[14] Economics Minister Krieger Vasena was sacrificed in an attempt to appease the unions, and in June 1970 Onganía himself was removed by his military confreres because he rejected a "political plan" under which he would share power with the joint chiefs.

First, the junta put General Roberto Levingston in power, a colorless figures without any political following of his own. He lasted less than a year. In March 1971 the leader of the army and the dominant figure in the military, General Alejandro Lanusse, took power in his own right and determined that the only way to break the Gordian knot of Argentine politics, the "impossible game," was to bring back Perón. Within a week political parties had been legalized and Lanusse announced that he would turn over power to a constitutional government within three years.

For the next year negotiations were conducted between representatives of the government and one or another of Perón's personal emissaries, either in Buenos Aires or in Madrid. While rumors circulated, factions in the military expressed their opposition to the process or to specific terms in the negotiations by declaring units or installations in rebellion. At the same time, increasingly militant groups perpetrated acts of terrorism either against members of the military or against members of the Peronist coalition they considered too reactionary or too closely linked to the military.[15]

Most of Lanusse's energies were directed at preparing the transition to a civilian regime. His foreign policy was altered to suit that purpose. He called for nationalization of the economy and supported policies to that end by Economic Minister Aldo Ferrer. He declared Argentina's adherence to ideological pluralism, a direct reversal of the policy of the Onganía junta that had sought an ideological alliance with the military regimes of the region against communism. Lanusse met Chile's socialist president, Salvador Allende, in the provincial capital of Salta in July 1971, where they agreed to seek a peaceful, political solution to the dispute over the Beagle Channel and signed a Declaration of Salta in which they pledged joint efforts to expand trade, transport, tourism, and the exchange of technology. Lanusse also authorized Foreign Minister Luis de Pablo Pardo to renew contacts with Cuba, with a view to resuming formal diplomatic relations with the Castro government. That goal was not consummated until the next government. Similarly, the Lanusse government reached a settlement with the government of Uruguay over the limits between the two nations in the River Plate delta, which the Perón regime accepted and signed in a treaty.

Through this chaotic period, the United States played almost no role whatsoever. The internal drama was played out without outside interference. President Nixon sent former Treasury Secretary John B. Connally on a tour of Latin America to discuss international trade and explain the import of Nixon's recent trips to China and the Soviet Union. He met with Lanusse, Pablo Pardo, and economic officials on 12 June 1972 to express U.S. concern about Argentina's nationalistic tendencies on foreign investment.

The delicate negotiations with Perón were not completely successful. Perón decided that he would not run in the March 1973 elections and, instead, backed his personal representative in Argentina, Héctor Cámpora, who easily beat the fragmented opposition. He took office in May under extremely difficult conditions. The Peronist movement was divided into at least four different factions, each of which claimed to interpret the wishes of the Líder (Leader) and considered the others as traitors who should be ignored or eliminated. Surrounding Perón was a group of advisers who had remained close to him during his lengthy exile. Chief among this group, known as the "family," was his new wife, María Estela Martinez de Perón, known as Isabel, and Lopez Rega, his personal astrologer and bodyguard. In the wings were old cronies and politicians who had served Perón during his previous reign. They were known as the "classic Peronists" and were, for the most part, politically conservative, nationalistic, Catholic, and prominent in the party machinery.

The other two factions were themselves highly fragmented. They were the unions, collected in the General Labor Confederation but split into three fragments, each of which claimed direct access to Perón. These groups had suffered severe losses in the bloody violence since 1970. The fourth major faction was a set of radical groups, almost all on the Left, comprised of students and young professionals and a few younger union activists, espousing a curious combination of Marxism and Peronism. As the transition to constitutional government approached, these groups fought bitterly and publicly for their right to claim recognition as the true interpreters of the Líder's policies.

Perón deliberately manipulated the four groups, not wanting any one of them to achieve a modicum of power independent of his person. He chose to let Héctor Cámpora run for the presidency in the first election in March, and made plans for his own return. To everyone's surprise, Cámpora won by a sufficient margin to obviate the need for a runoff. His cabinet was a coalition of moderate and conservative groups, including Lopez Rega as welfare minister, José Gelbard as economics minister, and Juan Carlos Puig as foreign minister. Presidents Allende and Dorticos attended the inauguration ceremonies, as did Secretary of State William Rogers.

Cámpora's first speeches and actions were dramatic and nationalistic. He pushed an amnesty bill through the congress, praised the guerrilla groups that had "fought violence with violence," and called for closer relations with the nations of Latin America to reduce the oppression of imperialism. At the same time, however, he and Perón called for an end to terrorism and for national unity, and indicated that the more radical of the guerrilla groups, like the ERP, the FAR, and the Montoneros, would have to submit to government control or face the prospect of repression.[16]

The Cámpora team had little time to do more than prepare the basic outlines of a foreign policy. Puig, whose writings on international relations had given him an international reputation, was a strong advocate of building an autonomous position for Argentina in world affairs through identification of Argentine interests with Latin America and the Third World. At the OAS meeting in Lima in June, Puig sided with the most progressive regimes in the hemisphere against the United States and spoke out on the need to reform the international system and to control the influence of multinational capital.[17] Except in its pugnacious tone, this policy fit well with the policies of economics czar Gelbard, who was a founder and leader of the CGE, the entrepreneurs' association said to represent domestic capital, though he and his principal advisers all had strong links to international capital. To both Puig and Gelbard it was indispensable to expand the base of Argentina's economic and political relations in order to reduce the nation's dependence on the United States. Their intention was to open relations with the Eastern bloc, expand relations with Asia, and improve the nation's relations with its neighbors.

Taken as a whole, the policy, as stated in speeches by Cámpora, Puig, and Subsecretary of Foreign Relations Jorge Vazquez and later in the writings of Puig, was a statement of the reformist tendencies within Peronism. It never represented the majority opinion within the movement, and in tone and substance it was not a true reflection of the Líder's views. Especially in its strident tone and its sharp hostility to the United States, it went counter to Perón's views of the world, which had become more pragmatic and settled since his ouster in 1955, and it did not capture Gelbard's attitudes toward the Western powers. The policy lacked support from the foreign service professionals and from the congress. As soon as Cámpora left office, just seven weeks after he had been inaugurated, Puig was fired, and the policy began to change.

Throughout the transition Perón insisted that his movement was unified behind his leadership. If there were differences, he said on many occasions, they were honest differences over how to achieve the movement's common goals and would be resolved once he was returned to power. During his exile, he had considered it useful to have several people speak for him, reining in one or another as it suited his convenience. So it was to be with Cámpora. He never had liked advisers or followers who displayed too much independence or leadership. But if anyone doubted there were serious fissures in the Peronist movement they were dispelled forever on 20 June 1973, when two million people gathered at Ezeiza International Airport near Buenos Aires to welcome their Líder home. Fighting erupted between heavily armed gangs of right-wing goons and equally armed bands of the Peronist Youth. Dozens were killed and hundreds wounded in the chaos that ensued. The plane carrying Perón was diverted to a nearby military airfield and he was taken directly to his home in the suburbs of the city. The next day, in a televised address, he denounced all violent groups in language that made it clear he would brook no further deviance. He said, "Each Argentine, whatever he thinks and feels, has the inalienable right to live in peace and security. Whoever violates that principle no matter what side he is on, will be a common enemy that we must fight without pause."[18] Cámpora made his own televised address on 25 June in which he called for an end to guerrilla activity. The ERP was only driven to more violent response and the struggle escalated. Lopez Rega organized secret paramilitary groups within the police, known as the Argentine Anticommunist Alliance, to eliminate the Left within the movement.

Whether he wanted to or not, Cámpora stepped down on 13 July to allow Perón to return to power in new elections. He was replaced by the president of the senate, Raul Lastiri, who happened to be Lopez Rega's son-in-law. The new elections were won easily by Perón, who took power in his own right on 12 October 1973. By this time he was in failing health, and he died in 30 June 1974, to be replaced by his wife and vice president.

The foreign policy of the Peronist regime was a reflection of the evolving conflict within the movement itself. The regime gradually moderated its rhetoric and its positions on critical issues within the hemisphere. More remarkably, Perón himself led the move toward closer relations with the United States and applied the brakes to the tendency toward greater autonomy for Argentina in the international system. The central thrust of the nation's foreign policy, as it had been for nearly a century, was to guarantee the nation's insertion in the world market. Only now the market had changed, as had the international system. Gelbard was the chief architect of the nation's effort to diversify its markets and broaden its industrial base and, in that way and not by hostile rhetoric, to increase its influence in world affairs. The two principal measures through which Gelbard would restore Argentine economic well-being and its international influence at the same time were the opening to the Eastern bloc and massive economic credits to Cuba.

In August 1973, while Lastiri was still president, Gelbard announced a

$200 million credit to Cuba. This was later increased to $1.2 billion. The beauty of the deal, from the Argentine point of view, was that the largest item in the credit was for the purchase of nearly $300 million worth of automotive equipment, nearly all of which was manufactured by subsidiaries of U.S. firms. This was neither a casual nor deliberately hostile act, as it has often been interpreted by observers in the United States. Gelbard's chief adviser, Julio Broner, who had succeeded him as president of the CGE, was part of the automotive industry himself and had close, amicable links to U.S. capital. He and his associates had no difficulty with the Cuban deal—they had negotiated it. In one deft gesture they had given the Argentine automobile industry, painfully vulnerable to economic cycles and scarcely competitive in the international market, a powerful boost and had all but ended the economic blockade of Cuba.

The U.S. government at first reacted in a hostile manner and then took six months to discuss the measure, finally authorizing the U.S. firms in Argentina to do business with Cuba. They had little choice, really. How could a corporation doing business in Argentina refuse to obey Argentine law, and refuse to do business with a foreign country, especially when that business meant the difference between profitable operation and a loss? Secretary of State Kissinger recognized the special role Argentina was playing as an intermediary between Cuba and the United States. In just ten years, the cold war had changed enough so that Argentina's links with Cuba, forged without public posturing hostile to Washington, could be accepted there with relative equanimity.

Gelbard's opening to the East was a long-term project designed to establish the nation's autonomy in international affairs. To make it work, Argentina would have to reestablish harmonious relations with the United States so that it had relatively constant access to the major sources of credit over which the United States exercised effective control, such as the IMF, the World Bank, the Inter-American Development Bank, and the private banking sector in the United States. It was an ingenious policy, certainly the most coherent and pragmatic since Saenz Peña's vision of Argentina's insertion in the world market a century earlier. It was a pragmatic and realistic adaptation to the world system and held great promise as a plan for national development. It failed largely because Perón died and his widow could not contain the internal conflicts within the movement or within the government.

After Perón's death Gelbard resigned and Lopez Rega increased his influence over Isabel. He was largely responsible for the growing wave of state terror against those he considered subversives, and he conducted an extremely idiosyncratic foreign policy without always keeping the foreign ministry informed. He visited Libya without informing Gelbard, and negotiated a huge exchange with Quaddafi. He encouraged a rapprochement with the new military dictator of Chile, Augusto Pinochet, and with the military in Uruguay and Brazil, and he moderated assertions that Argentina's destiny was identified with the Third World and the nonaligned. Under Isabel it was made perfectly clear that Argentina sided with the United States. The tendency toward an autonomous position, with hostile posturing toward the United States that had been apparent during the Cámpora administration, was stifled.

Once again the economy, as it had in the early 1950s, failed to help Perón accomplish his goals. Argentine exports increased 65 percent from 1972 to 1973, only to fall in 1974 and 1975. At the same time, deteriorating terms of trade virtually erased the favorable balance of trade. The foreign debt was growing by leaps and bounds. At the end of the military government in 1972, it was $5.4 billion; under Cámpora it expanded to $6.4 billion, and soared to more than $10 billion by the end of 1974. No wonder the economics ministers wanted to maintain cordial relations with the lending institutions, public and private, in the United States.

In the final analysis, it was the internal disorder and her incompetence that doomed Isabel Perón. The internal chaos reduced the capacity of the government to act or to project its influence internationally. Perhaps inspired by the Argentine Anticommunist Alliance, each of the military forces employed its own secret service to combat "subversive elements," and the army intensified its campaign against armed bands of insurrectionists, especially in the province of Tucumán. The killing and disappearances increased on both sides through 1975 and 1976, eventually reaching the intensity of a civil war. The rule of law became a mockery; the economy was in turmoil. Kidnappings of businessmen and politicians for ransom were common, and hardly a night went by without some bombing in the federal capital. Prices skyrocketed, with inflation reaching an annual rate of nearly 1,000 percent. The supply of basic commodities became irregular as retailers simply refused to sell goods whose prices the government attempted to control, and workers struck every time they wanted to adjust their wages to the levels of the cost of living. The military, led by army Chief of Staff Jorge Videla, assumed control of the government again on 24 March 1976, declaring that this time it would not relinquish power until it had accomplished a total restructuring of society to secure Argentina its rightful position in world affairs. This process would begin with the total extirpation of subversive elements from the body politic by whatever means necessary.

As with the government led ten years earlier by Onganía, this was not to be a caretaker government, content to rule until the civilian politicians had settled their differences sufficiently to allow for another round of elections in the impossible game. This was to be a regime that would define national goals, formulate policies to reach these goals, and employ the entire administrative capacity of the state to execute the policies. Unlike previous military regimes, this bureaucratic authoritarian state was from the beginning inextricably linked with international capital, even while it professed nationalism and a geopolitical stance on international affairs, positions previously associated with support for economic independence and hostility toward economic liberalism.

Like Onganía and Perón, the Videla junta turned the management of the economy over to a superminister who would guide the nation out of its stagnation. In this case it was José Alfredo Martínez de Hoz, perhaps the country's most prominent proponent of international liberal capitalism. Martínez de Hoz set out to revive the economy by stimulating the traditional export sector and by encouraging a flow of foreign capital into the country. Developmentalist critics of the regime's policies were either shouted down in the muzzled and controlled press or hounded into silence and exile, or worse.[19]

If we can say that it is logical or natural for a military regime to define its objectives in geopolitical terms, it is not at all clear why such a regime should include in its ideological baggage a free-market economic model of the Milton Friedman type. None of the military leaders was an economist; they handpicked José ("Joe") Martínez de Hoz as their economic czar to purge the economy in the same way that they were prepared to purge the society of its antinational, Marxist, subversive cancer with a powerful diuretic, at whatever cost to the body politic. The subtleties of the economic debate did not interest most of the military leadership. They associated protected industries. Keynesian pump priming, and nationalist economic policies with populist politics, Peronism, and other unnatural acts, although most of them had a keen appreciation of strategic industries.

Irrespective of the inherent defects of the free-market model, a subject far from the purpose of this book, it seems clear that the junta never contemplated the contradictions between the long-term economic and strategic requirements of a national-security regime and the painful process of reinserting the Argentine economy into the international market on the basis of a supposed comparative advantage in the production of some agricultural staples. The link seems to have been the persistent myth of the importance of the Argentine economy to the international economic system and the belief that Martínez de Hoz's policies would restore Argentine competitiveness in the market and, with it, the nation's prestige.[20]

Uniformed officers were put in charge of all the vital state-owned entities, the deficits of which were considered by some economists to be the greatest single impediment to bringing inflation under control. Army officers were put in charge of organizations such as the Yacimientos Petrolíferos Fiscales (YPF), the state-run steel factory, and the aluminum complex in Puerto Madryn because they were considered essential to the nation's security—the job of the armed forces—and because it was believed that their deficits were more than likely the result of civilian inefficiency or corruption. Whatever the management capacity of military technocrats, in the short run most of them displayed a passion for protecting their new turf and all but denied to the new minister of economics any influence over their corporate behavior. Rather than force a confrontation, Martínez de Hoz chose to ignore the anomalous situation, but the contradictions between his noble pronouncements on the cleansing of the economy and the continued stagnation of the state sector, which some estimated to be as high as one-third of the gross domestic product, could not be ignored forever.

For its part, the military, hardly students of the finer points of monetarist policy, ceded Martínez de Hoz a certain political and chronological space to accomplish his objectives. With the hefty exception of the state-run sector, Martínez de Hoz was given a free hand to cleanse the economy as long as he accomplished the military's primary economic objective: to accumulate within twelve or twenty-four months enough foreign reserves to permit the modernization of the armed forces, now responsible not only for national security and for the bloody crusade against internal subversion but also for the realization, once and for all, of the nation's historic destiny. Like so many of its predecessors, civilian and military, the junta was obsessed with international prestige.

From our perspective, it appears obvious enough that the contradictions between the economic consequences of the military's geopolitical schemes and the implications of the regime's official economic model would reappear sooner or later. Both in the months before and after the golpe, to both parties to the arrangement, the potential benefits of success were considered far greater than the risks of failure. Besides, economic success would have a political multiplier effect of sorts by doing more than anything else the regime could accomplish in the short term to forge a national consensus among the fragmented groups within the society, a consensus that would legitimate the regime and its national model of reconstruction with one fell swoop.

For a time the strategy looked as if it was right on the money. Martínez de Hoz took his after-dinner show on the road to banks and manufacturing associations throughout the developed world where he was lionized and promised support. Agricultural production reached levels not achieved since the 1930s. Some even saw the hand of God in the fact that between 1976 and 1978 the country enjoyed three bountiful harvests in a row, a phenomenon with few precedents in the twentieth century. In the midst of this economic surge, the nation hosted and won the World Cup in soccer. For a short while at least, everyone was an Argentine.

Just as predicted, the surging exports facilitated the accumulation of hard-currency reserves, which paved the way for nothing short of an orgy of shopping in the arms markets of the world, a buying spree that accelerated in the last months of 1978, as tension built between Argentina and Chile over the Beagle Channel, and extended well into 1979. (The Beagle channel dispute between Chile and Argentina centered on three tiny islands in the channel between Tierra del Fuego and the Chilean island of Navarino at the southern tip of South America. Chilean control over the islands implied access to the Atlantic, a principle Argentina would not accept.) Estimates of the amount spent on sophisticated hardware soared into the billions, and the wildest of them rang true as missile-firing corvettes steamed proudly into the navy base at Puerto Belgrano and wave after wave of Mirage jets were sighted entering Argentine air space.[21]

The division of responsibility for government policy-making whereby a superminister was assigned the task of bringing the economy back to health was imposed on the military by its sense that the war against subversion was its top priority and that it was work that fell to the military and not to civilians. The doctrine of national security became the doctrine of permanent war.[22] War was declared on the guerrilla groups. As General Ibérico St. Jean, appointed governor of the province of Buenos Aires, is alleged to have put it, "First we will kill the subversives; then their collaborators; then their sympathizers; then those who are indifferent; and finally, the timid." Military men were put in charge of the provincial and national police forces. Each service arm and each branch of the police had its own secret service that carried out operations independent of the others. For a while the judiciary was involved and due process was followed in a small number of cases. Increasingly, the secret services operated on their own without apparent supervision and without coordination. Each service had its own center for interrogation and torture; each had its favored places of incarceration. Thousands and thousands of Argentines were picked up on the streets or taken from their homes in the dead of night by armed men who claimed to represent the state, driving unmarked Ford Falcons. The overwhelming majority of those seized in this manner were never heard from again; they "disappeared." On occasion, some would reappear, having been tortured and interrogated, to go into exile or to retreat into silence, as a warning to others.[23]

These were the measures that constituted the all-out war on subversion, the dirty war. If there were excesses, they were defended as necessary to defeat an implacable enemy who violated all the norms of civilized government and who threatened the very existence of Western civilization. Besides, as many if not most Argentines said in referring to a friend or relative who was "disappeared" by the security forces, "Por algo habrá." There must have been something that he did, otherwise, why would the security forces pick him up? The saddest feature of the dirty war was that the vast majority of the Argentine people became silent accomplices in state's destruction of civil liberties.

Many Argentines acquiesced in the dirty war or closed their eyes to its horrors because they were tired of the chaos, tired of the instability, and, most profound of all, tired of their society's collective failure to achieve its promise. The majority of them, even those who had been deeply hostile to Perón in his first tenure as president, had turned to him, almost in desperation, as their last chance to achieve social unity and political stability. He had failed, and now they were willing to allow the military to put their house in order. For some, the imposition of a strong government was a golden opportunity. They were frustrated with the continued failure of their country to achieve the greatness they considered its destiny. Members of the junta expressed the deep nationalist drive in the soul of most Argentines for status and influence in the world. It was their obsession. The subversives were doubly evil, representing an abhorent ideology and denying all Argentines their due as citizens of a significant country.[24]

The activities of the paramilitary death squads and the pattern of torture and disappearances had become a foreign policy question even before the golpe in March 1976, as leaders of a number of Western nations indicated their displeasure with the way in which the rights of individual citizens were trampled in Argentina. As the state terrorist activity increased after the golpe, organizations such as Amnesty International kept up a steady drumbeat of criticism of the military government's complicity in kidnapping, disappearances, torture, and the assassination of civilians. At first, the military government brushed aside such criticism by saying that if such atrocities occurred they were the unwarranted but inevitable excesses in a military campaign against an armed internal enemy who fought dirty.

The significance of human rights violations in Argentina's international relations increased dramatically when Jimmy Carter became president. He had determined that his administration would distinguish itself from the Nixon administration by emphasizing its moral propriety, both in the conduct of public affairs and in the definition of public policy. In foreign affairs the United States would distinguish among foreign nations not merely by whether they professed opposition to communism, but also by the way in which they ruled their people. Democratic nations were considered better friends of the United States than authoritarian states. Under a new law passed by Congress, an Office of Human Rights was created in the State Department. Three regimes that had been considered friends of the United States, Iran, South Korea, and Argentina, were singled out for special attention.

Argentina got most of the attention as, after a short period of general condemnation, criticism of Iran and Korea was muted and all but silenced in deference to the strategic importance of those countries. Suddenly, Argentina became news in Washington, and for the wrong reasons. As part of her campaign and in the normal conduct of her business, Patricia Derian, director of the State Department's Office of Human Rights, made public pronouncements about human rights abuses in Argentina. Very soon her every utterance received front-page coverage in Buenos Aires. In response to this pressure, the official line of the Argentine government about the dirty war began to change as it became increasingly important to show the world that stability and order had returned, particularly as the government set its sights on the World Cup in soccer in June 1978, which it hoped to turn into a showcase of Argentina's progress since the golpe.

The official position on the human rights violations was that reports in the foreign press were grossly exaggerated or that it was the lamentable but understandable overzealous reactions of patriotic elements to the general malaise of subversion in the society and to the terrorism of revolutionary guerrillas who kidnap and kill civilians and military personnel. Those who supported the military regime believed that the U.S. government allowed Derian to make her public charges because, as one prominent businessman asserted, they "do not believe that Argentina is an important nation and therefore condemn her for alleged human rights violations, while excusing Russia and China." This policy "reflects a total lack of reality or understanding of the holocaust Argentina has undergone in recent years." He went on, "On March 24, 1976, Argentina ended a prolonged period of misgovernment marked by various populist regimes, and it entered an era of reconstruction on which the Republic should be refounded. The process has been hindered by internal and external difficulties of all types [among which is]: A world campaign organized by European and Argentine leftists which is being fostered in the U.S. to run down the international image of Argentina and which publicly supports self-exiled leaders of Argentine terrorism."[25]

Parallel to the new government's efforts to eradicate subversion, and designed to strengthen its hand, was a tendency in 1976 and 1977 toward some form of cooperation among the military regimes in the hemisphere. The junta seems to have decided that any form of isolation was too costly for Argentina in its weakened condition. Until its national strength could be restored, Videla dampened Argentina's international aspirations and accepted, at least temporarily, a subordinate position to Brazil in South American power politics, played out in public in negotiations over two potentially competitive hydroelectric projects on the upper reaches of the River Plate basin, both involving Paraguay.[26]

In 1978 Videla attempted to play the role of mediator within the military in the dispute with Chile over the Beagle Channel, a position that cost him dearly among the younger officers, the air force particularly, and among the nationalists in the population at large who welcomed a chance in November to teach the Chileans a lesson, once and for all. Argentina came within days or hours of going to war with Chile. The armed forces were mobilized, coffins were shipped to the south, and the national radio played martial music for long periods. Videla opposed the war, but his officers were determined to get satisfaction for the supposed violation of Argentine sovereignty in the channel, and even senior members of the government were uncertain if they could afford to back down without losing support within the military and from the population at large. Videla finally won the discussion, convincing his colleagues that they would best defend the nation's honor by restoring internal order and disdaining all interference in the internal affairs of the nation.[27]

Because his regime was so closely identified with economic liberalism, historically associated with antinationalism, and because he curbed the hawks and the geopoliticians on the channel and hydroelectric competition, Videla stacked his nationalist chips on one issue, an issue on which he refused to compromise, negotiate, or allow anyone to outflank him: the rejection of international criticism of human rights violations in Argentina. By 1979 the refutation and rejection of the international "campaign" against Argentina had become an obsessive issue in foreign policy and had spilled over into areas of political and economic policy.

The issue of human rights had assumed significant proportions by 1978. The accusation touched the very heart of the military's sense of its mission and threatened its long-term objectives. This brought the question of human rights violations into increasingly higher relief, until it seemed to block out or color all other questions. Argentines could not understand why Americans persisted in their attacks. They never perceived that the statements or attacks were coming from the office of the State Department charged exclusively with the evaluation of human rights all over the world, not from the secretary of state or from the president. As had happened so many times in the past, the U.S. government had unthinkingly stumbled upon an issue that was peripheral to its concerns but absolutely vital to the Argentine government. The asymmetry extended into the bureaucratic politics of decision-making in both governments.

In the United States Office of Human Rights Director Derian also held the rank of assistant secretary of state. To buttress her position, she was the wife of the president's press spokesman, and one of the highest ranking women in the administration. When she drafted a statement on Argentina, she only had to clear it with Undersecretary of State Warren Christopher. As a courtesy, she shared the contents with the assistant secretary of state for Latin American affairs. The Argentine desk officer often had very little time to make a case for modifying the statement, if he considered such a case needed to be made. Each year, the annual report on human rights conditions in Argentina had to be drafted jointly by the desk officer and the Office of Human Rights. In such a situation, Derian had all the influence. The officer who opposed her did so at great risk to his career.

By the end of the Carter administration it was clear to State Department professionals that increasing the pressure on the Argentine government did not necessarily produce the desired results. By contrast, it was the firm conviction of desk officers in the division at the time that such pressure was highly effective in Chile. It was their opinion, expressed in interoffice memoranda to the chief of the division, that the most effective way of dealing with the problem in Argentina was to reduce the public pressure on the military and increase informal efforts in the country to release individuals known to have been disappeared. This was the strategy used by the Canadian government, with some success, and the practice of various U.S. consular officials, who stretched their authority to win the release of prisoners.[28] For her part, Derian remained unsympathetic to views suggesting that peculiar conditions in Argentina might indicate an approach different from the one she had adopted. She was utterly ignorant of the history of U.S. relations with Argentina and once admitted that she never had heard of Spruille Braden. At the end of the Carter administration she claimed her policy had been effective, and that state terrorism in Argentina was declining. The decline in disappearances after 1979 was more likely the result of the fact that the military felt they had won the war on terrorism and that there were few subversives left, if any.[29]

The asymmetry of purpose and differing perspectives on the issue made meaningful dialogue difficult and increased the friction in dealings between the two nations. A high-ranking official of the ministry of foreign relations, who had done a tour of duty in the Washington embassy during the Carter administration, declared at the end of 1978 that he was sick and tired of the human rights issue. That was all he had worked on while he was in Washington. He had had as much difficulty explaining the U.S. position to his superiors as he had in dealing with the State Department. Without for a moment defending state terrorism or offering any of the excuses for it that were common among apologists for the military, he wished the issue would go away so that the two countries could get down to more serious business.[30]

Of course, the issue would not go away as long as the climate of repression persisted in Argentina and the defense of human rights remained a high priority of U.S. foreign policy. And the tension between the two nations persisted as long as each government continued blind to the perception of the issue by the other. It was as if one party considered the question too important to negotiate while the other considered it too unimportant for serious, high-level negotiation. Like Woodrow Wilson, Cordell Hull, or Spruille Braden before them, Carter and Derian did not comprehend Argentine reluctance to comply with their requests or demands because to them the issue was so clearcut—a case of black and white. They did not appreciate how their pressure was turned into a matter of protecting the independence of the government from outside interference. Videla's ability to withstand the external interference on this issue was the measure of his legitimacy among his military colleagues. As had happened so many times in the past, U.S. pressure on the Argentine government played into the hands of groups hostile to the government who represented positions even less friendly to the United States.

The Videla government's problem was compounded by the fact that, in one sense at least, the issue *was* black and white. Human rights were systematically violated in Argentina. The problem was how to explain such violations in a country that claimed to be fighting to preserve Western Christian values. Following upon the broadly based popular euphoria induced by the Argentine victory in the World Cup, there was a rising clamor in the local press to the effect that those who criticized Argentina did not know the real situation and intentionally distorted reality for their own ends. One glossy newsweekly ran a story on police brutality in the Philadelphia rent strike, suggesting broadly that the United States had no right to criticize conditions in Argentina. A woman's weekly ran a page of cut-out postcards showing bucolic scenes of parents playing with children or soccer stadiums crowded with orderly fans. The facing page ran the addresses of members of the U.S. government and officials in the United Nations and in Amnesty International to whom the postcards were to be sent. In December 1978 the campaign entitled *La Verdadera Argentina* (The Real Argentina) was repeated, by popular demand.

The following year, the Argentines decided to take their public relations efforts to the United States. They hired a U.S. public relations firm, and launched a monthly bulletin from the embassy in Washington, *Argentina*, distributed to people considered influential in the public and private sectors. They established strong ties to conservative groups in the United States with which they had or expected to have ideological affinity. The Heritage Foundation, in Washington, and Senator Jesse Helms proved to be extremely cooperative.[31] The next year they hired a private publishing firm, the Southern Cone Publishing & Advisory Services, Inc., which took over the job of distributing materials on real-life Argentina, including a new monthly newsletter, *Argentine Report*, and conducted seminars that brought Argentines and Americans together to discuss matters of public policy.[32]

While no one in the Videla government would defend violations of human rights, per se, there were high ranking members of the military and a few in second echelon government positions who were quite willing to do so. These men cared not one whit for the form or substance of political democracy. They were concerned with capturing once and for all the greatness that had eluded Argentina. Given such a premise, criticism of Argentina from abroad, however correct from a logical or a moral standpoint, was merely another obstacle to that broad goal.

Videla's dilemma was to drive for the national goal with all the energy of the hardliners while maintaining as broad a coalition as possible of civilian elements without whose support his rule would be severely weakened. His dilemma was reflected in the self-censored press, as the media grasped for a new vocabulary or new set of categories with which to defend or explain their country and the military government at the same time they defended such timeless Western and Christian virtues as democracy and human rights. Phrases such as "responsible democracy" and "organic democracy" had been clichés by the end of 1978, shorthand allusions to "irresponsible" and "inorganic" forms, which presumably characterized the polity during the chaos, inefficiency, and social tensions of the civilian regimes that went before the golpe in 1976. Certainly until 1980, the majority of the Argentine people was disposed to accept the regime, with its horrible repression, as the best possible alternative. For this acquiescent majority, external pressure on their government prompted a hostile reaction and self-defense. In terms of the political forces at play, the internal situation was remarkably similar to the debate on neutrality in 1941. Pressure from the United States had the unwanted effect of providing political legitimacy to the worst elements in the regime, including the butchers and psychopaths such as General Ramon Camps, who personally tortured the newspaper editor Jacobo Timmerman.

Martínez de Hoz's emphasis on the traditional export sector restored to prominence the traditional foreign policy goal of maximizing the sale of the nation's exportable surplus at the best price available. Argentina would sell meat and wheat to anyone who would buy. By 1980 the Soviet Union had become Argentina's best customer, taking 35 percent of its exports and 80 percent of its grains. When the United States called for a worldwide embargo on sales to the Soviet Union because of the latter's invasion of Afghanistan, Argentina refused. In 1980 and 1981 Argentina was virtually the Soviet Union's only supplier of foodstuffs outside the Eastern bloc. And this was a regime whose raison d'être was a campaign without quarter against communism and communist subversion. The foreign policy of the nation was in total disarray.

The U.S. presidential campaign of 1980 was of more than passing concern to people in Buenos Aires. Early in his candidacy, Ronald Reagan criticized Carter's emphasis on human rights. It was common knowledge that Reagan admired Jeane Kirkpatrick's arguments in favor of close relations with authoritarian regimes that declared themselves opposed to communist subversion. That must have warmed the hearts of the junta. Ironically, once the external pressure was removed, following Reagan's election, the Argentine government lost the issue that had provided a rallying point for popular support. Within a very short period of time, cleavages among the civilian supporters of the regime assumed increasing saliency. The debate over economic policy divided the military, the industrialists, and the financial community. Even the muted press became outspoken in its criticism of the regime's policies. Where singleness of purpose, decisiveness, and internal cohesion had characterized the government, now vacillation and indecisiveness became noticeable. Roberto Viola had replaced Videla in 1981 when the latter reached the end of the "term" set by the original junta. Martínez de Hoz left the government at the same time, as the signs became unmistakable that his economic miracle was coming apart.

Such was the apparent success of the economic model that it contributed to the restoration after 1980, in large measure, of the international reputation of the military regime, so badly tarnished by the blood of thousands upon thousands of disappeared, tortured, and jailed citizens. As the international pressure on the regime relaxed, it opened an internal political space and accelerated the process of political accommodation, a relaxation of controls. As Argentines returned from their summer vacations in February and March 1979, the generals seemed content with their success over the subversives and with their new equipment, the people seemed content with having won the World Cup and with the increasing purchasing power of their currency abroad (middle-class Argentines flooded into Europe and the United States to buy the latest consumer durables and luxury items), and the international bankers seemed content with their great friend "Joe" Martínez de Hoz. But the aura of well-being was chimerical. The economic situation began to deteriorate almost immediately, revealing that only under ideal economic conditions could the regime manage the contradictions between its economic and its geopolitical models.

The contradictions within the regime did not have an immediate impact on its foreign policy. The absence of normal political activity and of channels through which to express dissent had created for the regime a sense of independence that led the junta to give free rein to its grand geopolitical designs without the inhibition confronting any democratic regime, of listening to dissenting voices. In fact, it appears as if the military leadership did not even bother to go through the normal exercise of listening to competing scenarios within the bureaucracy or to collect systematically information available within the bureaucracy that might affect the selection of policy options. This became painfully clear during the Malvinas crisis. As one foreign diplomat reported:

> One can sympathize with Argentine frustration at negotiations with Britain. Frustration, however, is not a good counsellor. In fact, the Argentines would have come out well ahead of the game if they had had enough sense to accept a diplomatic settlement after their occupation of the islands. Unhappily they became intoxicated with their own rhetoric quite apart from the usual difficulties the military government had in making up its collective mind. Moreover, by then Argentina had accomplished the impossible. They had reawakened the British Imperial spirit. The Argentines did Mrs. Thatcher an immense political favor.[33]

Part of the problem derived from the nature of the regime and its peculiar mode of formulating policies. Although there have been few systematic studies of decision-making under the Argentine military government,[34] and most of the information we have about public administration during the 1976–82 period is anecdotal,[35] three propositions can be made without much fear of contradiction concerning the period up to the Malvinas war. First, there was no formal political opposition to the regime, and there were no organized groups that systematically subjected the actions of the government to public discussion and whose criticism represented a factor that the government had to take into account in formulating policy. Second, there were no institutions of intermediation in the society to fulfill the role of articulating the interest of groups or sectors in the society and making them known, in a systematic fashion, to the government. Labor unions and labor centrals, such as the Confederación General de Trabajo (CGT), might be considered an exception, although their role was anything but systematic. Third, there were serious impediments to freedom of expression among the mass media. Incidents of government censorship, in the form of pulling specific issues of a periodical off the newsstands or closing down an offending news organ, together with a pervasive, deadening self-censorship, left the mass media opaque and timid from 1976 to 1981. The radio and television newscasts were anodyne, and the large-circulation dailies were either sympathetic to the regime and wished to avoid public controversy or focused their critical energies on fringe issues, such as the level of tariffs or the deficits of public corporations. Only the English-language daily, the *Buenos Aires Herald,* made a practice of commenting openly on the political events of the day, and that earned for its managing editor, Robert Cox, threats against his life that drove him into exile.

The combination of these three elements over a period of time had the effect of virtually eliminating any mechanisms through which the government might hear alternate scenarios or consider heterodox perceptions in the course of formulating policy. This seemed to work to strengthen the junta while it was under pressure from the Carter administration and while state terrorism was most virulent. As the dirty war came to an end and Reagan replaced Carter, this peculiar administrative pattern worked to undermine policy coherence and was instrumental in the decisions that led to the disasterous Malvinas war.

The junta stated repeatedly that the armed forces were united behind decisions and policies of the government, but that is not the same thing as eliminating discussion during the decision-making process. The absence of free expression, together with reiterated insistence by the junta that the armed forces were united, led observers to assume that authoritarian regimes are monolithic and unified state actors. Nothing could be more misleading as far as the Argentine government was concerned. The insistence on the unity of the armed forces was a reaction both to the sad history of internecine conflict among the military groups in power and to the stark fact that they took power in 1976 in the midst of chaos. Their claim of having ended that chaos and of having repaired the sociopolitical fragmentation that characterized Argentina in the years leading up to the golpe represented one of the principal sources of their legitimacy. To solve the nation's problems, once and for all, the junta declared their unified support for a "process" that required the faithful adherence of all groups in the society for the benefit of the nation. In the first months following the golpe, the process was defined largely in terms of what the military was against—anarchy, clumsy mismanagement in government, galloping inflation, economic stagnation, leftist revolutionary guerrilla movements in the city and in the countryside, and a breakdown between the civilian government and the military authorities in their efforts to wipe out the guerrillas. Once the dirty war against subversion had been won, definition of the process in political terms proved more difficult and subject to severe disagreement among the military leaders.

In formal or institutional terms, the unity of the armed forces translated into unity in the junta and the right of any one of the services to veto any policy with which it was not in agreement. This was known as the *veto compartido* (shared veto) and often led to situations very much like government by committee, which created massive administrative bottlenecks. To protect the junta from the appearance of disagreement, bargaining and trading off often was relegated to subordinate bodies, particularly the Comité de Acción Legislativa (Legislative Action Commission), and to a vast, shifting array of ad hoc subcommittees on which each service was represented. If disagreements could not be reconciled within any of these bodies on matters not impinging directly upon the national interest, the decision was postponed. This occurred most frequently in the discussion of personnel files. On one occasion the nomination of a senior career diplomat to an important post ran into some unspecified difficulty in committee and never emerged. The post remained unfilled for months, until the gentleman solved the problem by withdrawing his name from consideration. Similar embarrassing impasses attended a number of staff appointments in various ministries of the government.

The insistence upon formal unity within the junta also had more deadly consequences. Once a question of policy was placed before the junta and had been decided, it was made public as an act of the state as represented by the unified armed forces. Differences of opinion within the junta sometimes were expressed after the fact by the minority service by shooting down a representative of the majority services on the streets of Buenos Aires, in broad daylight. It was as if one of the armed forces, having just lost a vote in the junta, gave notice publicly that its interests had not been represented and that it was exacting a price for its continued cooperation.[36]

Bottlenecks in the decision-making process and discontinuities in the process of bureaucratic politics were made worse by the traditional military distrust of the civilian experts upon whom they had to rely for information and advice on a wide variety of policy issues. This problem was particularly acute in the Ministry of Foreign Relations, where the career staff often appeared to be at odds with its military superiors.[37] The military often acted independently of the Foreign Ministry, especially in Central America, and Martínez de Hoz never cleared his movements or his statements with the Cancillería.[38]

Argentina long has had the reputation of conducting its foreign affairs in an unprofessional manner and of coming to the diplomatic bargaining table ill-prepared.[39] Not too long ago, a former foreign minister indicated that he had been unable to find critical background papers in the ministerial archives and that it was his common experience to attend international meetings without the benefit of briefing memoranda summarizing the historical antecedents for the issue under discussion, the sort of memoranda that dot the records of the Brazilian and Chilean foreign ministries, not to mention the National Archives in Washington or the Public Record Office in London.[40]

But the dilemma of the military government was not a lack of professionalism among the diplomatic corps nor a lack of information. Systematic interviews among senior foreign service officers, especially those who had held posts in the Argentine embassies in Washington, London, or Brasilia, made plain that the leadership in Palacio San Martin was provided with an ample supply of information about events in other countries and perceptive reports on the attitudes of those countries toward conditions in Argentina and policies of the Argentine government.[41] The problem was the lack of channels for that information to reach the decisionmakers in the cabinet and the junta. Censorship in the press, the often murderous manner in which the armed services carried on their political dialogue outside the government, and the severe repression of public political activity virtually eliminated mediating mechanisms in the society and in the government bureaucracy itself, through which the nation's leaders could assimilate information vital to their decision-making function. The information was there; what was lacking was the means to bring it to the attention of the decisionmakers and the context in which it could be evaluated to determine its consequences for the nation's policies.

By December 1981 the military felt compelled to reassert its intention to redefine national goals. General Leopoldo Galtieri, the new chairman of the joint chiefs, replaced Viola as president, and Roberto Alemann was named minister of economics amid assertions of renewed dedication to the market mechanism. "The time for words and promises has ended," said Galtieri, "the time has come for action." But the action to which Galtieri referred was not a new attempt to restructure political activity nor a new attack on stagflation or speculation; it was an invasion of the Malvinas Islands.

The war between Great Britain and Argentina over the Malvinas was strange in several respects. Everyone involved saw it coming months in advance, and yet no one could or would stop it; there is a quality of inevitability about the onset of hostilities. No one doubted who would win the military phase of the struggle, and yet that knowledge neither helped reduce the level of violence nor caused either party to alter its behavior. Many observers also sensed a laboratory quality to the conflict. Military planners around the world watched the battle with enthusiasm bordering on glee to learn how their latest weapons systems would perform under fire. The battlefield seemed so far away from the normal arena of interstate conflict that many observers felt detached from the fighting, coldly uninvolved, so that the immediate repercussions of the fighting were scarcely felt outside the war zone. Had the war dragged on longer, such geopolitical isolation might have broken down. In sharp contrast to the war in Vietnam, the actual fighting took place off-camera. It was the diplomatic maneuvering instead that was shown on television around the world, with a great deal of the diplomatic bargaining conducted on-camera. Because of the ever-present television crews, both sides were exposed as manipulating the information released to their populations, although only the Argentine leadership claimed to be winning the war when the news available to the public indicated otherwise. The outcome of the struggle benefited no one, and a solution to the underlying conflict may be as far away as it ever was. That result makes the loss of life even more tragic and senseless.[42]

As a study in crisis management, the Malvinas conflict is a nightmare. The

Argentine leadership completely misread or miscalculated British resolve and entered the crisis firmly convinced that the British would not and could not mount a military response to the invasion sufficient to dislodge Argentine troops without unacceptable military losses. So convinced were the Argentine leaders of this notion that they never formulated, much less implemented, plans to defend the islands against such a response. To the very end, the junta appeared stunned by the fact that the British fleet had bothered to come all the way into the South Atlantic.

The assumptions on which the decision to invade the islands was based reads like a list of nostalgic yearnings rather than the calculations of rational leaders. The Argentine leadership believed that

- their old natural ally, Great Britain, would not take amiss the invasion of the islands;
- the European nations would consider Argentina as one of them;
- the U.S. government would treat Argentina on a par with Great Britain given the support Argentina was providing in the conflict in Central America, thereby pardoning and forgiving all of the historical difficulties that had come between them;
- Argentina was a leader among the Latin American nations and that the other nations in the region would support Argentina in its anti-imperialist gesture;
- in any dispute, a democratic government and a nondemocratic government were essentially the same in the eyes of third parties.

The Argentine leaders lived in a world of dreams created in the course of a century of distorted perceptions of the world and of a tradition of acting without taking account of the possible consequences of their actions. In the case of the Malvinas war, their misperceptions proved tragic. The soldiers who lost their lives on the islands or who went to the bottom with the *General Belgrano* paid the consequences.

The leaders were supported in their view by the man they appointed to lead their foreign ministry in this crisis, Nicanor Costa Mendez, who convinced them that he understood the British, the North Americans, and the ways of international affairs. In the end, he revealed that he understood none of them, and he remains one of the heavies of the drama.

One cause of these gross miscalculations was the fact that the decisionmakers were remarkably ignorant of the U.S. political system and of how decisions are made in the United States. That error led them to take some careless remarks by Senator Jesse Helm's legislative assistant and by Secretary of State Haig's personal emissary, General Vernon Walters, as ironclad assurances by the U.S. government that in return for support in Central America the United States would back Argentine efforts to recapture the Malvinas—

even if force were necessary—and that the United States would make sure that the British did not overreact.[43]

While it would be an exaggeration to say that the United States played an insignificant role in the run-up to the conflict, it certainly did not play a dominant part. The squabbling within the Reagan administration, especially between U.N. Ambassador Jeane Kirkpatrick and Secretary of State Haig, did not help, and no one benefited from the charade of Haig's exhausting shuttle from Washington to Buenos Aires to London and around again. His ineffectiveness is clear demonstration of how out of touch with things in Argentina the State Department had become over the years. No one, except perhaps a few of the Argentine leaders who (hanging on to what Vernon Walters may have told them) doubted that, when push came to shove, the United States would side with the British and that the Argentines were doomed to defeat. In fact, Haig spent most of his time after the first round of talks trying to convince the Argentines of the inevitability of such a defeat. David Gompert, who accompanied Haig on his mission, summed up the situation: "It took extraordinarily poor judgment to invade the Falklands, and it is unlikely to happen again. But the fury in Argentina will not go away. . . . If frustration and miscalculation caused the war, rigidity assured that it would run its logical military course."[44]

One of the bitterest complaints of the Argentines is the "betrayal" by the United States and, more specifically, the material support given to the British during the conflict. This argument holds that a poor country could not possibly fight against the two strongest democratic powers in the world and that this realization led to a certain defeatist attitude on the part of the nation's leaders. Yet most of the Argentine leaders knew that the United States would not get involved militarily. Furthermore, no evidence exists that the disappointment felt by the military leadership affected their prosecution of the war or even their diplomatic strategy. On the other hand, in fairness to the Argentines, it is necessary to admit that U.S. aid was far from insignificant to the outcome of the engagement. It was critical to the British cause. The use of U.S. intelligence satellites enabled the British to monitor the movements of Argentine surface vessels. Would the Argentine navy have ventured out of port after the *Belgrano* was sunk if the United States had not been monitoring its vessels? We cannot know the answer. The use of Ascension Island certainly speeded the arrival of the British fleet at the war zone. Had the fleet not arrived when it did, it would have had to deal with foul weather in the South Atlantic and might have had to alter its war plan.

One of the critical consequences of the war was the mortal blow dealt to the military regime and the inexorable pressure placed on the military to turn the government back to the civilians. As this distance, it is tempting to say that—perhaps even with the terrible loss of life—the war was worthwhile because it rid the nation of the dictatorship that had taken far more Argentine lives than those lost to British guns. By exposing the military's lamentable lack of professional skill, the war completed the process of public disillusionment begun with the horrific bloodletting of the dirty war and deepened by the increasingly obvious failure of the regime's highly touted economic plans, which had been the excuse for many of the harsh repressive measures of the successive juntas. Almost as soon as the fighting stopped the process of political transition began.[45]

In political terms, the Malvinas crisis was for Galtieri what the human rights issue was for Videla. As long as he held firm and did not appear to retreat, he won considerable leeway in handling the delicate process of "political opening" during the military crisis. However, the crushing failure of the military adventure together with revelation of the government's systematic deception of the public during the conflict and the internal squabbling among the armed forces over the conduct of the campaign eliminated Galtieri's room for political maneuver and shattered the chimera of national unity. In keeping with the historical pattern, this embarrassment of the "moderates" searching for an accommodation with the United States strengthened the most nationalistic forces within the military. Their leader was General Lami Dozo, chief of the air force. Capitalizing on the prestige won in combat by his courageous pilots and the seething discontent among the junior officers in all three forces, Lami Dozo made a bold bid for power in July. He called for the formation of a party to "defend the objectives of the process of national reconstruction." The army, led by General Cristino Nicolaides, still had enough force to block the move, and Lami Dozo withdrew from the junta and retired from active duty.

In economic terms, the war tied Economics Minister Alemann's hands and led to his early resignation. The fight against inflation suffered a mortal blow, and free-market advocates were forced to take a back seat to those who insisted on maximizing the sale of Argentine products to the Soviet Union, even if that required barter agreements, to those who wished to rearm the nation and strengthen domestic production of critical material, and to those who argued that the hostile action of the United States and the Common Market required at least a minimum amount of national industrialization for the ultimate protection of the nation's sovereignty.

The kaleidoscopic changes in cabinet personnel and the constant public wrangling among the military after the defeat in the war indicated that the "proyecto político" of the military government was in complete disarray. This only served to hasten the return to civilian rule and to quicken the pace of efforts by civilian political parties and interest groups to formulate their positions on important issues confronting the nation. The more disorganized the authoritarian groups, the more coherent appeared the civilian forces. The failure to recapture the Malvinas underscored the bankruptcy of the military proyecto, but it did not lend credence to any alternative model for national reconstruction. The military left the government; they were not forced out.

The United States played no significant role in the transition, but it did welcome the return to constitutional government.

As the Argentine people prepared to vote in 1983, their nation seemed in a sorry state. The economy was in shambles. Its foreign policy was in utter confusion. The nation appeared to have lost its way, to have lost its identity and become an international pariah. As individuals, Argentines professed to adhere to traditional personal, moral values, such as the family, the church, and interpersonal relations. But there still was no consensus on public policy issues. In the face of national failure Argentines had accepted as a price for their individual comfort and contentment depolitization and demobilization and a pervasive alienation from public affairs. This alienation—and the dete-rioration of mediating institutions—would be formidable obstacles on the road back to any kind of participatory political regime in the 1980s.[46]

NOTES

1. Guillermo O'Donnell, "El juego impossible," *Documento de Trabajo* (Buenos Aires: Instituto DiTella, 1972). See also Gary W. Wynia, *Argentina in the Postwar Era* (Abuquerque: University of New Mexico Press, 1978); and Richard D. Mallon and Juan Sourreille, *Economic Policy Making in a Conflict Society. The Argentine Case* (Cambridge, Mass.: Harvard University Press, 1975).

2. On this period see, among many others, Gustavo Ferrari, "Constantes de la política exterior argentina," *Economic Survey, Suplemento Especial,* no. 1370 (2 February 1973); Juan Carlos Puig, "La política exterior argentina y sus tendencias pro-fundas," *Revista Argentina de Relaciones Internacionales* 1, no. 1 (1975); Roberto Etchepareborda, "Presencias nacionales en el exterior. Elementos de la política de los estados," *Respuesta Argentina,* supplement (July 1974); and Dardo Cúneo, "Argentina's Foreign Policy," in *Latin American International Politics,* ed. Carlos A. Astiz (Albany: State University of New York Press, 1969).

3. The term is from Carlos Escudé, *La Argentina ¿Paria Internacional?* (Buenos Aires: Editorial Belgrano, 1984).

4. *Siete Dias,* 14 July 1978.

5. Edward S. Milenky, *Argentina's Foreign Policies* (Boulder, Colo.: Westview, 1978), chapter 4; Felix Luna, *De Perón a Lanusse, 1943–1973* (Buenos Aires: Planeta, 1972); Wynia, *Argentina: Illusions and Realities* (New York: Knopf, 1986).

6. Alvaro C. Alsogaray, *Bases para la acción política futura* (Buenos Aires: Editorial Atlantida, 1969).

7. Guillermo O'Donnell, *Modernization and Bureaucratic-Authoritarianism* (Berkeley: University of California Press, 1973).

8. See, among others, *Primera Plana,* 16 October 1967, 3; *Economic Survey* 12 February 1968.

9. Oscar Braun, *Desarrollo del Capital Monopolista en Argentina* (Buenos Aires: Editorial Tiempo Contemporaneo, 1970) and Guillermo Martorell, *Las inversiones extranjeras en la argentina* (Buenos Aires: Galerna, 1969).

10. Enrique Oteiza, "El brain drain intelectual y el desarrollo," *Documento de Trabajo* (Buenos Aires: Instituto DiTella, 1969).

11. The concern for geopolitical issues was reflected in the founding of a journal dedicated exclusively to their public discussion. *Estrategia*, founded by General Juan Enrique Guglialmelli, published articles by Argentines and by foreigners. He was particularly anxious to disseminate the work by Brazilians, both to show Argentines what serious discussion of the issues was like and to alert his compatriots to the menace from the north. He was especially concerned with the work of the chief Brazilian theoretician General Golbery, whose *Geopolitica do Brasil* has become something of a classic. On the Brazil–Argentine rivalry in Uruguay, see my "Uruguay: the Quintessential Buffer State," in *Buffer States in the International System*, ed. John Chay and S. R. Ross (Boulder, Colo.: Westview, 1986).

12. On U. S. relations with the Brazilian regime see Jan Knippers Black, *United States Penetration of Brazil* (Princeton, N.J.: Princeton University Press, 1985); and Riordan Roett, *Brazil: A Patrimonial State* (Boulder, Colo.: Westview, 1982).

13. The geopolitical issues in the South Atlantic have been the special province of Carlos Juan Moneta for many years. His evaluation of the situation during the Onganía regime as well as a chapter by me on Argentine-Brazilian relations can be found in Moneta, et al., *Geopolítica y Política del Poder en el Atlántico Sur* (Buenos Aires: Pleamar, 1983). To appreciate the degree to which these geopolitical concepts permeated the thinking and writing about Argentina's international position, see *La Nación*, 1 June 1978, 5, 12 October 1978, 8 and 16 November 1978, 8; *Somos* 3, no. 112 (1978):11, 56; and *Carta Política*, no. 60 (1978):5.

14. On the wave of violence see María Matilde Ollier, *El fenómeno insurreccional y la cultura política (1969–1973)* (Buenos Aires: Centro Editor de America Latina, 1986); on the Cordobazo see Horacio González Trejo, *Argentina: Tiempo de Violencia* (Buenos Aires: Carlos Perez Editor, 1969).

15. The negotiations are described in Joseph A. Page, *Perón: A Biography* (New York: Random House, 1983), chapters 47–50.

16. For various views of this period see Juan Corradi, *The Fitful Republic. Economy, Society, and Politics in Argentina* (Boulder, Colo.: Westview 1985); Frederick C. Turner and José Miguens, eds., *Juan Perón and the Reshaping of Argentina* (Pittsburgh: University of Pittsburgh Press, 1983); and Wynia, *Argentina in the Postwar Era.*

17. For a review of foreign policy during this period see Carlos Juan Moneta, "La Política Exterior del Peronismo, 1973–1976," in *Foro Internacional* 20 no. 2 (1979). Juan Carlos Puig's most interesting book from this period is *Doctrinas Internacionales y Autonomia Latinoamericana* (Caracas: Universidad Simon Bolivar, 1980).

18. The episode is recounted in detail in chapter 52 of, Page's biography of Perón.

19. Marcelo Diamond, an economist and industrialist, wrote frequently on economic subjects for *Clarín*. At the end of 1979 he received a series of anonymous telephone calls from agents of the secret police suggesting that he take an extended vacation or else. These calls were used to warn people that one agency or another of the secret services was after them.

20. The power of these myths is discussed in Carlos Escudé, *Patología del nacionalismo. El caso argentino* (Buenos Aires: Editorial Tesis, 1987).

21. A recent report by the Banco Central (*Informe Mensual*, August 1983) commented dryly that the accumulated foreign debt included a "miscellaneous cate-

gory of $15 billion that undoubtedly corresponds to arms transfers during this biennium" (i.e., 1977–79). On the Beagle Channel dispute, see Lanus, *De chapultepec al Beagle*; Juan E. Guglialmelli et al., *El conflicto del Beaglo* (Buenos Aires: El Cid Editor, 1978) and Manuel Malbran, *La cuestión del Beagle* (Buenos Aires: Emecé, 1973).

22. Juan Corradi, "The Culture of Fear in Civil Society," in *From Military Rule to Liberal Democracy in Argentina*, ed. Monica Peralta Ramos and C. H. Waisman (Boulder, Colo.: Westview 1987), 113–30.

23. The literature on this painful episode is growing. The most comprehensive summary of horrors is *Nunca Mas* (Buenos Aires: Comisión Nacional sobre la Desaparición de Personas, 1984). See also Eduardo Luis Duhalde, *El estado terrorista argentino* (Barcelona: Editorial Argos Vergara, 1983). Perhaps the most famous case of an imprisoned Argentine is that of Jacobo Timmerman, editor of the newspaper *La Opinión*. He survived to recount his experiences in captivity in *Prisoner without Name, Cell without number* (New York: Knopf, 1981). There also are reports by OAS and U.N. commissions on human rights and annual reports by the State Department on the condition of human rights in Argentina. See, for example, *Informe de la situación en Argentina* (Washington, D.C.: OAS, Comisión Internacional de Derechos Humanos, 1980).

24. See, for example, Francisco Carlos Pelerano, *Argentina: Los Grandes Desafíos* (Buenos Aires: Editorial F.E.P.A., 1979); Ricardo Zinn, *La segunda fundación de la República* (Buenos Aires: Pleamar, 1976); V. R. Beltran, ed., *Futuro Político de la Argentina* (Buenos Aires: Instituto diTella, 1978); and Carlos Floria, ed., *Reflexiones sobre la Argentina política* (Buenos Aires: Editorial Belgrano, 1981).

25. Ricardo Zinn, *Argentina: A Nation at the Crossroads of Myth and Reality* (New York: Robert Speller & Sons, 1979), 1–2.

26. Juan Archibaldo Lanús, *De Chapultepec al Beagle: Política Exterior Argentina, 1945–1980* (Buenos Aires: Emecé, 1984), chapter 6.

27. On the Beagle see Manuel Malbran, *La cuestión del Beagle*, Juan E. Guglialmelli et al., *El conflicto del Beagle* and Lanús, *De Chapultepec al Beagle*, chapter 10. For a scathing attack on what he calls negative nationalism, see Escudé, *La Argentina ¿Paria Internacional?*

28. The decision-making in the department is reconstructed from interviews with the parties involved during September 1980. I was a scholar-diplomat in the State Department at that time. The Canadian policy was described to me by Ambassador Dwight Fulford, in an interview on 15 April 1978. Consular officers in the U.S. and Canadian embassies accounted for more than 250 individuals whose lives they saved by accompanying them out of their place of detention and granting them safe conduct out of Argentina.

29. Interview with Patricia Derian, 5 September 1980.

30. Interview, Buenos Aires, 8 December 1978.

31. See various issues of *Argentina*, 1979; interview with Ambassador Jorge A. Aja Espil on 16 October 1979.

32. Several seminars were held at the Wye Plantation, outside of Washington, during 1980–83. Some of these were known as El foro argentino-norteamericano.

33. Interview on 11 August 1982.

34. Among the most useful studies of how the regime functioned is Oscar Oszlak,

"Public Policies and Political Regimes in Latin America," paper presented at the Woodrow Wilson Center for International Scholars, Washington, D.C., 9 March 1983.

35. See, for example, *Mercado*, 30 November 1978, 16–17; *La Opinión*, November 1978, 9–11; *Tribuna de la República*, November 1978, 8–12; *Confirmado*, 30 November 1978, 56–60; and *Clarín*, 9 April 1983, 2–3.

36. The civilian editor of *Confirmado*, said to be an army spokesman, was shot dead in the Barrio Norte in August 1978 by plain-clothes agents of another service following a bitter debate over financial policy. Similarly, when Videla announced that the government would crack down on paramilitary death squads acting without government authorization, uniformed troops kidnapped the head of the Department of Pediatrics of the Hospital de Niños while he was attending clinic, as if to express their dissent from the president's decision.

37. Heraldo Muñoz ("Reflections on the Malvinas Conflict," discussion paper, Woodrow Wilson Center for International Scholars, Washington, D.C. 1982) suggests that this was true throughout the southern cone and was exacerbated by the Reagan administration's search for allies in the crusade against communism.

38. Interview with Oscar Camilion, who was foreign minister in 1981, 22 July 1986.

39. See, for example, the laments of two former foreign ministers, separated by half a century, Estanislao S. Zeballos, *Conferencias de Williamstown* (Buenos Aires: Editorial G. Kraft, 1927); and Miguel A. Cárcano, *La política internacional en la historia argentina*, 2 vols. (Buenos Aires: EUDEBA, 1969).

40. Interview with Cárcano on 28 January 1970.

41. Interviews conducted in October 1980, August 1981, and October 1982. This perception is confirmed by a report done for a private Argentine foundation at the time of the conflict evaluating the Argentine diplomatic corps. The author found that the diplomats displayed all of the negative characteristics of a professional service—cliquishness, loyalty to a cohort, insensitivity to domestic contextual factors—as well as the positive characteristics of such a group.

42. The literature on the Malvinas is vast. It is reviewed in my "The Malvinas War of 1982: An Inevitable Conflict that Never Should have Occurred," *Latin American Research Review* 22, no. 3 (1987). Material in these paragraphs is drawn from that essay.

43. When I asked the Argentine participants in those crucial meetings if they had understood where these messengers fit into the complex pattern of U.S. decision-making and what influence they might have been expected to wield over policy formulation, their response indicated that they viewed the United States as some unitary actor whose representatives pronounce unambiguous declarations as if they were the words of some anthropomorphic being. The Argentine leaders heard what they wanted to hear and did not allow reality to alter their views.

44. A. R. Coll and A. C. Arends, eds., *The Falklands War: Lessons for Strategy, Diplomacy, and International Law* (Boston: Allen & Unwin, 1985).

45. The nature of the transition to democracy and the persistent denial by the military that it had erred at any point in the dirty war raises the difficult question of whether it learned anything from the war. Carlos Moneta concludes that it has learned nothing from its experience. Not only is the military looking forward to the

next campaign to liberate the Malvinas, it also considers its so-called political and economic defeats or mistakes merely the result of not having applied its solutions firmly enough or long enough. Judging from the interviews that Moneta conducted with military leaders in 1984 and 1985, their view of the world is just as myopic as it was in 1981, and their lack of understanding of world affairs is every bit as pronounced today as it was then. See Moneta, with E. López and A. Romero, *La reforma militar* (Buenos Aires: Editorial Legasa, 1985).

46. See Edgardo Catterberg, "Cambio y continuidad política en Argentina. Algunas pautas de opinión pública," and Joseph S. Tulchin, "Desintegración social e inestabilidad política," in *Iberoamérica en los Años 80. Perspectivas de cambio social y político,* ed. Enrique Baloyra and Rafael Lopez Pintor (Madrid: Centro de Investigaciones Sociológicas, 1984).

chapter 9

REINSERTION INTO WORLD AFFAIRS

The central foreign policy issue for the new democratic regime of Raúl Alfonsín was the reinsertion of the country into the international arena. In the forty years since World War II Argentina had suffered a severe identity crisis. It had not demonstrated any self-confidence in its role in international affairs and had changed foreign policies and its basic posture on international issues more frequently than Diego Maradona scored soccer goals. The country reached bottom after the Malvinas war when, in the words of Carlos Escudé, it had been converted into the world's pariah, frustrated in its principal goals, alienated from its traditional allies, enmeshed in quarrels and disputes with its neighbors, bereft of logical and loyal friends, and without comprehension of the world around it.[1]

Its every move in international affairs seemed clumsy and confused. Was Argentina a country that defended Western and Christian values, or was it the country that had most violated the human rights of its citizens? Was it a country closely tied to the United States, helping it in the semi-clandestined struggle in Central America, or a nonaligned nation and the country, after Cuba, with the largest commerce with the Soviet Union? Was it a country of pacifist principles or an aggressor ready to go to war with its neighbors or with European powers in order to settle territorial disputes that were not resolved in its favor? Was it all of these? None? How was the nation going to define itself before the rest of the nations of the world?

The new government came to power with a very positive public image and was welcomed with enthusiasm by the rest of the nations in the hemisphere. It was as if the transition to democracy in Argentina was a case freighted wih special significance. As a result, the Alfonsín government, and Alfonsín personally, enjoyed privileged international status. This status created political space for the regime within which it operated to establish its new image. At the beginning of its mandate the government had the luxury of formulating its international policies without strong inhibiting pressures, and, for a short while, it appeared as if Alfonsín would restore the nation's influence in the world.

But the political space, like a political honeymoon for a new administration in domestic politics, proved ephemeral. Critics argued that Alfonsín misspent this political space and failed to define clearly the new role for democratic Argentina within the world community. Even benevolent observers became increasingly skeptical about the foreign policy of the Alfonsín government as time went on. By the end of the administration foreign policy was unravelling and public debate on international issues was increasingly infused with proposals and rhetoric that referred nostalgicly to a nation that might have been.[2]

The government had some important successes, especially at the outset, and was able to reassert a constructive international position for the nation, culminating in the election of Foreign Minister Dante Caputo as president of the U.N. General Assembly in 1988. On the other hand, there were several instances in which the government was unable to accomplish its goals, and a few, perhaps most significant, in which its policies were not in keeping with its stated ethical values and its moral goals. Most disturbing, in its confrontational tone and inflated rhetoric, on more than one occasion, the government appeared to imitate the military government it had succeeded, a disgraced government that had showed itself to be ignorant of the world, irresponsible in its actions, and totally insensitive to the international consequences of its actions.

How can we explain this contradictory record by a government that insisted so often on the moral and ethical differences that separated it from its predecessors? Contemporary Argentine critics have suggested that it was a deep-seated confrontational tendency in Argentine foreign relations or considered it the result of an excessive idealism peculiar to this government. Another explanation, put forward by political analyst Carlos Floria, is that Alfonsín misunderstood the fact that his was a transitional government whose primary goal ought to have been to shore up or restore a weakened political system. Such a government, because of its inherent weakness and the potentially disastrous consequences of its collapse, ought not to attempt an aggressive foreign policy.[3]

A long view of Argentine foreign relations such as that presented in this volume suggests that it is a century-old tradition of exceptionalism that attributes to Argentina a position of significance and prestige in world affairs and that assumes and accepts confrontation with the United States. Though no longer valid, this tradition continues to influence, even distort, the view of the world held by Argentines and their leaders. That meant that the government could assume positions of inflexible morality—*principismo*—without regard to the consequences of its actions. The actions of the Alfonsín administration suggest that this tradition continued to influence the foreign policy of Argentina and to have had a powerful effect in defining the nation's reinsertion into the world system.

The nation's traditional policy, formulated to deal with its insertion into the world market in the nineteenth century, became increasingly disfunctional after World War I, when U.S. hegemony in the hemisphere was no longer contested, and contributed to a major crisis in relations between the two nations during World War II. The assumptions underlying that traditional policy persisted, distorted, and complicated the reinsertion of the nation into the world system following the disaster of the Malvinas war. Whether it wished to or not, the Alfonsín government could not reinsert the nation into the world arena without previously or simultaneously defining its relations with the United States. The lack of resolution in its relations with the United States blocked the evolution of a new international role. Given its obsession with Central America and the distractions of the Irangate scandal, the Reagan administration was not a useful partner for Argentina in this difficult transition stage. It had little time or energy for Argentine affairs. Unless and until Argentina can resolve its long-standing differences with the United States, its foreign policy will continue to be characterized by contradictions, a confrontational tone in the face of minor crises, and a *principismo* that is little congruent with other aspects of the international comportment of the nation.

This will not be easy. Accommodation with the United States is and has been for many years a highly charged matter in domestic politics. In the short run, better relations can be achieved only by making them less significant. It is worthy of note that from the beginning of the administration to the end, prominent figures like Economics Minister Grinspun and Caputo himself sought to make political capital out of tweaking Uncle Sam's nose in public, which only served to make establishing the bases for a new policy more difficult. It is a noble tradition, made famous by Roque Saenz Peña and Manuel Quintana at the first Pan-American Conference in Washington in 1888–89 when it had been a coherent expression of Argentine insertion in world affairs.

The challenge for the democratic government of Raúl Alfonsín was to define a new role for Argentina in the international system. To do this, as both the president and foreign minister admitted publicly, it was necessary for the country to define its purpose. To declare that it was a democratic country was a first step, but it was not sufficient in and of itself. Without a clear sense of self and of its possibilities in the world, it was difficult or impossible to project a clear image to the world. In this effort political instability and economic stagnation were serious obstacles. The links between internal cleavages and international behavior created painful difficulties.

From the first moment, in his inaugural address, and right to the last, President Alfonsín maintained the same priorities in foreign affairs. He declared unequivocally that Argentina was a Western nation, nonaligned and developing. By this he meant that the nation was historically, culturally, and politically associated with the countries of the West, but that it was not going to form part of any military bloc. He added that the posture of the nonaligned was not or should not be passive. They are or would be affected as much as the members of the military blocs by a nuclear war or any conflict between the great powers. Therefore, the nonaligned nations had the right to fight for disarmament and the denuclearization of the world.[4]

The term *developing nation* signified two important things. In saying it, the president recognized the nation's economic reality. Whatever the potential of the country might have been, it was critical to recognize its present reality—vulnerable, weak, insecure. Some calling themselves realists insist that Argentina is a poor country, a Third World nation, and should behave as such.[5] Alfonsín did not want to identify Argentina in this fashion. He believed that to admit publicly that the country was not yet developed was a sufficient dose of cold water for the moment. The second significance of the term *developing nation* was political. With it, Alfonsín intended to link Argentina with nations in the Southern Hemisphere, which implied an actual or potential opposition to the countries of the Northern Hemisphere. As such it was a powerful rejection of the nation's traditional posture and a brisk breath of fresh air. Neither Alfonsín nor Caputo ever spelled out how an underdeveloped nation could play a significant role in world affairs, nor how a Western nation could assume an aggressive neutralist position and still exercise considerable influence over the major powers.

The principal goal of the new government was to maximize the autonomy of the nation in its project of reinsertion in world affairs. To achieve this goal, the leaders stated that they would maintain contacts with as many states as they could, to broaden the nation's linkages with the world, and to facilitate cooperation among the nations of Latin America. Caputo realized that these measures might create tension with the United States. Using the same argument they used in discussing Argentina's potential role in the arms race, Alfonsín and Caputo insisted that Argentina, along with the other nations of Latin America, has the right and perhaps the duty to take part in the quest for peace in the hemisphere because conflicts are going to affect all the nations in the region. With this argument the Argentine government, always in conjunction with other governments, supported efforts to resolve Central American conflicts.[6]

On the face of it, a policy of cooperation with Latin America and support for peace in Central America didn't appear confrontational or unrealistic, but certain signs of ambiguity and echoes of the past were disquieting. In his inaugural address Alfonsín reiterated some Yrigoyenist refrains of international moralism. Three years later, in his lecture at the Universidad de Buenos Aires, Caputo declared that Argentina supported ethical values in its foreign policy. Although his policy is pragmatic, he said, "it is realistic to support principle and the moral position. Ethics, morals, principles, have practical force." Later he mixed morality with a touch of realpolitik: "I believe that a country like ours that is never going to be a military power, nor wishes to be a military power, which has a long way to go before it is even an economic power, can be a moral power."[7]

The problem with these declarations is that it was not clear what it means to be a moral power or a moral nation. It is not a familiar category in political science or in diplomacy. What we do know from the government of Woodrow Wilson in the United States is that international morality is not always understood in the same manner or shared by all the participants. Wilson showed that military power together with ethical fanaticism could be dangerous and that actions self-defined as moral could have consequences quite different from those anticipated.[8] The history of Yriogyen's foreign policy suggests that morality disconnected from power is a romantic, irresponsible gesture, whose international impact generally is null and even can damage the nation's own interests.

Perhaps what Caputo had in mind was that when a nation recognizes that it does not have the military and economic power to exercise influence over other international actors if only to defend itself, then to define itself as a moral power and to have others recognize it as such can give the country greater influence than it otherwise might have. In that case the question becomes, "Moral force for what purpose?" Here Caputo was clear: Argentina would attempt to maximize its international autonomy and to reinsert itself in the world in such a manner as to favor its economic development and the well-being of its people. Its moral force should facilitate accomplishment of these goals. The danger in this posture was that it was remarkably like earlier versions that attempted to claim an exaggerated influence for the nation in world affairs on the basis of its high moral positions.

When it assumed office, the central problem facing the civilian government in December 1983 was the monstrous external debt and economic stagnation. Assigned the task of dealing with this problem was an intimate friend of the president, Bernardo Grinspun. A man of strong personality, never timid in expressing his opinions, Grinspun represented the international face of the new government. Critics have argued that Grinspun was unnecessarily confrontational.[9] Certainly, he was confrontational in his posture and truculent in his public statements, but the issue is whether this posture won space for the new government and accomplished its purpose.

The first statement by the new minister was that the foreign debt inherited from the military government was monstrous and that the new government could not pay it, that the new civilian government certainly would not undermine democracy by exacting payment of the military's debt at the expense of the Argentine people. From the start the other participants in the international dialogue were patient in their dealings with the Argentines. The U.S. government discreetly abstained from commenting on Grinspun's bellicose rhetoric. Instead, its first responses were positive, constructive, and concrete.[10] Major figures in the banking world and public officials in the U.S. government visited Buenos Aires as if it were some sort of political Mecca. All expressed their support for the new democracy; no one complained about the stance assumed by Grinspun. The latter was occupying the space accorded to the new democracy and making the best of a difficult situation. We know now that while the public declarations by Grinspun and others indicated that no progress was being made or would be made on the question, negotiations were going on behind the scenes paving the way for a settlement.[11]

Grinspun knew that paying the debt was both economically and politically impossible in 1984, and he took advantage of the situation to win greater support for the government on other controversial issues. Alfonsín was determined to bring the question of the Pope's proposal concerning the Beagle Channel before the public at the earliest opportunity. Through public opinion polls conducted by his government, he knew that a majority of the public favored a peaceful and reasonable solution to this vexing problem.[12] He was convinced that Argentina had to accept the Pope's plan, which recognized Argentina's primacy in the Atlantic while granting most of the islands in dispute to Chile. But he also knew that the nationalists, civilian and military, were capable of undermining the most reasonable proposal by sticking an antinational label on the government. Such a label would make it impossible for him to govern and ease the way for an alliance between the most reactionary elements among the labor unions and the military to join forces in destroying the nascent democracy. Grinspun's tactics protected Alfonsín's nationalist flank. The government's nationalist credentials were undeniable when, almost on a daily basis, the economics minister appeared on the front pages of the daily papers defying—or appearing to defy—the creditor nations. Beyond the referendum over the channel itself, Alfonsín knew that his capacity to effect domestic reforms would be conditioned or constrained to a significant degree by specific international problems, such as the channel and the Malvinas. If it couldn't resolve those disputes or at least make some progress toward solution, the government would be held hostage by extremist groups, no matter how small they might be.

Alfonsín's policy had other purposes. By calling for a popular referendum he minimized the risks of nationalist attacks and simultaneously reaffirmed the popular character of the regime; he fortified the image of the nation as a peaceful force among nations; and he demonstrated that the government had the capacity to defuse conflicts without having the costs of the solutions fall on the shoulders of the population. In this sense Grinspun's policies were wonderfully apt for the domestic political situation in which the government began its term in office. In addition, they constituted an opportunity to design a strategy in regional politics. The idea of a "Debtors' Club" appealed to Caputo and to Alfonsín. Grinspun's rhetoric was useful in establishing better relations with the nations of Latin America.

Grinspun's policy had another advantage: it was a shrewd negotiating technique. In 1984 the creditor nations did not have a concerted policy on the debt. The major banks really feared that their clients, among them Argentina, were not going to repay their debts. During 1983 and 1984 the financial press spoke openly about the possible bankruptcy of some giant banks, and there even were persistent rumors of the collapse of the international banking system. Grinspun offered a solution to the impasse. Obviously, it was not an agreeable option for the banks, but it imposed upon them the necessity of coming to an agreement among themselves.

Once the banks had come to an agreement, and once they had reached an understanding with the governments of the developed nations, it was necessary to change the Argentine position on the international debt question. The referendum on the Beagle Channel was held in November; Alfonsín's visit to Washington was announced in January 1985; Grinspun resigned in February. It was time for another policy and a less aggressive personality, one not committed to a heroic stance. It was clear that the solution to the problem was going to be long and would entail considerable difficulties for the Argentine people. It was clear, also, that such solutions required amicable relations with the international agencies. Such harmony was impossible with Grinspun.

The negotiations with the IMF and the World Bank continued for two more years. The Argentine government admitted from the very beginning that any solution to the crisis would have to include some form of understanding with the IMF. It was only a matter of the terms of that understanding. The nature of that agreement, in turn, would determine the contours of the settlement with the private banks. Once Grinspun left office, Argentina's international economic policy had no confrontational tone. The subsequent spokesmen for the Argentine government in economic matters, Juan Sourrouille, Mario Brodersohn, and Adolfo Canitrot, were frank and direct, but never aggressive. In the long run they were much more successful than Grinspun and paid a lower cost in terms of international tension.[13]

In its relations with the United States the new Argentine government was open in recognizing the historical difficulties between the two countries. Caputo told *Newsweek* during a visit to the United States, "We share with the United States the values of individual liberty and social justice. On the other hand, Argentina is also a nonaligned nation and that is an area of discord. In addition, Argentina is a developing nation, not an industrialized one, and that is an area of conflict of interest."[14] One of the areas in which Argentina was willing to disagree publicly with the United States has been the situation in Central America. From his first conversation with President Reagan to his last, in November 1986, Alfonsín did not let an opportunity pass without informing the North American leader that his policy in Nicaragua was in error. Caputo's public statements carried the same message.

But these disagreements over Central America were markedly different from earlier episodes. There was nothing confrontational or quixotic about the manner in which they were expressed. Nor can they be called romantic gestures or mere rhetoric; the words of the nation's leaders and their actions were congruent. More important, they acted in concert with the majority of the nations of the hemisphere, an association that strengthened other positions taken by the government in support of hemispheric cooperation, something that the previous Argentine posture of presumed leadership in the hemisphere never contemplated. Further, the Argentine position was actually quite moderate in the context of the debate over Central America. While there certainly were strong ideological elements to their position and a fairly uncritical posture toward the Sandinistas, the Argentines did not support the Sandinistas to irritate the United States. They declared their support for pluralist democracy in Nicaragua and argued in favor of the participation of the democratic opposition in a clean and open contest for power.

Given the historical nature of conflict between the two nations, the most positive element in the disagreement was that the Argentine perspective was not idiosyncratic, for it was shared by the majority of nations in the hemisphere and in Europe and by many people in the U.S. government itself. In this case, it was the White House that lost touch with reality and that had become obsessed with its own perspective. The Argentine position reminded those surrounding President Reagan that their vision was not shared by friend and foe alike.

It is worth repeating that the policy of Argentina in the Central American dispute was realistic and moderate both in its analysis of the situation and in its diplomacy—Argentina did not attempt to push its position on the United States by itself; it always acted in concert with other Latin American nations. This is important because in the long run, the most significant foreign policy initiative of the Alfonsín government was the rapprochement with Brazil and other countries of Latin America. If the proposed integration goes forward, it will increase the autonomy of both nations more than any moral gesture or neutrality policy. By the time Alfonsín left office in July 1989 in the midst of the worst economic crisis in the twentieth century, there had been more talk than action. The test will come when technical teams from the two countries get together to work out details and when specific measures are instituted that may expose the weaknesses of industries or sectors that have lived for years behind the walls of one form of protection or another. Effective identification as a Latin American nation may be the only way Argentina can reinsert itself in world affairs without first coming to terms with the United States.[15] A cynic might point out that much has been written in the past about how cooperation among the Latin American nations is the most efficacious way to protect themselves against the imperialism or the hegemony of the United

States. It remains to be seen if this latest effort will be more than pious rhetoric.

If Argentina's economic integration with Brazil is a challenge to the United States and other industrialized nations, then Alfonsín picked a good moment for such a move. From 1985 to 1988 the Reagan administration paid little attention to the bilateral cooperation between Brazil and Argentina, or to how such cooperation might curtail U.S. influence in the hemisphere in the long run. In private, U.S. officials responsible for following the events on a day-to-day basis were convinced little would come of the integration effort. They admitted that even if there was much progress, their superiors would not pay any more attention than they did already, which was very little indeed.[16] This lack of attention—and the nations of Western Europe did not appear to be any more interested in what was going on in Latin America than was the United States—made it easier for Brazil and Argentina to advance their schemes for cooperation.

Of course, the lack of attention on the part of the industrialized nations had a negative aspect as well. They might have done more in helping Argentina's new civilian government in its herculean efforts to re-create the bases for democracy.[17] It was a form of isolation, an isolation not wished for by the Argentines. In the concrete case of the dispute over the Malvinas, the lack of support by the industrialized nations, especially the United States, hurt Argentina. When the European nations turned their backs on the dispute still open between Argentina and Great Britain, the Argentine government felt compelled to act on its own and precipitated the most serious confrontation of the Alfonsín regime. The open wound of the Malvinas represented the sword of Damocles over the collective head of the Alfonsín regime, complicating its internal and external capacity to act. The Argentines could not allow the matter to rest, even for a short period, and yet without support they were not capable of bringing the British to compromise. The official position of the United States in the dispute was that it was the friend of both parties and would not become involved. As in the period before the war of 1982, that ostensibly evenhanded posture favored the British.

The government of Margaret Thatcher had insisted for years that the hardline it adopted in refusing to negotiate the issue of sovereignty over the Malvinas was due to the fact that the Argentine government was a dictatorship that could not possibly respect the rights of its citizens. Under such circumstances, how could anyone expect that the British would facilitate the transfer to the islands to such a regime? The other part of the great public opinion campaign conducted by the British to justify their steadfast refusal to negotiate with the Argentines was that they had to respect the interests of the inhabitants on the islands. But no one doubted the democratic character of the new Argentine government in 1983 nor its passionate defense of human rights. And still the British remained totally inflexible in the face of repeated attempts by the Argentines to reopen a wide dialogue on the future of the archipelago. The new airstrip was opened in 1986 at the cost of $1 billion. The cost of "Fortress Falklands" was extremely high, as predicted. But Prime Minister Thatcher did not budge.

Constantly frustrated in its efforts to open a dialogue with Great Britain, the Argentine government became slightly desperate in 1985. The tone of its diplomacy became confrontational. Sinking the Taiwanese fishing boat and signing contracts with Russian and Bulgarian fishermen to fish in these very troubled waters could not have had any result other than the one it had. When great Britain responded by declaring an exclusion zone around the islands, the Argentine government stimulated the latent nationalism of the Argentine people through a series of public declarations of outrage. The initiative nearly got out of hand. There was a brief moment of near-hysteria in Buenos Aires. This was not the kind of support the regime had desired or anticipated. The most charitable explanation of the government's headstrong behavior is that the government felt itself hemmed in by the internal national-ist groups and could not allow the British initiative to pass without some strong protest. Caputo stated that his actions were designed to isolate Britain diplomatically, but they had the opposite effect, winning sympathy for the British and antagonizing Argentina's friends, none of whom wanted to see further bloodshed over the islands.[18] Critics of the Alfonsín government argued that this confrontational behavior showed that the old myths that have distorted Argentine foreign policy had not been laid to rest and that in manipulating those myths Caputo demonstrated that he had failed to fashion for the nation a policy appropriate to its new station in the world.

The worst feature of the crisis was that the United States did nothing to relieve the tension. The United States' official position continued to be that it had no position on the matter. The least it could have done to strengthen the fragile democracy in Argentina was to have encouraged its British allies to soften their rigid position even a little. The slightest movement by the Brit-ish, however insignificant in the long run, would have been interpreted in Buenos Aires as a great triumph for the government and would have been the most effective way to disarm the extreme nationalists on the Left and on the Right, expanding the political space available to the government. Though hard to prove, it is not unreasonable to suggest that the rebels led by Colonel Aldo Rico were either emboldened by the government's failure to move the British or angered by that failure as they revolted during Easter Week, 1987, forcing Alfonsín to deal directly with the rebels and lose face in accepting several of their demands.[19]

But the Reagan administration no longer seemed capable of constructive action in its dealings with the Argentine government. Representatives of the government repeatedly stated how much they favored democracy in Argen-tina, how much they wanted the new government to succeed. On more than one occasion Treasury Department officials called for greater flexibility on the part of the banks in negotiating with the Argentine government so that the

Argentine democracy was not compromised, but it did not seem to have much effect. Certainly, the prestige of the executive was not involved. Since the Iran-contra affair, if not before, the executive appeared detached from international situations that were not in crisis or that did not directly threaten the U.S. national interest. Without the active participation of the U.S. government at the highest level, the impasse over the Malvinas was not likely to change. Ironically, such direct involvement by the United States would have reduced the autonomy of action so earnestly sought by the Argentines. Whether from the strength of his conviction or from the internal pressure, Alfonsín could not leave the Malvinas issue alone. He felt compelled to act. And yet without support from the United States or from the European nations his actions only served to make a bad situation worse.

Foreign Minister Caputo stated that in its reinsertion in the world, Argentina sought autonomy of action. Of course, international autonomy never can be absolute. It is defined in the context of international relations. For that reason, it was necessary for Argentine to redefine its relations with the United States, Europe, Latin America, and the Third World. The brusque changes in policy and the lamentable episode in the Malvinas reduced the confidence of the international community in Argentina. A critical element in the reinsertion was the restoration of that confidence, to reestablish the sense of responsibility of the nation as an actor in the international system. The lack of confidence was another element in the heavy, sad legacy of the military regimes. There were indicators that Alfonsín did not recognize this legacy or refused to be bound by it. Throughout his administration he acted and made statements as if he were representing a nation without such a past, without such a legacy, declarations that were counterproductive and that restricted rather than broadened the government's autonomy in international affairs. Autonomy in international affairs was not an intrinsic characteristic of the restored democracy; it had to be won or earned anew.[20]

A clear case of a foreign policy action that confused other international actors instead of clarifying the Argentine reinsertion was Alfonsín's 1986 visit to Cuba. It appears to have been a challenge to the United States in the best Yrigoyenist style—without positive results and without potential benefit, but with serious negative consequences. It was added as a technical stop after Alfonsín's visit to Russia and Western Europe. From one point of view, it is possible to see both visits as part of a single strategy. But that was not the Argentine purpose. The dramatic increase in trade with the Soviet Union since 1980 was understood in Washington. It was recognized as crucial to the economic well-being of Argentina. As long as relations with the Soviet Union were restricted to the economic, for the most part at least, Argentina's reinsertion did not get tangled in the web of cold war tensions. That was not the same with Cuba. Alfonsín never would say that Cuba is a pluralist and open democracy. His visit apparently was designed to augment his international contacts, as Caputo had announced. But to what end? Was it, as in so many instances in the past, a gratuitous gesture seeking prestige, without obvious benefits for the nation? As Caputo himself said, augmenting international contacts doesn't make any sense if it doesn't lead to a specific and concrete objective.

Another posture that complicated Argentina's reinsertion in the world was its calling for disarmament by the great powers. Such a policy was consistent with Argentina's posture as a moral nation, but it was not perceived as the Argentine government wished because it came too soon after the period in which Argentina was one of the world's most heavily armed nations, and one of its most bellicose. Again, Alfonsín was caught up in the legacy of the military governments. While Alfonsín personally did not have to prove his democratic and pacifist credentials, the nation did have to pass through a period of reconstructing its international confidence and goodwill.

Linked to the theme of disarmament is the persistent refusal of the Argentine government to join the international antinuclear movement. Again, Alfonsín declared that the Argentine purposes were entirely peaceful—and no doubt they were. But it was not Alfonsín whose word was questioned; the doubt and uncertainty about Argentina's foreign policy objectives rested in the historical memory of the developed nations.[21] Furthermore, the position taken was inconsistent with that of a moral nation. A moral and ethical nation must be cleaner than other nations. Refusing to participate in or to take the lead of the antinuclear movement made little sense in the context of Argentina's reinsertion in the world as a moral and nonaligned nation.

The key to Argentina's reinsertion in the world was its relations with the United States. Given the history of relations between the two countries, it was difficult if not impossible for Argentina to accept a bilateral relationship in which it was to play the subordinate role. But there was no other viable option open, at least in the short run. A U.S. government interested in Latin America could facilitate or ease Argentina's reentry in the community of nations. The Reagan administration showed itself incapable of playing a positive role. The Argentines' only viable option was the Latin American option. At the same time, to define itself primarily as a Latin American nation and to define its new role in the world as a member of the Latin American community was still to define itself in terms of its relationship with the United States. Much was said in the 1980s of the relative deterioration of the economic hegemony of the United States. While the decline of U.S. power on a global scale was more evident with each passing day, in the Latin American context this decline was certainly relative, and it was questionable that it had reached the point at which it might have facilitated the independence of action of any of the nations in the hemisphere. Argentina, weakened by three decades of political instability and economic stagnation, would have had considerable difficulties in asserting its autonomy of action without first having won it. You have to walk before you can run.

But if a stern, realistic approach suggested a rapprochement with the

United States, there is little evidence that the Alfonsín regime accepted it. In this sense it remained a prisoner of the rhetoric and the posturing of the nation's traditional diplomacy. The democratic government's most serious foreign policy flaw was its inability to define clearly its conception of Argentina's position in the world. The government defined an ideal position for itself, but it did not indicate how it intended to achieve that position or goal. Without that clarification, the foreign policy of Argentina will continue to be characterized by inflated rhetoric, gestures disconnected from the international behavior of the country, confused signals in disputes, and a reduced capacity to influence other nations in international forums. Without a clear image of what Argentina is, its position in the international system will be ill-defined and its international influence will remain severely reduced.

Without a clear sense of itself, the Alfonsín government, like so many civilian and military governments before, continued to be a prisoner of old policies and old rhetorical positions. These policies emerged from a totally anachronistic vision of the nation's role in world affairs—a vision of a near-great power with significant influence on world affairs through the export of foodstuffs and through a universally recognized potential. According to this vision, the nation enjoyed great influence without counting on the accretion of power in the conventional sense. Whether such a role in world affairs actually existed in the past is a matter for discussion, but clearly it does not exist today. In the context of high internal political tension and economic debility, the Krausean rhetoric of the president and the public declarations of the foreign minister served mainly to confuse friends and others. Worse, it diminished the efficacy and the impact of the government's policies and, in certain cases, actually stimulated internal or international tension.

In the short run, Argentina will increase its international autonomy more by a low-profile foreign policy. The lower profile fits better with the country's current level of economic and political resources. More important, it will help reconstruct the tattered fabric of relations with the United States. Perhaps most important of all, it will serve to make foreign policy less salient in the internal political debate, defusing it to some degree and actually weakening the extremist elements arrayed against the democratic regime. The people's vision of their future is important to the internal debate. Until recently, that vision has been inflated and unrealistic, distorting public discussion of foreign policy and putting severe constraints on any government. The government's task is to modify the vision to fit the realistic possibilities of the nation—the nation of today, not the nation of yesterday.

Chancellor Caputo said that one of the Alfonsín government's objectives was "to disconnect internal conflicts from world conflicts."[22] The visit to Havana and the treaty with the Soviet Union to fish in the troubled waters of the South Atlantic could not have been calculated taking that disconnection into account. On balance, the Alfonsín government merits passing grades for its foreign policy. It ruled at a time that would be extremely difficult for any

government. The relations with the United States were better at the end of
the Alfonsín regime than at any time in the past fifty years, and the capacity
to improve them still further is in the hands of the Argentine government.[23]
In that sense it enjoys far more autonomy than most of its predecessors in this
century. We shall see in the next few years if the Argentines have discovered
how to take advantage of their historic opportunity to create a realizable
future for their nation.

NOTES

1. See Carlos Escudé, *La Argentina: ¿Paria Internacional?* (Buenos Aires: Editorial Belgrano, 1984).

2. The benevolent commentaries of Roberto Russell can be followed in the various issues of *America Latina/Internacional* (Buenos Aires). For an early, optimistic view see his "La nueva política exterior argentina: rupturas conceptuales," *Ideas en Ciencias Sociales* 1, no. 2 (April–June 1984):46–54. Escudé's criticisms are in *Argentina democrática,* ed. Manfred Mols and Enrique Garzon (Buenos Aires: Sudamericana, 1988).

3. Escudé, *¿Paria Internacional?*; Russell, "La nueva política exterior argentina"; Carlos Floria, *La transición a la democracia en la Argentina* (Buenos Aires: Planeta, 1988). Roberto Starke, who is studying this period, shares Floria's view.

4. Alfonsín's speeches are reprinted in the public press and are summarized in two useful publications that give the Argentine version or vision of the government's policies: *Tres Años Ganados: Balance de gestión del gobierno democrático desde el 10 de diciembre de 1983 hasta diciembre de 1986* (Buenos Aires: Secretaría de Cultura de la Nación, 1987), and *Reseña de la obra de gobierno* (Buenos Aires: Secretaría de Cultura de la Nación, 1985). Foreign Minister Caputo's speeches are collected in *Discursos del señor ministro de Relaciones Exteriores y Culto Dr. Dante Mario Caputo* (Buenos Aires: República Argentina, 1987).

5. See, among others, Guido DiTella, "La política económica," in Garzon and Mols, eds., *Argentina democrática.*

6. For a sample of Argentine principles in foreign policy, see Alfonsín's speech before the 39th General Assembly of the United Nations, 24 September 1984; Caputo's talk to the National Press Club, Washington, D.C. 12 April 1984; Caputo's lecture to the Jornada Académica, "Treinta meses de política exterior en democracia," 4 June 1986; and Caputo's speech before the 41st General Assembly of the United Nations, 22 September 1986. Among the early analyses of the new government see Manfred Wilhelmy, "Argentina: política exterior del gobierno democrático," and Roberto Russell, "La política exterior argentina en 1984," in *Las políticas exteriores latinoamericanas frente a la crisis,* ed. Heraldo Muñoz (Buenos Aires: Grupo Editor Latinoamericano, 1985); Russell, "La nueva política exterior argentina"; and Carlos Perez Llana, "Mirar creativamente al mundo," *Creación* 1, no. 1 (June 1986). The quarterlies *Cono Sur* (Santiago, Chile) and *America Latina/Internacional* (Buenos Aires) have shrewd commentaries by Carlos Portales and Roberto Russell in nearly every issue.

7. In *Discursos del señor ministro.*

8. For a comprehensive review of Wilson's foreign policy see Roberto Schulzinger, *American Diplomacy in the Twentieth Century* (New York: Knopf, 1984); and Michael Hunt, *Ideology and American Foreign Policy* (New York: Columbia University Press, 1986).

9. Carlos Escudé, "Un analisis crítico," in Garzon and Mols, eds., *Argentina democrática.*

10. *New York Times,* 13 January, 1 April, and 1 June 1984. The only exception in the public press was an editorial in the *New York Times,* 30 March 1984, accusing both the private international banks and the Argentine government of "playing chicken."

11. Interview with a former member of the economic team, whose name is withheld upon request.

12. I am grateful to Dr. Edgardo Catterberg, former pollster of the Alfonsín government, for sharing these data with me.

13. Interview with an official of the World Bank who conducted negotiations with the Argentines in 1984–85. His name is withheld by request. Even before Grinspun left the president made it clear that he would not take part in a debtors' revolt. When Alan Garcia visited Buenos Aires in December 1984 and delivered a ringing call to arms before the Argentine congress, Alfonsín was quick to throw cold water on the scheme (*La Nación,* 16 December 1984, 1:7–8; 17 December 1984, 51–52.

14. *Newsweek,* 9 December 1985.

15. For two analyses of the cooperation with Brazil, see Monica Hirst and Miguel Lengyel, "Integración argentina-brasileña. Un paso histórico," and Eduardo Basualdo y Claudio Lozano, "Integración argentino-brasileña. Una visión crítica," both in *Cono Sur 5,* no. 5 (October–December 1986).

16. Interviews with desk officers and other State Department officials, who requested anonymity.

17. This is not intended to deny that James Baker, as secretary of the treasury, frequently applauded the efforts of the Argentine economic team, which gave them a little more breathing room with which to work. It argues that the U.S. government easily could have done more within the framework of its policy, with little or no additional cost.

18. *El Pais,* 14 October 1986, 1:3–4. For a summary of the Argentine press, see Southern Cone Publishing Company, *Ten Days Report. Argentina* (October–November 1986).

19. There is no doubt that this episode weakened the president and opened the way for subsequent military uprisings that further eroded his prestige, both at home and abroad. See *Somos,* 12 October 1988, 4–7 and the *New York Times,* 25 January 1989, 1:3–4.

20. Escudé, "Una analisis crítico."

21. On the nuclear issue see Daniel Poneman, "Argentina," in *Limiting Nuclear Proliferation,* ed. Jed C. Snyder and Samuel F. Wells, Jr. (Cambridge, Mass.: Ballinger & Co., 1985).

22. Speech of 4 June 1986.

23. Caputo campaigned successfully for president of the U.N. General Assembly, and one Argentine analyst noted that it was significant that the United States did not campaign against Caputo or for the British candidate, the ambassador from Barbados. See Fundación Carlos Pellegrini, *Marco Externo,* August–September 1988, 14–15.

CHRONOLOGY

1810 *Cabildo Abierto* (open town meeting) is held 25 May in Buenos Aires, launching the movement for independence from Spain.

1816 Formal independence from Spain is declared 9 July in Tucumán by the United Provinces of the River Plate.

1823 President James Monroe delivers his message to Congress, which includes the foreign policy statement known as the Monroe Doctrine, on 3 December.

1824 Caesar Rodney arrives in Buenos Aires in May as first representative from the United States to the United Provinces. He dies soon after his arrival.

1829 Lewis Vernet named governor of the Malvinas Islands in June.

1831 The U.S. vessel *Harriet* is seized in November by Vernet and is taken to Buenos Aires, accused of illegal trespass in the waters around the Malvinas. In December the *U.S.S. Lexington* levels Argentine settlement on the Malvinas in retribution and takes hostages to Montevideo.

1832 The British take possession of the Malvinas in December, claiming sovereignty under the name Falkland Islands.

1852 Urquiza overthrows dictator Juan Manuel de Rosas.

1889 First Pan-American Conference is held in Washington, D.C., 2 October–19 April 1890.

1914 Hostilities begin in Europe on 2 August, throwing Argentine financial markets into disarray.

1917 The United States enters the war 2 April on the side of the Allies.

1920 Second Pan-American Financial Conference is held in Santiago, Chile.

1928 Fifth Pan-American Conference is held in Havana, Cuba, in February, at

179

which Argentine Ambassador Honorio Pueyrredón delivers a stinging attack on U.S. imperialism.

1929   Lord D'Abernon leads a British trade mission to Argentina in March that signs an agreement with the Argentine government calling for mutual trade preferences between the two nations.

1930   *Golpe de estado* removes Hipólito Yrigoyen from power on 6 September and replaces him with a military man, José F. Uriburu.

1932   British dominions hold conference in Ottawa at which Argentine trade is denied special privileges within the Commonwealth.

1933   Roca–Runciman Pact is signed in April; under it Argentina is granted quotas for its exports to Great Britain.

1939   Nations of the hemisphere gather in Panama in September for the Meeting of Consultation after German battleship *Graf von Spee* caught and crippled by British warships in the River Plate delta 13–15 December.

1940   Argentine government offers its proposal for "nonbelligerency" to the U.S. government on 19 April. Argentine President Roberto Ortiz is forced to leave office 3 July because of illness, ceding power to the vice president Ramón Castillo, a strong proponent of neutrality. Nations of the hemisphere gather for second Meeting of Consultation in Havana, Cuba, 21–30 July.

1942   Hemispheric meeting at Rio de Janeiro is called in February to discuss Japanese attack on Pearl Harbor.

1943   Army overthrows Castillo government 4 June.

1944   Army replaces Pedro Ramírez with Edelmiro Farrell in January, Juan D. Perón appointed vice president and minister of labor.

1945   Hemispheric nations meet 15 February–6 March in Mexico City to discuss postwar problems. After being arrested, Perón turns the tables on his opponents within the military and reemerges to reclaim leadership of the government on 17 October in a public demonstration organized by Eva Duarte, his consort.

1946   Perón wins presidential election 24 February. Argentine gold assets are unblocked in the United States in May.

1947   The United States imposes restrictons on sales of ships to Chile and Argentina after they draft an agreement that all trade between them will be restricted to their own vessels. The United States stops shipments of coal to Argentina. Inter-American Conference for the Maintenance of Continental Peace is held 15 August–12 September in Rio de Janeiro; it produces the inter-American defense treaty.

1950   U.S. purchases of Argentine grain double. Argentina receives $125 million loan to shore up reserves. Argentina endorses United Nations' right to intervene in Korea.

1951   State of siege is declared in Argentina and is lifted in 1955.

1955   Argentina signs contract with Standard Oil of California in March for oil exploration in Patagonia. General Eduardo Leonardi leads overthrow of Perón in Liberation Revolution (Revolución Libertadora) on 16 September. General Pedro Aramburu leads coup against General Leonardi on 13 November. Confederación Nacional de Trabajo CGT (National Worker's Confederation) is placed under military control.

1961   President Arturo Frondizi tries to mediate in conflict between the United States and Cuba; cultivates Kennedy administration and later talks with Ernesto "Che" Guevara; is forced to stop efforts by pressure from Argentine Army.

1962   29 March coup ousts Frondizi; José María Guido is installed.

1963   Arturo Illia (UCRP) wins election for president 7 July.

1965   Argentina supports U.S. invasion of Dominican Republic.

1966   General Juan Carlos Onganía leads coup against Illia 28 June.

1968   Popular revolt against military regime is staged 28 May at Córdoba.

1970   General Alejandro Lanusse deposes Onganía 8 June and appoints Roberto Marcelo Levingston, former military attaché to the United States, as president.

1971   Joint chiefs of staff dismiss Levingston 23 March. General Lanusse sworn in as president.

1973   Héctor Cámpora takes 49 percent of vote as candidate of Peronist alliance (FREJULI) in March. Perón arrives in Argentina 20 June. Scores are killed as fighting erupts among crowd waiting for his arrival. Cámpora is unseated in July after Perón withdraws his support. Presidency is passed to Paul Lastiri, Chamber of Deputies president.

1974   Perón wins 61.4 percent of the popular vote 23 September to be elected president; his wife, María Estele (Isabel) Perón, is elected vice president. Juan Perón dies 1 July; Isabel Perón rises to presidency.

1976   Armed forces remove Isabel Perón from presidency 24 March. Military junta consisting of General Jorge Rafael Videla, Admiral Emilio Massera, and Brigadier Orlando Ramón Agosti appoint Videla as president 31 March; he is inaugurated in May.

1978   Patricia Derian as representative from the United States pushes President Videla to be more observant of human rights. The United States stops exports of nuclear material and technology to Argentina and urges other countries to do the same.

1978   Soccer's World Cup is held in Argentina in June; Argentina emerges as world champion.

1982   Argentine troops occupy the Falklands/Malvinas Islands 3 April. The United States suspends shipments of military hardware to Argentina 30 April, condemns Argentina 1 May for the "illegal use of force" in seizing the islands, imposes sanctions on Argentina, and offers aid to Britain. General

Mario Benjamín Menendez surrenders to British 14 June. President Leopoldo Galtieri resigns 17 June in wake of Falklands defeat. General Reynaldo B. Bignone is appointed president 22 June and announces the restoration of civilian political activity.

1983   Raúl Alfonsín of the Unión Cívica Radical wins an absolute majority of votes 30 October in his bid for the presidency and assumes office 10 December. Military junta is dissolved 9 December.

1984   Argentina's foreign debt hits $48 billion.

1986   Argentina wins soccer's World Cup.

1989   Carlos Saul Menem (Peronist) wins presidential election 14 May and receives the presidential sash 9 July. It is the first time in Argentine history that the presidency has transferred from one elected president to another from an opposing party. State of seige declared by President Alfonsín 28 May in response to food riots throughout nation. Inflation tops 100 percent a month in June–July and reaches 150 percent a month in July. Foreign debt hovers around $60 billion.

BIBLIOGRAPHIC ESSAY

The history of relations between Argentina and the United States has not produced an extensive bibliography. The magisterial survey by Harold Peterson, *Argentina and the United States 1810–1960* (New York: State University of New York Press, 1964), is now badly out of date, and students will find it difficult to use. Much more lively is the study by Arthur P. Whitaker, *The United States and Argentina* (Cambridge, Mass.: Harvard University Press, 1954), although it is marked by the obsession with Perón so common among U.S. students of Argentina during that period. Comparable surveys by Argentines are nonexistent.

This is not to suggest that Argentine scholars have not been concerned with their nation's relations with the United States. Their concern has tended to be focused on one or another of a few episodes, such as the Malvinas Islands occupation in the 1830s, the persecution of Argentina by the United States during World War II, and the triangular relations between Argentina, Great Britain, and the United States in the period after the Great Depression. On the other hand, it is not far off the mark to suggest that surveys of Argentine international relations in the twentieth century deal to a great extent with relations with the United States. The best of these are Alberto Conil Paz and Gustavo Ferrari, *Política exterior argentina 1930–1960* (Buenos Aires: Huemul, 1964), and Juan Archibaldo Lanús, *De Chapultepec al Beagle* (Buenos Aires: EMECE, 1984), although both, as their titles indicate, focus on the modern period. The most interesting corpus of work by a single Argentine scholar on the foreign relations of his country as they concern the United States is by Carlos Escudé. His books include *Patología del nacionalismo* (Buenos Aires: Editorial Tesis, 1987), *Gran Bretaña, Estados Unidos y la Declinación Argentina 1942–1949* (Buenos Aires: Editorial de Belgrano, 1988), *La Argentina vs Las Grandes Potencias. El precio del desafío* (Buenos Aires: Editorial de Belgrano, 1986), and *La Argentina: ¿Paria Internacional?* (Buenos Aires: Editorial de Belgrano, 1984).

Aside from these few books, most students of Argentine foreign policy have focused on the relationship with Great Britain or on why Argentina should not pay attention to the United States. Of interest are H. S. Ferns, *Britain and Argentina in the Nineteenth Century* (Oxford: Clarendon Press, 1960); Gustavo Ferrari, *Conflicto y paz con Chile* (Buenos Aires: Editorial Universitaria de Buenos Aires, 1968); and Roger Gravil, *The Anglo-Argentine Connection* (Boulder, Colo.: Westview, 1985). The best statement of the Argentine world view shaped by the generation of 1880 is still Thomas F. Mc-Gann, *Argentina, the United States, and the Inter-American System 1880–1914* (Cambridge, Mass.: Harvard University Press, 1957).

Probably no episode in the relations between Argentina and the United States has received greater attention than the conflict created by Argentina's policy of neutrality. In addition to the works of Escudé, the most useful are Mario Rapoport, *Gran Bretaña, Estados Unidos y las clases dirigentes argentinas: 1940–1945* (Buenos Aires: Editorial de Belgrano, 1980); Michael J. Francis, *The Limits of Hegemony. United States Relations with Argentina and Chile during World War II* (Notre Dame, Ind.: University of Notre Dame Press, 1977); and Randall B. Woods, *The Roosevelt Foreign Policy Establishment and the "Good Neighbor": The United States and Argentina, 1941–1945* (Lawrence: Regents Press of Kansas, 1979). The German side of these events is available only in Ryszard Stemplowski, *Zaleznosc i Wyzwanie* (Warsaw: Ksiazka i Wiedza, 1975), parts of which are summarized in Spanish as "Dependencia y Desafio: Argentina ante las rivalidad de las potencias anglosajonas y el III Reich." Ronald Newton has completed a major study that should be published soon. Several years ago, Guido DiTella and Donald Watt put together a conference on Argentine foreign relations during World War II. Callum MacDonald contributed to that volume, as did Escudé, Rapoport, Stanley Hilton, and myself. The conference volume is due to be published by Macmillan in 1990.

There is remarkably little serious scholarship worthy of mention on the modern period. The notable exception to this general statement is the outpouring of work on the Falklands/Malvinas War of 1982. I reviewed more than thirty titles in the essay "The Malvinas War of 1982: An Inevitable Conflict That Never Should Have Occurred," *Latin American Research Review* 22, no. 3 (1987). Little of note has been published since, although Virginia Gamba and Peter Beck are preparing a binational study that should make a significant contribution.

To get an accurate picture of Argentine foreign policy during the 1960s and 1970s, the student must refer to two journals in Spanish that ceased publication early in the 1980s. *Estrategia*, as its title implies, was concerned with geopolitical issues, especially the military and strategic competition with Brazil, and *La Revista Argentina de Relaciones Internacionales* was an effort to bring important works on international relations to an Argentine public. The most acute observer of Argentine foreign policy in the 1960s and 1970s is Carlos Juan Moneta. His essays have been published in many journals and collections, such as the volume edited by Heraldo Muñoz and myself, *Latin American Nations in World Politics* (Boulder, Colo.: Westview, 1985), and his own *Geopolítica y Política de Poder en el Atlántico Sur* (Buenos Aires: Pleamar, 1983). More recently, FLACSO, in Buenos Aires, has begun publishing a quarterly newsletter that provides excellent analysis of contemporary affairs, *America Latina/Internacional*. Together with *Cono Sur* (published by FLACSO, Santiago) and *Estudios Internacionales*, it provides the student with a rich store of information and instant analysis of foreign affairs.

Published studies by United States scholars of U.S. relations with Argentina since Perón's ouster in 1955 are remarkably few. One is Edward S. Milenky, *Argentina's*

Foreign Policies (Boulder, Colo.: Westview, 1978). Information about Argentina's position in world affairs and some consideration of foreign policy can be found in such studies of Argentine politics as Gary W. Wynia, *Argentina in the Postwar Era* (Albuquerque: University of New Mexico Press, 1978). This is the best. As far as U.S. policy is concerned, a little information about Argentina can be found in such monographs as Stephen Rabe, *Eisenhower and Latin America* (Chapel Hill: University of North Carolina Press, 1988); Samuel L. Baily, *The United States and the Development of South America* (New York: Franklin Watts, 1976); Cole Blazier, *The Hovering Giant: US Responses to Revolutionary Change in Latin America* (Pittsburgh: University of Pittsburgh Press, 1976); Michael Shafer, *Deadly Paradigms* (Princeton: Princeton University Press, 1988); and R. Harrison Wagner, *United States Policy toward Latin America: A Study in Domestic and International Politics* (Stanford: Stanford University Press, 1970).

Primary sources for the period are limited and terribly one-sided. As is so often the case in the history of the United States' relations with other nations of the Western Hemisphere, the best source of information is U.S. government archives, and Argentina is no exception to this rule. Even though Argentina's archives for the period prior to World War I are open to scholars, the archives of the Ministry of Foreign Relations are in lamentable condition and contain very little information of value to the historian. Access to archival material for the period after World War II is severely limited. The same is true for private collections. There are a few for the period prior to 1930, and very little after that. For government statements, scholars must rely on newspapers or on official collections published irregularly by the administration to advertise its foreign policy. Examples from different periods are General Juan Sebastian Garré et al., *Política Internacional Argentina* (Buenos Aires: Circulo Militar, 1966), and República Argentina, *Discursos del señor ministro de Relaciones Exteriores y Culto Dr. Dante Mario Caputo* (Buenos Aires: Presidencia de la Nación, 1987). Alberto Ciria makes an interesting effort to show his countrymen how the United States viewed Argentina in the period after World War II in his *Estados Unidos nos Mira* (Buenos Aires: Ediciones La Bastilla 1973).

By contrast, the U.S. government collected paper in profusion for the period from World War II on. In addition to the obvious material familiar to the historian of international affairs—cables, minutes, background memoranda, interoffice discussions, and the like—there is a wealth of primary material on Argentine history and foreign policy forwarded by representatives of the U.S. government and filed in the National Archives. While some of the material is tendentious and must be checked against other sources, much of it is of great value. A good sample of the official correspondence is published in the annual volumes of the *Foreign Relations of the United States.*

Despite the fact that presidents of the United States rarely focused their attention on Argentina for prolonged periods of time, the presidential libraries contain a great deal of information about relations with Argentina because they include so many papers submitted for the president's information. Collections in the Roosevelt Library have been used extensively by those studying the tension between Argentina and the United States during World War II. The Eisenhower and Johnson collections are being put to good use in general studies of the period, although no monographs on Argentine affairs have been published yet. Similarly, the Kennedy papers are only beginning to be explored for information on inter-American relations.

Memoirs and biographies of major figures in the relations between the two countries reward reading with snippets of information and insights, not with concerted attention to the subject of bilateral relations. Certainly the most entertaining is the memoir of the British ambassador to Argentina, Sir David Kelly, *The Ruling Few* (London: Hollis and Carter, 1952). Kelly's trenchant remarks about U.S. policy and diplomacy are no less biting in his published recollections than they are in his dispatches, which are available in the Foreign Office Records of the Public Record Office in London.

Among U.S. figures whose memoirs are worth perusing are Spruille Braden, *Diplomats and Demagogues* (New Rochelle, N.Y.: Arlington House, 1971); John Moors Cabot, *First Line of Defense: Forty Years' Experiences of a Career Diplomat* (Washington, D.C.: School of Foreign Service, Georgetown University, 1979); and Jesse H. Stiller, *George S. Messersmith* (Chapel Hill: University of North Carolina Press, 1987).

Argentines whose memoirs contain information about relations with the United States includes Miguel Angel Cárcano, *Churchill–Kennedy* (Buenos Aires: Ediciones Pampa y Cielo, 1966), and Lucio M. Moreno Quintana, *Misiones en Londres y Ginebra* (Buenos Aires: privately printed, 1946).

INDEX

Achilles, 66
Adams, Brooks, 20
AID (Agency for International Development), 123
Ajax, 66
Alemann, Economics Minister Roberto, 154, 157
Alfonsín, President Raúl, 163–66, 168–77
Allende, President Salvador, 136, 138
Alliance for Progress, 120, 121, 124
Alvear, Ambassador María de, 8, 11, 44, 48, 49
Alves, José de Paula Rodrígues, 67
Amnesty International, 145, 149
Anchorena, Tomás Manuel de, 9, 10
Aramburu, General Pedro E., 120
Aranha, Osvaldo, 73
Argentina, 6
  asymmetry of purpose with the U.S., 147, 148
  autonomy of action, 105, 108, 111, 138, 166, 173, 174, 176
  development, 16, 18, 19, 25
  dependence, 33, 38, 41, 47, 48, 55, 56, 58, 59, 110
  desire for prestige, 174
  dirty war, 144, 145, 157, 161
  foreign debt, 167–69
  Foreign Ministry, 64, 153
  governing elite, 63, 83, 88, 111
  international autonomy, 175
  manifest destiny, 18
  military, the, 111, 122, 132–35, 146, 147, 150, 156, 157, 173
  military government, the, 149
  military junta, the, 151–53, 155
  National Congress, 68
  nationalism, 63
  neutrality, 40, 63–70, 76, 83, 84, 87, 90, 109
  nonbelligerency proposal, 66, 67, 69–75, 78
  oligarchy, 51, 105
  struggle to reduce U.S. hegemony, 108
  territorial dismemberment, 6
  territorial integrity, 13
  United States trade agreement with, 74
  worldview, 19, 20, 23, 25–27, 29, 31, 34–36, 38, 40, 41, 46, 47, 53, 55, 63, 76, 83, 84, 88, 89, 95, 99, 108–10, 126, 127, 140, 142, 144, 155, 163–65, 175
Argentina at the San Francisco conference, 109

Argentine Anticommunist Alliance, 139, 141
Argentine Report, 149
Argentine Rural Society, (Sociedad Rural Argentina), 52
Armour, Ambassador Norman, 65, 67, 69–71, 74, 78, 79, 85, 86, 87, 90, 104
ATLAS, (Asociación de Trabajadores Latinoamericanos) 107

Baldomir, Alfredo, 73
Balestra, Juan, 16
Bay of Pigs, 124
Baylies, Francis, 10–12
Beagle Channel, 133, 137, 143, 146, 168, 169
Becú, Carlos A., 32
Betancourt, Rómulo, 119
Blaine, Secretary of State James G., 22
Bliss, Ambassador Robert Woods, 51
Blue Book, 63, 77, 93, 94
Bolivia, 135
Bonaparte, Joseph, 4
Bosch, Foreign Minister Ernesto, 51
Braden, Spruille, 63, 91, 95, 100, 104, 107, 133, 147, 148
Bramugila, Foreign Minister Juan, 107, 108
Bravo, Leopoldo, 109
Brazil, 26, 27, 32, 56, 72, 73, 81, 96, 104, 111, 117, 126, 134–36, 140, 146, 153, 170, 171
Briggs, Ellis O., 92, 93, 95
Brodersohn, Mario, 169
Broner, Julio, 140
Bruce, James, 106, 108
Bryan, Secretary of State William J., 35
Buchanan, President James, 12
Buenos Aires Herald, 152
Bunsen, Sir Maurice de, 38, 39
Byrnes, Secretary of State James, 92, 94

Cabildo Abierto, 4, 8
Cabot, Chargé d'affaires John Moors, 94, 98

Camilión, Oscar, 120
Cámpora, Héctor, 137, 138, 139, 141
Camps, General Ramon, 149
Canitrot, Adolfo, 169
Canning, Foreign Minister George, 7
Cantilo, Foreign Minister José Maria, 64, 65, 67, 68, 73, 74, 120
Caperton, Admiral William, 37, 38
Caputo, Minister Dante, 164–67, 169, 170, 172–77
Cárcano, Miguel Angel, 120, 130, 161
Carnegie, Andrew, 22
Carta Politica, 159
Carter, President James (Jimmy), 133, 145, 147, 148, 150, 152
Caseros, 13
Castillo, Ramón, 63, 75, 95
Castro, Fidel, 109, 117–21, 123, 137
CGE (Confederación General de Empresas), 138, 140
CGT (Confederación General de Trabajo), 107, 137, 151
Chapultepec conference, 90–92, 94, 102
Chile, 72–74, 77, 82, 83–85, 105, 133, 136, 140, 143, 146, 147, 153, 168, 173
Christopher, Warren, 147
Churchill, Winston, 87
CIA, 123
Clay, Henry, 8
Clayton, Wil, 90, 91, 102
Club de Progreso, 32
Codovilla, Victorio, 109
Colombia, 117
Comité de Acción Legislativa, 153
Confirmado, 161
Connally, Treasury Secretary John B., 137
Connolly, Tom, 91
Coolidge, President Calvin, 48
Cordobazo, 136
Cortesi, Arnold, 90
Costa Mendez, Nicanor, 155
Count de Polignac, 7
Cox, Robert, 152
Cronista, Comercial El, 43

Cuba, 121, 122, 124, 137, 139, 140, 163
Cuban missile crisis, 122

D'Abernon, Lord, 41, 50, 51
de la Plaza, President Victorino, 24, 33, 36, 44
Declaration of Salta, 137
Derian, Patricia, 145–48
descamisados, 105
Diamond, Marcelo, 159
Diario, El, 44
Dillon, Douglas, 119
disappearances, 140, 145, 150, 148
Dominican Republic, 124, 126
Dorticos, President Osvaildo, 138
Duarte, Eva. See Eva Perón
Dulles, Secretary of State John F., 111
Duncan, Silas, 10, 11

ECA, (Economic Cooperation Administration), 95, 106, 107
Economist, The, 51
Eddy, Montague, 89
Eisenhower administration, 113, 117, 119, 122, 124
Eisenhower, Milton, 113
Época, La, 38, 40, 43, 44
ERP, (Ejércitio Revolucionario Popular), 138, 139
Escudé, Carlos, 163
Espil, Ambassador Felipe A., 54, 57, 58, 67, 70, 75
Estrategia, 159
European Economic Community, 88
Exeter, 66
EXIM Bank, 71, 72, 110, 111

Falklands. See Malvinas
FAR (Fuerza Armada Revolucíoniaria), 138
Farrell, General Edelmiro, 87, 88, 91, 92
Feis, Herbert, 58
Ferdinand VII, 4, 6, 7
Ferrer, Economic Minister Aldo, 136
Figueres, José, 119

Fiske, John, 21
Fliess, Alois E., 17
Floria, Carlos, 164
Florida territory, 4–6
Forbes, John, 8, 9
Fortress Falklands, 172
Franco, Francisco, 108, 134
French and Indian War (1756–63), 2
French, 7, 8, 12
Frondizi, Arturo, 119, 121, 122, 124–26, 130, 135
Fulford, Dwight, 160

Galtieri, General Leopoldo, 154, 157
García Uriburu J., 31
Gelbard, José, 138–40
General Belgrano, 155, 156
General Labor Confederation. See CGT
George Washington's Farewell Address, 2
Golbery. See Silva
Gompert, David, 156
GOU (Grupo de Oficiales Unidos), 87
Goulart, Jango, 122
Graf Von Spee, 66
Great Britain, 3–5, 17, 31, 32, 82; declining role in world affairs, 31, 41, 47, 50, 84, 87, 96; blacklist during World War I, 36; Board of Trade, 31, 38, 83; Foreign Office, 31, 35, 40, 51, 53–55, 84, 87; imperial conference in Ottawa, 52, 53, 55; influence in Argentina, 32, 88, 89
Great War, The, 30, 46, 50, 64, 165
Grinspun, Economics Minister Bernardo, 165, 167–69, 177
Groppo, Finance Minister Pedro, 70
Guani, Foreign Minister Alberto N., 73
Guido, José Maria, 125
Gulf of Tonkin, 125

Haig, Secretary of State Alexander, 155, 156
Harding, President Warren G., 46, 48

Harriet, 9, 10
Havana conference, 79
Havana, 175
Helms, Senator Jesse, 149, 155
hemispheric defense, 93
Heritage Foundation, 149
Hickenlooper amendment, 126
Hoover, Herbert, 48
Huemul Project, 108
Hughes, Charles Evans, 48, 49
Hull, Secretary of State Cordell, 54,
    56–58, 63, 71, 82, 84–89, 91,
    92, 95, 148
human rights, 148–50, 157, 171

Ibañez, General Carlos, 107
Illia, Arturo, 125, 126, 134
IMF (International Monetary Fund),
    111, 140, 169
IAPI (Instituto Argentino para la
    Promoción del Intercambio), 106
Inter-American Conference Caracas,
    111
Inter-American Conference on Prob-
    lems of War and Peace (Mexico
    City 1945). *See* Chapultepec Con-
    ference
Inter-American defense conference at
    Rio de Janeiro, 95, 100
Inter-American defense meeting in
    Rio, 81, 82
Inter-American Development Bank,
    118, 119, 140
Inter-American Economic Conference
    in Buenos Aires, 118
Inter-American Financial and Eco-
    nomic Advisory Committee, 66
Inter-American Treaty of Reciprocal
    Assistance, 100–101
Ivanissevich, Dr. Oscar, 106

Jackson, Andrew, 10, 11
Jefferson, Thomas, 4
Jockey Club, 106
Johnson, Andrew, 12
Johnson, Lyndon B., 123–25
Jones, Jesse, 72

Justicialismo. *See* Peronism
Justo, General Augustin P., 52, 55, 56

Kellogg, Secretary of State Frank B.,
    48
Kelly, Ambassador David, 87, 90
Kennan, George, 102, 117
Kennedy, John F., 119–26
Khrushchev, Soviet Premier Nikita,
    118, 123
Kirkpatrick, Jeane, 133, 150, 156
Kissinger, Henry, 125, 133, 140
Korea, 110
Korea, war in, 101
Krause, Karl, 39, 40, 175
Krieger Vasena, Adalberto, 134, 136
Kubitschek, Juscelino, 117

Lami Dozo, General Basilio, 157
Lanusse, General Alejandro, 136
Lastiri, Raul, 139
Lavalle, Juan, 9
League of Nations, 40, 46, 47
Levingston, General Roberto, 136
Livingston, Secretary of State Edward,
    10
Lonardi, General Eduardo, 111, 120
London Wheat Conference, 50
Lopez, Carlos Antonio, 12, 13
Lopez Rega, José, 137–40
Lord Cochrane, 6
Luce, Henry, 123, 130, 143, 144
Lleras Camargo, Alberto, 117

Macleay, Sir James, 53
Madison, James, 4, 5
Mahan, Captain Alfred Thayer, 20, 35
Malbran, Manuel, 53
Malvinas Islands, 1, 8–12, 108, 133,
    134, 136, 151, 152, 154–57, 161,
    162, 168, 171–73
Malvinas, Spanish settlement, 8
Malvinas war, 163
Mann, Thomas, 92, 123, 124
Marshall, Secretary of State George,
    95, 100
Marshall Plan, 95, 104, 107, 108, 127

Martínez de Hoz, José Alfredo, 142,
143, 149, 150, 153
Maza, Manuel Vicente de, 11
Messersmith, George, 94, 95, 100
Miller, Secretary of State Edward G.,
105, 110
Millikan, Max, 117
Miranda, Francisco de, 4
Miranda, Miguel, 107
Mitre, President Bartolomé, 13, 33
Mitre Law, 89
Molina, Minister Luis B., 37
Molinari, Diego Luis, 36, 37, 44
Molotov, Vyacheslav, 109
Monroe, James, 6–8
Monroe Doctrine, 7, 12, 40, 104
Monte Protegido, 36, 37
Montoneros, 138
Morgenthau, Henry, 82
Morrison, DeLesseps, 121
Murature, Foreign Minister José Luis,
31, 33, 35

Nación, La, 23, 33, 43, 159
Naón, Rómulo, 31, 32, 37, 44
Nazis, 69, 71, 73, 75, 92, 93
New York Post, 94
New York Times, 90, 177
Niagara Falls Conference in 1915, 32
Nicolaides, General Cristino, 157
Ninth International Conference of
American States in Bogotá, Co-
lombia, 104
Nixon, Richard, 117, 125, 133, 135,
137, 145

O'Brien, Edward, 24
OAS, (Organization of American
States), 111, 119, 124, 126
Organization of American States, meet-
ing in Bogotá, 1960, 108, 118
Organization of American States, meet-
ing in Caracas, 111, 113
OAS meetings on democracy, most no-
tably in San José, Costa Rica, 120
Odria, General Manuel, in Peru, 107
Oliver, María Rosa, 24

Olney, Richard, 14
Onganía, General Juan Carlos, 125,
126, 131, 134–36, 141, 142
Operation Pan-America, 117, 119,
121
Opinión, La, 161
Oriana, 36, 37
Oribe, Manuel, 13
Ortiz, President Roberto, 55, 62–71,
73, 74, 79, 120, 126
Ovey, Sir Esmond, 83

Pablo Pardo, Foreign Minister Luis de,
137
Pan American Union, 23, 32, 49, 90
Pan-American Conference in Havana
in 1928, 49
Pan-American Conference in Washing-
ton, 110, 122, 165
Pan-American Financial Conference,
31
Pan-American Financial Conference
in 1920, 41
Pan-American Scientific Congress, 68
Panama declaration, 65, 66, 68
Paraguay, 135, 146
Parish, British Chargé Woodbine, 9
Patrón Costas, Robustiano, 85
Paz, Hipólito Jesús, 107
Pearl Harbor, 63
Perlinger, General Luis, 89
Perón, Colonel Juan D., 75, 87, 89,
90, 92, 93, 96, 99, 100, 104–11,
113, 118, 120, 121, 125, 128,
129, 132, 133, 136, 137–42, 144
Perón, Evita, 93, 107
Perón, María Estela Martinez de (Isa-
bel), 137, 141
Perón's rhetorical nationalism, 100
Perón's Third Position, 105, 106, 109,
111
Peronism, 105, 119, 120, 125, 128,
132, 142
Peronist, 121, 125, 137, 139
Pierson, Warren Lee, 72
Pillado, Ricardo, 24, 33
Pinochet, Augusto, 140

Poinsett, Joel Roberts, 4, 5
Point Four, 111
Polignac memorandum, 7
Polk, James K., 12
Prado, Peruvian President Manuel, 122
Prebisch, Raul, 118
Prensa, La, 18, 43, 44, 52, 77, 78
Prestes, Luiz Carlos, 109
principismo, 37, 39, 40, 49, 50, 75, 165
Pueyrredón, Foreign Minister Honorio, 37, 38, 48, 49
Puig, Juan Carlos, 138

Quadros, Janio, 120, 135
Quincy, 73
Quintana, Manuel, 22, 24, 49, 165

Radical party. *See* UCR
Radicals, 52, 78, 110, 125
Ramírez, General Pedro P., 85–88, 93
Reagan, President Ronald, 133, 150, 152, 156, 165, 169, 170–72, 174
Rico, Colonel Aldo, 172
Rio de Janeiro defense conference, 1947, 93–95, 102–104, 110
Rio meeting, 84
Rivadavia, Bernardino, 7, 8
Robertson, Sir Malcolm, 52
Roca, President Julio, 32, 38, 75
Roca, Vice President Julio A., 54
Roca-Runciman Pact, 50, 55, 56, 58, 59, 89
Rockefeller, Nelson, 88, 91, 92, 95
Rodney, Caesar A., 8
Rogers, Secretary of State William, 138
Roosevelt, President Franklin D., 54, 56, 57, 64, 68, 70, 81–83, 86, 87, 92
Roosevelt, Theodore, 24
Rosas, Governor Juan Manuel de, 10–13
Rostow, Walt W., 117, 123

Ruiz Guiñazú, Enrique, 75, 76, 81, 82, 83
Russia, 173

Saavedra Lamas, Foreign Minister Carlos, 53–56
Saenz Peña, Roque, 16, 22–24, 26, 38, 39, 41, 48, 49, 110, 140, 165
Saldías, Adolfo, 23
San Francisco conference, 91, 92
San Martin, José de, 6
Sarmiento, Domingo F., 17
Seward, Secretary of State William H., 14, 20
Silva, Golbery do Couto e, 159
Siete Dias, 133
Slacum, Consul George W., 9, 10
Smoot-Hawley Tariff, 51
Social Progress Trust Fund, 119
Sociedad Rural Argentina, 17, 52
Somos, 159
Sourrouille, Juan, 169
South Africa, 136
Southern Cone Publishing & Advisory Services, Inc., 149
Soviet Union, 101, 109, 117, 118, 122, 123, 126, 150, 157, 163, 173, 175
Spaeth, Carl B., 92
Spain, 1, 3, 4, 5, 6, 7; imperial rivalry with Great Britain, 1
St. Jean, General Ibérico, 144
Stalin, Josef, 109
Standard Oil of California, 111
Stettinius, Edward, 89, 91, 92
Stimson, Henry L., 37, 44
Storni, Admiral Segundo N., 85–87
Strong, Josiah, 21

Taylor, Maxwell, 122, 123
Thatcher, Margaret, 151, 171, 172
Timmerman, Jacobo, 149, 160
Tomaso, Secretary of Agriculture Antonio de, 53
Toro, 36, 37
Tower, British Ambassador Sir Reginald, 26

Treaty of Versailles, 47
Trujillo, Rafael, 119
Truman, President Henry S., 94, 100, 102, 104, 106
Turner, Frederick Jackson, 20

U.S.S. Lexington, 10, 11
UCR (Radical party), 35, 38, 40, 44, 63
UCRI (Intransigent Radical party), 119
UCRP (People's Radical party), 125
Unión Industrial Argentina, 32
Unión, La, 43
United Nations, 91, 111, 149
United Nations, Conference on World Trade in Havana, 108, 110
United Nations, Economic Commission for Latin America, 118
United States
  beef lobby, 56
  congress, 57, 58, 65, 70
  Department of Agriculture, 48, 49, 56–58, 72
  Department of commerce, 58, 72
  Department of State, 71
  Department of State, Office of Human Rights, 145, 147
  Department of the Treasury, 72
  fear of Soviet Union, 100
  foreign policy, 84
  good neighbor policy, 63, 104
  grain trade with Spain, 5
  hemispheric dominance, 100
  manifest destiny, 18
  military leadership, 88, 91
  military strategists, 101
  policy of containment, 113
  purchase of the Louisiana Territory, 4
  State Department, 35, 48–51, 56–58, 65–67, 69, 70, 72, 73, 81, 83, 85, 87, 88, 91–95, 100, 101, 104, 106, 107, 110, 111, 120, 121, 123, 133, 145, 147, 156
  social Darwinism, 21

Texas beef lobby, 54
trade with Spain, 4
wartime relationship with Great Britain, 82
Uriburu, General José F., 51, 52
Urquiza, Justo José de, 13
Uruguay, 66, 68, 72, 73, 75, 88, 107, 135, 137, 140
Uruguayana, 120

Vandenberg, Arthur, 91
Vazquez, Subsecretary of Foreign Relations Jorge, 138
Vernet, Lewis, 9–11
veto compartido, 152
Videla, Chief of Staff Jorge, 141, 142, 146, 148–50, 157
Vietnam, 122, 125, 154
Viola, Roberto, 150, 154
Voorhees, P. F., 12

Wallace, Henry, 57, 58, 82
Walters, General Vernon, 155, 156
War of the Triple Alliance, 13
Washington Post, 90
Webb, James W., 13
Webster, Daniel, 11
Welles, Under Secretary of State Sumner, 57, 66, 67, 70, 71, 73, 75, 77, 80, 82, 83, 87, 88, 95, 104
Wilson, President Woodrow, 35, 37, 39, 46, 84, 148, 167, 177, 199
World Bank, 111, 140, 169
World Cup, 148, 150
World War I. *See* The Great War
World War II, 165

YPF (Yacimientos Petrolíferos Fiscales), 142
Yrigoyen, Hipólito, 32, 36–42, 44, 49–51, 108, 125, 126, 135, 166, 167; administrative style, 38

Zeballos, Estanislao S., 18, 26, 33, 73, 161

About the Author

Joseph S. Tulchin was educated at Amherst College, Peterhouse Cambridge, and Harvard University. He taught at Yale before joining the faculty of the University of North Carolina at Chapel Hill, where he is now on leave from his position as professor of history and director of the Office of International Programs. He is director of the Latin American Program of the Woodrow Wilson International Center for Scholars, Washington, D.C., and has served as associate editor and editor of the *Latin American Research Review.* Over the past twenty-five years, he has published more than ten books and fifty articles on U.S. foreign policy and Latin America.

Tulchin first visited Argentina in 1962 and has returned nearly every year since.